Civilisations and Social Theory

Volume 1 of Social Dialectics

Also by Anouar Abdel-Malek

Nation and Revolution: Volume 2 of Social Dialectics

Spécificité et théorie sociale (edited)

L'Armée dans la nation (edited)

La Dialectique sociale

Renaissance du Monde Arabe (co-edited with
A.-A. Beläl and H. Hanafi)

Sociologie de l'Impérialisme (edited)

Idéologie et renaissance nationale: l'Egypte moderne

Kultûr Emperyalismi (with G. and A. Dino,
P. N. Boratav)

Anthologie de la littérature arabe contemporaine,
volume 2: Les Essais

Egypte, société militaire

Peuples d'Afrique

Books in Arabic

Al-Fikr al-'Arabi fî Ma'rakat al-Nahdah

Al-Gaysh wa'l-Harakah al-Wataniyyah

Al-Mougtama'al-Miçrî wa'l-Gaysh

Dirâsât fî'l-thaqâfah al-wataniyyah

Madkhal ilâ'l-falsafah

Maktabat al-afkâr

Civilisations and Social Theory

Volume 1 of Social Dialectics

Anouar Abdel-Malek

State University of New York Press
Albany

14-12-81.

First published in the U.S.A. by
State University of New York Press, Albany

Printed in Hong Kong.

For information, address State University of New York
Press, State University Plaza, Albany, N.Y., 12246.

Library of Congress Cataloging in Publication Data

Abdel-Malek, Anouar.
 Social dialectics.

 Revised translation of La dialectique sociale.
 Includes index.
 CONTENTS: v. 1. Civilisations and social theory.
—v. 2. Nation and revolution.
 1. Nationalism and socialism. 2. Underdeveloped
areas – Social conditions. 3. Underdeveloped areas –
Politics and government. I. Title.
HX550.N3A2413   303.4'01   80-25061
ISBN 0-87395-500-5
ISBN 0-87395-502-1 (pbk)

To Antonio Gramsci

Great intelligence embraces,
Small intelligence discriminates.
Great talk is sparkling,
Small talk is verbose.

Tchuang-Tseu

Time is the field of human development.

Karl Marx

Dialectics, in effect, is a method of thinking, or rather a coherent sequence of intelligible methods, which help to melt certain rigid conceptions and to bring practice to dominant ideologies.

Bertold Brecht

Contents

Sources

The essays published in this book were first published as follows:

Part I   Positions

Part II   Dialectics of Civilisations

International, Institut Charles de Gaulle (21–23 décembre 1975), ed. Cujas (Paris: 1977), pp. 499–509.

Part III   The Concept of Specificity

11   'La notion de "profondeur du champ historique en sociologie" ', *Sociologie des Mutations*, ed. G. Balandier (Paris: Anthropos, 1970), pp. 51–62.

12   *The Concept of Specificity – Positions*, paper presented to Working Group 14 'Civilizations: One or Many?' at the 9th World Congress of Sociology, Uppsala (1978) roneo 17 pp.

13   *On the Dialectics of Time – Positions*, paper presented to the First Symposium organised by the Iranian Centre for the Dialogue of Civilizations on the theme 'Can the Planetary Impact of Western Thought Render Possible a Real Dialogue between Civilizations?', Tehran (20–23 October 1977), 13 pp.

Preface

The initial inspiration of the two-volume *Social Dialectics* – from its inception in the early 1950s to its publication in the original French edition in 1972 – lies and remains deeply rooted in the transformation of the world in our time, in the rise to contemporaneity of the Orient – Asia and Africa, together with Latin America. And this at a time when the division of the world into two systems and the emergence of science and technology are the twin driving forces behind the second stage of the Industrial Revolution.

The central difficulty facing social theory at the time of Yalta, the climax of Western hegemony, was how to generate ways and means of tackling the hitherto marginalised societies and cultures belonging within the non-Western civilisational moulds. Prepostulated universalism, as a recipe, simply would not do. It was neither able to interpret, from the inside, the specificities at work, nor was it acceptable to the major formative tendencies within the national schools of thought and action, deeply attached as they were to authenticity, efficacy and the primacy of self-reliance, to the sovereignty of the national power of decision. Thus it became necessary to engage in a critical examination and reassessment of the notions, concepts, categories, theories and systems of thought in which the Western world expresses its historic hegemony in intellectual terms. If it were to be effective, such a critical reassessment must necessarily be coupled with the restructuration of political and social theory through the presentation of a set of theses and concepts whose aim would be to organise a theoretical workshop where the necessary and inevitable dialectical contradictions and confrontations might forge a path to mediation and towards complementarity.

Such an endeavour could not but be strenuous and extremely complex. It was rendered still more difficult and urgent by the rising tide of the negative idea, deeply at work within the leading cultural centres of Europe and North America, and aiming at the erosion of the structuring forces of Western civilisation. Yet it refused to offer a viable and convincing alternative civilisational project, while throughout rejecting and reducing to marginality the Orient, the Three Continents.

Hence the nature and the tone of the present work.

The cultural, ideological, theoretical and political battles of the 1945–70 generation find their echo in these pages, as the problems are posed anew, taking as their starting point the Orient, the Three Continents, and the transformation of the world that results from the rising historical initiative of the hitherto marginalised nations, cultures and civilisations. It was necessary to give primacy to the constructive side, so to speak, of this task – to its historically positive character. Hence the presentation of a series of alternatives in the form of positions, in opposition to the negations of the prevailing negative idea and its epigones.

It was necessary, we felt, to clarify succinctly the historical and intellectual tone of this work, to underline that it is centrally a work concerned with the elaboration of a general conception of the interrelations between power and cultures at a time when the world is being transformed for the first time since the rise of Europe to hegemony in the fifteenth century.

One cannot fail to recognise at this point that the introduction of the dimension of cultures and civilisations into social theory requires a word of explanation – so far have we departed from the traditions and the tonality prevailing in the West until two generations ago. The functional, operational, quantitative approach to social reality, at the expense of the dialectical *Weltanschauungs*, has led to the prevalence of reductionism, the negation of specificity, the mechanistic belief in the predominance of the economic infrastructure and the cult of technology which leads to the control of minds and souls through the cosmopolitan mass media.

Yet the world is changing for all to see. *Volens nolens*, this transformation has to be accounted for from the inside: it must of necessity create the requisite conditions for a restructuration of social theory in our time. It was that which made this long journey necessary, always bearing in mind and drawing together a dialectical dialogue in depth between the central Western and Oriental traditions, in the hope of opening a path through nihilism and despair, the sterilisation of intellectual creativity, the impotence of the will, and above all the abdication of creative thought in the conflicting fraternity of mankind.

It is not a book of social theory, a theoretical book, a new stage in ideological epistemology, but rather a work in which the attempt to elaborate a more relevant, valid and significant body of social theory is constantly related, at each step and stage, to the real concrete world of our times, to its historically constituted specificities in their rich diversity and across their powerful contradictions. The work is largely based upon the marginalised specificities and contributions of the Orient, essentially within the Three Continents, though naturally enough with particular emphasis on the processes deeply at work within the Arab–Islamic, Afro–Asian civilisational circle. After all, how else could we approach it? That was the position of Max Weber in reflecting upon the feasibility of ensuring to the German Establishment its distinct, prominent place within the expanding European totality in the first quarter of this century; of Talcott Parsons, the late ideologist of the 'Great Society'; of C. Wright Mills, who attempted to voice an alternative model for the Western civilisational project; before them, of Auguste Comte and Emile Durkheim's desire to reflect the established ethos of the French bourgeoisie at the end of the nineteenth century; not to mention the work of Ibn Khaldoun and Machiavelli, Vico and Marx.

A non-temporal social theory can only obtain in the subjectivist epistemological productions of professional ideologists, divorced from the real concrete world, from the objective dialectics of human societies in given historical periods and places, and from the geo-historical formative influences deeply at work in the hidden part of the iceberg. This work originates from influences to which I have already referred; this will help to indicate its terms of reference, and its credentials, and at the same time I hope it will encourage the acceptance of its possible relevance to the many-splendoured array of formative influences that go to make up the cultural, intellectual, scientific and theoretical workshop best able to account for our human condition and prospective, and thus help all those concerned with the future of human rationality in this world to take meaningful action.

It seems superfluous to draw attention to the notions, categories and concepts around which most of the positions presented here are structured. Most of them are identified in the titles of chapters or sections. While it may now be premature, it would seem proper, at a later stage of this work, to provide a systematic presentation of both concepts and formative theoretical elements. It has been felt necessary, however, to draw attention to the historical framework from which the very position on the problematic of political and social theory and philosophy emanates, so that renewal, when it does occur, can be understood against its objective background, rather than as a mere manifestation of exceptionalism and non-conventionality.

Since the publication of the original volume in 1972, many works have appeared, and much work has been done, especially around the turning point of 1973. The inclusion of new essays at the expense of more specialised or regional pieces has become necessary, as the Spanish, Portuguese, Italian and Japanese editions of this book have shown. In the present English edition – which we are honoured to see published by our friends at Macmillan Press and the State University of New York Press, thanks to the clear-sighted support of Robert Shreeve, Steven Kennedy and Mike Gonzalez — the following chapters have been added to the original text of the first, 1972, edition: Chapters 3, 7, 8, 10, 12 and 13 of Volume One; and Chapters 3, 5, 8, 9 and 10 of Volume Two. At the same time little more than half the original text is now being retained within the framework of these two books, for various scientific and technical reasons.

Part I
Positions

1

The Historical Moment of Theoretical Work

In the historical evolution of human societies each phase, each period, each stage is one of transition. There is little purpose, then, in referring to the inevitable exigencies (the contradictions, ambiguities, incoherence or precoherence, the preformulated renewal) of the formidable period of transition in which we live; this alone cannot account for or justify the forms or directions, the obstacles to and perspectives for theoretical work in the different fields of human and social science. To assume anything else would lead us to opt for an idealist vision of historical evolution on which neofideism and all other dogmatisms rest.

In principle, there is nothing to prevent us from accepting the comforting theoretico-ideological framework. Unless we reconstitute the world under glass, in the cultivated settings that so appeal to scholars, where the contradictions and the challenges slip quietly by, we cannot hold to that haughty, didactic, conceited attitude; yet that is precisely the attitude of a majority of Western intellectuals.

How then can we account for the deepening gulf between the different theoretical interpretations of societal phenomena; how can we explain the continued and increasing complexity of the web of differences and contradictions? Through ideology, which contains and limits theory? At one level, it is useful, but it is not sufficient in itself. For we must also account for the internal differentiation between theoretical interpretations that explicitly belong within a single ideological universe; and we must explain the development of theoretical tendencies of the same, or even identical, line within each of the major theoretico-ideological interpretations. Does the explanation lie in a fashion, or in the weight of a dominant ideology? Perhaps; but even then there is something left, and it is important. How can we account for the (recently recognised) difference that stems from the impress of the different frameworks in which the genetic structuration of the theories has taken place – that is the national-cultural frameworks within the great civilisational spheres.

We shall return to these great questions, raised here by way of introduction. At the same time, it will be assumed that the problem of theoretical work must be posed within the frame of a concrete reality, that of the present and foreseeable future stages of historical evolution.

1.   The end of classical universalist humanism

It is irksome to have to accept the temporality, the finite character, the limitations in time and space of the ideas (and the beings) in which we place our faith and which structure our lives; they are, ultimately, our defence against the anguish of death. We see how great a problem that is the moment that we seek to pose questions at the level of generality; with the generous vision of universality, universalism, humanism, or the encyclopedist, scientific mediation. How can one imagine a universalism that is itself contingent, marked by historical necessity and historically determined as a world view? What is to be done if humanism, once rigorously analysed and situated in its context, proves to be a phenomenon of the same kind rather than a timeless ethical exigency?

There is comfort, certainly, in the example offered by the phenomenon of rationality, by the demand for organisational coherence in both the analysis and the interpretation of phenomena of all kinds which rationalism expresses. For rationality, once seen as a single, univocal process, is now recognised as a process at two levels, formal and dialectical, after Heraclitus, Hegel and Marx. If the structuring process at the heart of all thought can thus be differentiated; if the single, univocal and unilateral character of formal rationality and its systematic expression in formal logic can be thus relativised, then it will be possible to treat universalism and humanism in the same way.

But it is not possible at all: universalism and humanism in fact constitute a world view, which must account for the interaction of societies in the real world, for their struggles, for hegemony and dependence, progress and regression, revolution and reaction, war and peace. What has to be analysed is, fundamentally, the role of violence in the balance of power both between the different national socio-economic formations, and between the different classes and social categories within each of them. The demands of concrete-dialectical logic, of the social dialectics of the real world, in some ways prevent normal, formal logic from functioning as it should.

Despite Auschwitz, Hiroshima and Vietnam, humanism is thriving; the hegemonic centres of the West continue to adhere to it, rejecting with horror the eruptions of great social and national struggles as just so many lapses in the duties of humanism; sectors of the Western socialist movement, for their part, present their attempt at renewal as a struggle to restore to humanism its authenticity. So we are dealing with a deeply rooted defence of humanism throughout the public spirit of the West. What is its source?

This question poses the problem of the historical moment in which humanism emerged first in Europe, and later in the West as a whole. That historical moment is the time of European expansion leading to Western hegemony – that is, between the sixteenth and the twentieth centuries. It is the time of the great maritime discoveries; the first attempts at integration through the domination of the Orient; the sectional scientific revolutions preceding the Industrial Revolution; the Industrial Revolution itself; the victorious bourgeois revolutions against feudalism; the emergence of a socialist vision in the workers' movement; colonialism and hegemonic imperialism. Despite the spirit of Christianity, everything up till then had been marked by provincialism and sectarianism; in the world of that time – which was Europe, except for the eastern and western fringes beyond Moscow and Stockholm – faith was imposed on the infidel literally by fire and sword – through the Inquisition, the ghettoes and the pogroms. In the restrictive climate of a declining medieval Europe, before the Renaissance, nothing led anyone to look beyond their own world. That would only come with the rise of the social groups of the new, ascendant class – the bourgeoisie of the merchant and maritime banks, and then the manufacturing bourgeoisie – who, on the basis of a more vigorous work ethic as understood by Protestantism, undertook with firmness the task of rationalising both the world of economics and the world of ideas; for that work ethic corresponded to the implicit aspirations of these new social groups, and this ascendant class. Galilee became possible at last; the Renaissance, the *Aufklärung*, the *Encyclopédie*; revolutions. It was necessary to open other countries – the world – to the political and economic initiatives of Europe; at the same time, it had to be seen as possible to integrate them into the European framework that was being offered to them. Hence the postulated equivalence of the different units – peoples, classes, races, nations, cultures and territories – united within a unifying monad: universal humanity. Having reduced Central and South America, Europe established itself in North America. Thus the vision of one world became a real possibility; and the core, the power axis, the civilisational objective of that potential unity was quite naturally seen to be the West.

Less than two centuries separate the French Revolution and the Long March (1789 to 1949); yet they are two centuries in the course of which the combination of scientific and technical progress and the military and political power which aspired to impose its model on the spirit, the will and the very hearts of others, made it possible to realise the project of universalisation, at a rapid pace, in large sectors of the world. Humanism could be posed because, for the first time in the history of the world, a single hegemonic centre of power and culture had come to dominate the largest part of the world. The world seen from the West could now be presented as *the* world view. At least, nothing could prevent it at the level of hypothesis, it being understood that 'Man must prove the truth, that is, the reality and power, the this-sidedness of his thinking in practice.'

The praxis of the real world in the modern and contemporary era in which our theoretical work is located unfolds in a context of crisis from the point of view of the state of Western hegemony.

Within the hegemonic West itself, social dialectics take the form of class struggles in each of the Western countries as well as of wars between states; between 1939 and 1945 it took the form of a war between states which was (for the first time) an authentic world war, in the course of which whole states and peoples waged a war of national liberation against the coalition of fascisms. Meanwhile, at the meeting point between the classic period and that of the 1939–45 war, one of the European states – Russia – broke away and established a socialist power which in its turn would, in the course of the war, set up a constellation of socialist states in Central and Eastern Europe. The period of the concert of powers, from the Treaty of Vienna to Versailles, is no more. The West is certainly still hegemonic, but the centre of power has been displaced to the United States, leaving Europe weakened, divided into two blocs and, in recent times, deprived of most of its colonies and dependencies in the world.

This is the inner circle. The external circle – the dependent world – has experienced an even more remarkable evolution. We readily speak of 'decolonisation', an exclusively Western-centrist term. Yet the process under way since the beginnings of Western penetration in fact constitutes a process of civilisation in which the actions of national movements first against colonialism and then against imperialism are aimed at achieving national liberation; for that is the indispensable precondition for renaissance, or nation-building, according to whether it is ancient nations or new national state formations that are involved. There are two great

periods: the period of formal independence, where national revolution
seems sufficient to confront a colonialism of limited extent and
penetration; and the period of the combination of national revolution, or
national liberation if you prefer, and social, socialist revolution. The
simultaneous existence in our period of two historical phases interwoven
in very different ways according to region, specific historical evolution
and the actual relations of forces (and within each of these phases, one
of two great options – radical-national or national-revolutionary)
provides the key to that highly complex mosaic: what was yesterday the
dependent sphere, and is today the principal arena of liberation and
revolutionary movements.

The essential component of this movement on a world scale is the
resurgence of the Orient – Asia and Africa; its impact has contributed to
the development of the continental dynamics of Latin America, as well as
of social and political movements of a new type in the West itself. It is
enough to compare the condition of the Orient around 1850–70 with what it
is today; the China of the opium trade, in the wake of the greatest national
communist revolution in history, has become one of the three centres of
influence in the world, privileged and protected partner of the various
Wests; Meiji's Japan has become the world's third major industrial
power; the Arab and Islamic world, despite crippling contradictions, has
been able to restore the state and its culture, and to industrialise; black
Africa, in spite of its backwardness, is experiencing interesting populist
developments in a number of places; in Vietnam, post-Korea, hegemonic
imperialism came to know defeat and discredit. The Afro-Asian (later
Tricontinental) movement has expressed the reality and the aspirations of
this great activity. In recent years, significant calls to arms have come out
of China itself; the world is one, the revolution has penetrated the five
continents and moved them to activity.

The time has come when the East wind prevails over the West wind; the
Orient *is beginning to take the historical initiative*. But this initiative
itself is a dialectical process, interacting with the social dialectics of the
West, in retreat, in crisis, but not in decline. It is a matter, let us recall, of
taking the initiative, not of acting as a substitute. The time has come when
the world balance of power established for the last time by the West at
Yalta in 1945 cannot be sustained without the Orient. Thus we enter a
difficult historical period of which the whole of humanity is aware in a
confused way; the future perspectives have not been clearly set out by the
principal partners themselves, but it is very clear that the initiative lies
with Asia, rather than the Orient in general. No complacency can hide the

depth of the 'Asian drama', nor the drama of the Indian subcontinent, nor of the Arab renaissance or the shifting balance of forces in Africa. We shall return to this question.

There is one revealing testimony to this double movement, the crisis of the West, the renaissance of the Orient, the crisis of imperialist hegemony and the rise of liberation and revolutionary movements; the anxious, concerned attitude of the youth of the countries of the West, expressing itself through despair, Utopianism and a constant wandering.

In the West, it is the generation that formed the popular fronts, maintained resistance, pushed forward decolonisation, stood fast at Stalingrad, survived Nazism, accepted the consequences of Yalta, remodelled its project in the wake of coexistence, absorbed a Marxian economism and a deep psychopathology and was an incredulous and uneasy witness to the rise of China – it is this generation, which today runs business and holds the key posts in the cultural apparatus, that must measure the price of its survival and assume the limits that it imposes.

A new generation has (almost) come of age for whom Yalta is no more than a name on a map. It is discovering a world whose concrete dialectics are contained within the network of relations of forces between national states and power blocs. Within its own sphere this youth feels at one and the same time more powerful and more constrained. Its power stems from the combination of birth control policies since the Second World War, material progress in daily life in Europe thanks to American aid (reconstruction, food, housing, health, social security; leisure activities), and the extension of public and private freedoms (sexuality, religious freedom, political ideologies). Everything seemed possible, if only the obstacles could be cleared away. And the objective? None in particular – but there was a great openness, a thirst for innovation. Here Utopia was tainted with anarchism, under the direct influence of those political apparatuses devoted to undermining the concrete approach to the political fact, an approach that sees social dialectics unfolding within the framework of the real world, the world of classes and national formations ranged behind their state. This youthful generation denounces, often with justification, the attitude of resignation that marks the history of the generation of the great turning-point, a generation to whom justice has not been done.

The general atmosphere in the youth movements of the West is as we have described it. Their critical violence against the older generation is located at the phenomenal level, and rarely seeks out the cause of those obstacles and blockages they so correctly denounce. It is in that domain, however, that everything will come together; beyond their rage, the youth of the West pose fundamental questions that relate precisely to the great crisis to which we have referred, to that double movement which the West, naturally enough, finds great difficulty in thinking through rather Ⲭ than simply accepting.

Why the bloodshed and death in Vietnam, when the wolves could accept peaceful coexistence? Why disfigure the planet, when the means seem to be available to make it a human place to live in? Why a formalist, conservative order, when it is so easy to conceive of a new scale of dialectical and prospective values? Why a knowledge so remote from the real world, when that world so urgently searches for the paths to a future of justice and fraternity? Why the refusal to learn the lessons of that other civilisation – the Orient – with which we must negotiate and reach agreement? Why insist on brandishing universalist humanism when we are still building new charnel-houses – when we still speak of the other?

We have scarcely begun to measure the present and future impact of Vietnam on the conscience of the world. In the blood of our brothers, all hypocrisy, all crimes and denials of the future were exposed. The leap forward in Western consciousness, stemming from the roots – the youth, the workers – has violently shaken the tree. The joint action of the young and the workers has often been realised; despite the poisonous masks worn by certain factions, it has been possible to rediscover the route to mass action. For it remains true that it is the young – mainly workers and students – who have posed the fundamental questions in a world that had not yet been interpreted. But this is no longer the youth unified by its belief in the October Revolution of 1917 or the Long March. There have been too many problems, too many contradictions, too many traps, too many realisms. Put another way, the front of youth has been considerably extended, while the sphere of their beliefs has grown more limited.

The moment, then, is right for the emergence of a powerful movement going in search of new ideas; a new neofideism has been born, which is still a search and not yet a defined project. In the eyes of the young, the old faith, the old project, are well and truly dead; hence the mass character of their search, and hence the rejection that it encounters. For this time, what is at issue is simply ideology: the end of humanism, the rejection of universalism, precisely in the name of the world of peoples, cultures and civilisations in which, in a confused way, a majority of the youth and the workers seek to discover themselves through Utopianism and exoticism, and an openness to others.

2.   The formation of the contemporary dominant ideology

The history of the variations in the dominant ideology that have occurred during the recent periods in class society – of capitalist socio-economic formations within the general framework of national movements and hegemonies – unfolds against a background of idealist philosophy and liberal political theory, both of them conceived within the rules of rationality and formal logic. The critique of those conceptions, after Hegel, has been one of Marxism's most important contributions to modern and contemporary thought; this at the level both of method and of world view. Most of what we shall consider below stems from this school of thought – even the designation 'dominant ideology' itself.

On the basis of that history, we can now propose the following characterisation of *dominant ideology*: the dominant ideology constitutes the superstructural framework – ideas, theories, myths, beliefs – which, at the level of both implicit and explicit superstructure, provides a justification of the socio-political order; that order represents the mode of societal maintenance developed in one, or a group of, national socio-economic formations at a given stage of their historical evolution. On that basis, the dominant ideology is one element of a double structure; the other is the actual apparatus of *rationalised violence* – that is the state.

Is it possible under these conditions to speak of a dominant ideology in the contemporary period, in that multiplicity of contradictory move-ments, this flux which overflows all limits? The breakdown of the classic superstructural balance and the collapse of universalist humanism under the impact of the real world seem necessarily to imply that a unifying synthesis is no longer possible, at least at the present stage. Can we then continue to speak of a dominant ideology? Would it not be more accurate to speak of the different ideologies that command the allegiance of people? There is a considerable temptation here to opt for a rigorous prudence, and that in its turn would give credence to a pragmatism that has been momentarily concealed by the clamour of the great ideological struggles. The 'end of ideology' reconsidered and to some extent adjusted.

That option, however, confuses the end of one among many forms of ideology in general, and of a dominant ideology in particular – the end, that is, of a world restricted to a relatively limited rate of change – with the transformation of that ideological form into another, contemporary form. In reality, the plurality of contemporary pantheons can be seen as a breakdown of the superstructural universe into many parts. It will be clear that these multiple mirrors can be seen and interpreted as so many constituent facets of the ideological superstructure in general, and of the dominant ideology in particular. That is the classic problem of change in history.

Let us take this hypothesis as a starting-point, trusting that it will be verified in the course of this chapter. Where is the dominant ideology to be found? If it does fulfil the role that we have suggested, then it is in the field of the social dialectics of the real world that we must seek the formative elements of the problematic of the dominant ideology – unless, of course, we wish to maintain that the world of ideas develops through spontaneous regeneration.

The social dialectics of the real world in the contemporary era consist essentially of rapid and radical change on many levels and within a number of circles. Thus the problematic of the dominant ideology will emerge from a consideration of the specific characteristics of the real world in our time. And this can take various forms, though all of them will be ranged around two central options: conservation and change.

The option of conservation is the central element of the dominant ideology, of all dominant ideologies, given that every dominant ideology envisages its own maintenance. The issue here, then, is what response should be given to the great questions of the era of crises, of the double movement of history as we have described it – such as to ensure the maintenance of the *status quo*. And this is the issue in every epoch. Our epoch, however, has been situated and defined as the era of world integration and of great transformations at every level and in every area of the life of men in society. And the demand that the *status quo* be maintained – if one opts for it – will be pushed to its extreme; at this stage, the game admits of no unchangeable rules. Thus is defined a first dimension of this view; its fixism in the face of a world being thrown in all directions.

What should be one's attitude to that movement if one looks at it from the other point of view, that of change? It will be clear that it will not be possible to fix anything, in the strict sense. The problem consists in integrating change while carefully ensuring that it has no structural implications for the concrete movement of the real world. One can always turn back to the idealist philosophy of history, of course, particularly in its dialectical variant. But a century of Marxist critiques has sharply undermined its credibility in the interpretation of movement, though still retaining its conception of the progressive movement of history in the form of dialectical materialism. Further, the rhythm of history has intensified to such an extent that movement and change have come to take on an accelerated, phenomenal aspect.

This movement, then, must be approached in a positive way, in terms of a forward projection, or what might be called a *prospective interpretation*. The quest for roads to the future has not been easy. An attentive study of the concrete movement of societies will clearly show how difficult it became to establish any continuity between ideals, whether realist or Utopian, and the realisation of these ideals in the contemporary world. There have been too many inconsistencies: the impact of two world wars; the renaissance of the Orient; scientific and technological change; the hardening of national and state political forms. Eden was not at hand, and the new societies emerging from the great and complex struggles taking place at all levels and everywhere were not recognised as the realisation of their deepest aspirations. In these circumstances, the aim of disengagement became possible; the sought-after changes would now be realised through the subjective will of those who chose to promote them, rather than as a result of actions undertaken through praxis in the real world in the framework of the world balance of forces.

In a word, the problem was the following: how could an ideal change be 'produced'? The answer? On the basis of a 'production' of theory, of the 'production' of changes and revolutions in theory which are not realised through praxis. The arm of criticism, not as a substitute for the critique of arms but as its essential foundation. Thus the stumbling block of reality can be avoided, and any precise analysis of the real world denounced as positivism, empiricism or pragmatism. Everything becomes possible, on the basis of the intellectual will of the boffins; epistemology replaces revolutionary praxis and its theory, setting its face against history and a critical historicism that has been guilty of a failure to respond to the summons at the time and in the manner required; and rejecting politics and its demand for a concrete dialectical rationality, which can so easily lead to opportunism, reformism or despair in its many forms.

The contribution to the problematic of change that this vision offers is to erect functionalism into the logical step that takes history from the project to the act. Methodology; models and typologies; a dogmatic epistemology; everything can and should be foreseen, calculated and programmed. It should be possible to 'produce' anything. And one can see how vital it becomes to establish a panoply of possibilities – in 'theoretical' terms. The scientific attraction comes in the attention given to operational aspects, to the theoretically correct functioning of the social processes which are thus produced.

This brings us to the point at which the two approaches, through conservation and through change, meet; for both are at work within the attempts to deal with the central contradiction in the problematic of the dominant contemporary ideology. The question is, to what extent are these two approaches in conflict? Or are they, objectively speaking, in a relation of contradictory complementarity, or non-antagonistic contradiction?

Let us return to those who defend conservation. The defence of the *status quo* leads directly, as we have pointed out, to fixism; but it is no longer conceived in the unilinear manner of the Thomist model. Quite naturally, it is conceived on the basis of the advances in the natural, social and human sciences and in terms of a notion of totality – symbiotic or dialectical – which represents the structuration of a series of elements organically linked at the heart of a single phenomenon. In our time, fixism presents itself as fundamentally *structuralist*. Its particular advantage is that it masks the challenge of history and historicity, of the coming-into-being of human societies as the result of praxis. It presents a complex conception of reality, neither unilinear nor simplistic; its notions of totality and of structure – intangible givens, the 'being' of the world of phenomena – allow for pluralism, but within a fixist monism which is a- and anti-historical, a- and anti-dynamic, and a- and anti-revolutionary. It is, to be precise, the *neo-positivism* of our time, of the general crisis of imperialist hegemony, principally in the West, as the result of the rise of liberation and revolutionary movements in the world, and principally in the Orient.

It is very clear that the two approaches flow organically in the same direction. If structuralism constitutes the fundamental framework of the contemporary dominant ideology, it must nevertheless seek an accommodation with movement which, once achieved, can be integrated into its general framework. The accommodation consists in dreaming up a procedure which allows the theoretical possibility of change without rooting such change in the dialectical movement of the real world; for this is the object of the functionalist, of every functionalist programme. Seen in this way, *functionalism* completes the fixist neo-positivism of the structuralist school by adding a voluntarist element, a neofideism capable of winning hearts from processes from which it had disdainfully separated itself and maintained its distance. The formal contradiction, therefore, is not constitutive; the two wings of the contemporary dominant ideology thus complement one another admirably.

The convergence becomes clear if one looks closely at the cultural scene, particularly in Europe. There the epigones of Marxist structuralism, falling well within the general lines of the dominant ideology, are literally surrounded by groups of acolytes composed almost exclusively of (traditional, non-organic) left-wing intellectuals. The security of the Marxist profession of faith allows the structuralist lily to be regilded; and this structuralism, at last given the right to make laws for the proponents of revolution, will lay down (through writing and theoretical production) a set of unyielding prerequisites for politics, for the forces involved and for the lines to be followed in the non-Utopian realm. The dominant political class in the countries of the capitalist or hegemonic imperialist system are in no sense misguided; they open wide the gateways to emotional recognition, to fame; they provide the platforms and acknowledge these epigones as authorities. These prodigal sons are of great assistance to them at the moment of the civilisational crisis which is affecting the old hegemonic centres.

The diversion will be achieved in the name of Marxism. The boffins will take responsibility for trampling underfoot the social dialectics of the real world in the name of a prefabricated Utopia elevated to the status of scientific knowledge on the basis of epistemological 'production'. Fashion will add its weight; the proponents of critical rationalism, of which Marxism is an important component, will be denounced as conservatives whose gaze is fixed on the past, as positivists concerned only with pragmatic activity, or as dusty old fossils living out history in reverse. In every field of culture, and at all scientific levels, there is evidence of this convergence at the heart of the generalised counter-offensive of a hegemonic West in crisis. The surprising thing is that the compilers of anthologies have barely touched on it up till now; though it is true that the projectors of this theory lead us to look towards the distant future.

From this analysis of the contemporary dominant ideology, one can derive one general characteristic: that is, the *negative idea* – a refusal to acknowledge the real, praxis, the dialectics of the concrete. Structuralist neofideism, with its functionalist variants, makes it possible to sustain the cohesion of 'what is' in the face of movement, its specificity and its demands. And this negative idea is offered as the most general superstructural framework of the world that supports and sustains it, and in which it has been developed.

We come face to face with universalism once again. Since that world – the West – has thought and continues to think of itself as both the world and its centre, it has posed its dominant ideology in different periods as the ideology of all possible societies. And thus it is the crisis of the West that lies at the heart of the contemporary dominant ideology – the negative idea of structuralist-functionalist neofideism.

It follows that this dominant ideology no longer has a universal or a universalising character: consider the impact of these tricks and games on the Chinese Cultural Revolution, the rise of Japanese power, the universes of Islam or Buddhism, to quote only the most obvious. Elsewhere what is thought – on the basis of what is, of what is done, of 'the present as history' – is very different. The shadows hide what has been, in a recent past, renaissance, enlightenment or revolutionary Utopianism. In the renascent and revolutionary Orient other sources, both ancestral and new, are being worked on; studies and other testimony speak of joy, simplicity, asceticism, rigour, generosity and openness, solidarity and, of course, of a China and a Vietnam that have carried others along with them and nourished their thought. Out of such material, and other less malleable sources, new and different ideals are being formed, at whose core appears a positive, dialectical, activist mode of thought imprinted with tragic optimism and fraternity.

The contemporary dominant ideology is, therefore, the ideology of a single sector of the world which is still hegemonic, it is true; but the epoch that is now beginning will bring great changes in world history. For the negative idea is *provincial*. The authentic legacy of Western thought is to be found elsewhere, in the critical rationalism characteristic of the modern scientific spirit and the ideal of revolutions. That is the point of contact between the two civilisations; in this consists the promise of an authentic dialectical relation between them.

3. The theoretical project

3.1 The problematic field

Having begun by analysing the historical moment of the contemporary dominant ideology, we can now move on to the critical phase, and propose some elements of a theoretical project now in process of formation.

We should begin by setting the picture in order, starting with the question of the historical moment of theoretical work, seen in a positive, prospective light. First, the double movement which denotes the *breakdown of the world balance of power*, and whose significance must be precisely defined. We are not speaking here of tangible power – assessed in megatons, the production of chemicals, in statistics of patents granted, etc. – but of the *efficacy of power* itself, that is, its ability to lead the general movement of the history of human societies through the present stage of history and into the foreseeable future.

The efficacy of power must rely in the first place on the ability to set in motion the means and instruments of material and intellectual power in whatever framework they may be required to operate; for they will only succeed in shaping its future to the extent that they are able to develop its specific potentialities in an atmosphere of the greatest possible consensus between the masses of people directly concerned. In other words, power is not power in the act, but only the condition of that power; the transition from potential to actual power is never realised in an automatic, mechanical way. Between the potential and its realisation lies the stage, the step or, if you prefer, the level of consciousness, from analytical consciousness to theory. That has always been the way in history of those who have wished to resolve the difficult balance of the greatness of the project and the moderation of the means. Nowhere is this so clear as in the thought of Sun Tzu, who developed his *Art of War* five centuries before the Christian era; no one has posed the problem more clearly or attacked it better. And the evidence is there, in every domain, from war to mysticism, in invention, from the discoveries to aesthetics.

Let us return now to the double movement of the contemporary era. The crisis of the hegemonic West does not signify its decline. The West – and not just Europe – is always and will be for a long time to come the point at which the means and instruments of hegemony at every level, from nuclear energy to ideology, converge and are accumulated. None the less, the internal cracks grow deeper, and the possibilities of exercising that hegemony in the dominated and dependent sphere grow relatively fewer, for that has become the sphere of liberation, of revolutionary movements. It is this complex network of factors that explains the collapse of the universalist, humanist, civilisational project, which has been the core of Western culture since Antiquity (European Antiquity, let us be clear), through hegemonic imperialism and the first socialist revolution, to the nuclear age. That is the core of the crisis. Yet things can continue on their course; the maintenance of the system is not in question; decline cannot be measured by reference to very grave symptoms of a declining hegemony or its impact on the peoples who are in the ascendant. But who then takes the historical initiative?

It is at this point that the problem of the civilisational project is posed. If we consider the period of the ascent of Europe, and later of the West, it becomes clear that the latter has been able to form an image of man which stands at the centre of a philosophy of culture which has different stages, but which exists within a civilisational framework whose name and appearance is that of a universalist and rationalist humanism. Throughout this complex period, the Orient not only continued to exist, but continued to play a vanguard role in the movement. Until the fourteenth century, in Islam and the Arab world; until the sixteenth in China through its science and its civilisation. Only the West, however, has been able to achieve a synthesis between the progress of the economic and technological superstructure and that of a cultural project set at the heart of a civilisational project constructed in the image of the world at that time; the historical initiative belonged to it by right and not only, as a simple Manichaean view would have it, because of its manipulations or the fire power it had been able to concentrate in its hands, nor even as a result of chance.

This complex combination of factors seems to be concentrated in the contemporary Orient, principally in China and Japan, in the immensity of Asia where two-thirds of humanity, its people and its resources, are to be found. The economic thrust of Japan, which has for the last few years been the world's third largest industrial power, is easy to recognise; it is equally clear that that advance is the result of a synthesis, drawing together a mode of societal maintenance based on a strongly hierarchical, autocratic communitarianism on the one hand, and a highly disciplined integration of science and modern technology on the other. This has developed in Japan on the basis of a vision of an economy of potential and of means which allowed advancement on the broadest front. The attitude towards China evokes other resistances, arising from the feelings of repugnance towards Communism in any form; and this in turn reawakens recent memories of the struggle against the yellow peril. This is the standpoint of those whose starting-point is Western-centrism, and an obstinate refusal to see what the Cultural Revolution did face up to: how to pose the problem of the relations between civilisation and revolution; how to initiate a critical activity, at once theoretical and practical, against the ossifying state and party apparatus; how to solve quickly, but in a lasting way, the problems of transition from a society eroded by archaic forms and a famine economy to an economic and social change of exceptional quality, and this in a country that embraces a quarter of humanity; how to force hegemonic imperialism to stop, revise its general course and negotiate with a renascent and revolutionary Orient which, until 1971, had always been the butt of a general scorn. To these two poles should be added the examples of Korea and Cuba, and of Vietnam above all; for the holocaust inflicted by the imperialisms upon the small frame of that country at every level has endowed the Vietnamese tragedy with an exemplary status for the whole world, as far as the synthesis of reason, courage and will in our age is concerned.

These are the starting-points for our thesis that the renascent and revolutionary Orient has taken the historical initiative in the world that is now coming into being. We have come a long way from the calculations of the positivists; history, after all, is not mere accumulation, but a deployment of forces.

The breakdown of the world balance of power, however difficult it may be to accept, is an imposing process, and its depth, extent and complexity often mask a second process at work in the contemporary world, whose influence is equally powerful.

The *scientific and technological changes* that have taken place in this second half of the twentieth century are impressive and imposing. Its promise, as well as its dangers, are already emerging. The explosion of planet Earth, this vessel which has borne our millenarian wanderings through space, this lost, infinitesimal point in the expanse of the universes, is no longer merely a vision in the mind. Progressively, evolutionary Utopianism has begun to understand the proposition that all things have specific limits, and that the same applies to our planet. The demographic explosion, energy and food resources, the destruction of the environment, the liberation of sources of destructive energy which are increasingly difficult to contain within secure limits, are added to the corrosive effects of an evasion which encroaches upon the deepest well-springs of the personality.

Faced with this threat, scientific and technological change appears as the dawn of a promised salvation. Everything seems to be possible; and yet that very possibility is in part the source of the threat. And this is a second source of deep and persistent tensions which combines with the first; the accelerated pace of that transformation (it has taken barely two generations) is matched by the equally rapid breakdown of the world power balance. The result is that, simultaneously, the intellectual framework which, less than a century ago, still had pretensions to universality, is now rendered obsolete, and it becomes possible to contemplate an unforeseeably profound reshaping of the world.

The interconnection of these two processes is, literally, a constitutive element of the contemporary world. It is fashionable to assume that the transformation of science and technology is of interest only to the powerful – the Northern hemisphere, the hegemonic sphere. As for the rest . . . But as we have seen, this 'rest' is no longer 'third' as far as the capacity of the hegemonic powers, the ascendant countries, to maintain its marginalisation is concerned; nor are those powers able to control the implementation of the results of this scientific and technological transformation. In the middle term, for a generation or two, from now until the year 2000, the West will continue to concentrate in its own hands the essential inventive capacity and the capacity to realise it. But that will be at best a period of transition from the current hegemonic disequilibrium to a new balance. The scientific and technological revolution is not the West's affair alone (in fact, of certain parts of the West) but is a matter for the whole world.

Thus the structure of the problematic of the contemporary theoretical project is defined on the basis of the historical moment of our era. That is why this approach to the theoretical work leads to *critical-historicism* – in response to the haughty and sterile backward glance represented by the negative idea.

The problematic of the contemporary theoretical project can be precisely defined: to know objectively the process of interaction at work at the heart of the social dialectics of our time, whose two specific constituent elements – the breakdown and transformation of the balance of power, seen from the point of view of the historical initiative, and the scientific and technological revolution – make it necessary and possible to consider the social dialectics of the classical period (class struggles, humanist evolutionism) in new terms, at *a higher level*, within the framework of national socio-economic formations, nations, and of cultural spheres situated within the general framework of civilisations.

It is a matter, at the same time, on the basis of this new and increasingly profound awareness, of ensuring the effective insertion of this theoretical work into the dialectics of civilisations which are only now beginning to unfold, yet which command the future. This can be achieved by transforming the traditional intellectuals into organic intellectuals serving the people and their future.

3.2   *Social dialectics*

The position of the problem of social dialectics itself clarifies the question of its realisation, that is the theoretical project. Simultaneously, the realisation of the theoretical project alone will ensure that we fully structure social dialectics in the contemporary epoch of world history.

In other words, the theoretical project is not contained or given in its manifesto – after which, and on the basis of analysis of the position, one would attain the epistemology of the essence of the theoretical project. What can and should be posed at this stage of the theoretical work is the *general vision* of the work to be undertaken and thus of the *method* which has proved most fruitful; finally one must be able to point to those *clusters of possibilities* which seem the most complex and the richest in creative potential.

The theoretical work covers a process already under way (which for us began in 1960) and which will continue through a number of stages, with the present volume as its starting-point. Whatever criticism this work may provoke should be presented as part of this long march, rather than as a criticism of a single text which, outside its field of movement, must necessarily appear sectional.

We have already explained why we see social dialectics as an integral component of critical historicism, in fact as its contemporary expression and its authentic perspective. This necessarily raises the question of its relation to Marxism.

According to the conception which we have already presented on a number of occasions – notably in 1968 at the Unesco Colloquium on Marx, in Paris – Marxism represents the most advanced expression of critical historicism in the era of the industrial and bourgeois-democratic revolutions of Europe and America, that is within the framework of Western civilisation. Quite naturally, the stress is put on endogenous social dialectics, on the struggle of classes and social groups within nations long assured of their existence, and themselves grouped within the general civilisational framework which at that time could pass for 'the world' – despite the incursion of Hegel, and later of Marx and Engels, into a part of the Orient. With Lenin and Stalin, this Marxism becomes conscious of exogenous parameters: imperialism, the national question, the international balance of forces. That was the objective situation of the first socialist state at that time, in the wake of the 1914–18 war, face to face with itself and with a world either antagonistic or friendly and allied with it. It was then too that in a recently unified Italy coming to grips with the problems of political integration, social homogeneity and cultural identity, there was germinating a Marxist thought which extended and developed that contribution of Marxism-Leninism – so rich in promise rather than dogma – in applying it to the national specificity of its country, Italy. The Marxism of Antonio Gramsci, and in his footsteps, of Palmiro Togliatti, constitutes a specific and fruitful creative orientation of revolutionary Marxism towards the national socio-economic formations of European and Western civilisation. It is the alternative to the pseudo-renewal of rightist and reformist inspiration, as well as to the revolutionary verbiage that is either wilfully cosmopolitan or a worshipper of the other.

On the other side of the river, the history of the revolutionary movements continued its course. A prestigious line from Sultan Galiev, Tan Malakka and M. N. Roy to Mao and Ho Chi Minh, and particularly in its Indian, Indonesian, Philippine, Japanese, Egyptian and Sudanese expressions, though little known or understood, continued the elaboration of Marxism within the national liberation movements and social revolutions in the countries of the Orient. In these lands, which the European socialisms did not even take into account, a problematic was defined; later they were to become the favoured terrain of revolutions and of socialism, and Marxism inspired this national renaissance with a socialist orientation. That is in fact the fundamental inspiration of the epigones of Marxism in the Oriental lands. The world has been obliged to acknowledge Mao as the leader of a People's China. But there has been an attempt to reduce Vietnamese Marxism to an ethical and ascetic populism, a new evangelism of the poor. The others continue to be unknown, ill-considered or denigrated.

The theoretical work, of which this essay is a first element, as well as our earlier work on Egypt, its area of movement, its renaissance, its crisis and its future, must be considered as part of that line of convergence which understands Marxism as a vision of the world and as a method of analysing the dialectics of the real world; the Marxism elaborated by Gramsci and Mao in particular. Part of that line, not the repetition of the dogma or the letter, nor as exegesis. For there are other influences within this fundamental and central inspiration: Sun Tzu, Ibn Khaldoun, Hegel, Lefebvre and Needham, whose influence will often be found throughout these pages.

None the less, it is true that the fundamental inspiration at the level of theory is Marxism, in its many manifestations. The very choice of the term social dialectics to designate both the approach to the theoretical work and the first premise of that work points clearly to that continuity at the theoretical level.

That is its ideal, theoretical and ideological affiliation. But social dialectics is not the product of theory passed through epistemological exegeses. Other sources are also deeply at work there.

The first source has always been, is and will continue to be *a critical participant study of movements in the world*, participating in social dialectics through the whole span of its concrete expression and its interconnecting specificities.

This attitude towards the real has, until very recently, continued to provide the foundations of an imposing theoretical edifice, an encyclopedic, prospective vision of the world; this is the intellectual universe in which we still wander, and whose elements still provide us with the materials that enable us to continue to go forward. But we must repeat insistently that this universe has been dismantled. Hence the critical participant study in the movement of the world, in the social dialectics of the real world, is the only means that we still have at our disposal today (and into the foreseeable future) of reconstituting the cohesion of the ideal in the aftermath of the explosion. Then, on the basis of the critical and comparative study of the real in its dialectical movement, we can elaborate new syntheses, and these shall be the framework of the theories of the future.

There can never be any question of withdrawing in order to understand things better, the better to label and list the elements of the concrete reality; though that is how the wise men accumulate references and come to be good positivists. It is in essence a matter of reaching a knowledge in depth of the reality, the potentialities, the obstacles that exist in the real world, the better to ensure the continuation of the dynamic process into the future. And we know that neither exegesis, nor epistemological 'production' can prevail over the balance of forces at work in the real world. The levers of change lie elsewhere, in the development we have proposed.

The real world of the contemporary era, as it is revealed in actuality by scientific knowledge, praxis, is no longer the world of a single, endogenous social dialectic, as it might have been defined a century ago. In the clamour of struggles at the very heart of the West, a factor assumed to have been left behind, the fact of nation – the nationalitarian phenomenon as well as nationalisms – imposes itself as the fundamental matrix along which, willy nilly, endogenous social dialectics develops – that is, the struggle for power of classes and social groups. The resurgence of the dependent sphere – the forgotten Three Continents, but principally the Orient in Asia and Africa – has imposed the need to understand facts that had been kept silent since the period of Western expansion. The national socio-economic formations – the *nations* – are themselves located within the wider framework of the regional *cultural spheres* – Europe, the Arab world, Latin America, the Anglo-Saxon world, the Indian subcontinent. And these regional cultural spheres are themselves ranged at the heart of great *civilisations*, the two most important of which are the Indo-European and the Chinese civilisations; the mediating cultural spheres that lie between them testify to the difficulty and the continuity of the dialectics of civilisations.

Four circles of social dialectics, in place of the single circle of endogenous social dialectics. The simplistic, Manichaean world is no longer, though it once suited the electoralism of countries endowed and sated with possessions, and given to the division between heaven and hell, during that short period of calm that lasted from the Treaty of Vienna to the October Revolution, Yalta and the founding of Communist China.

Four circles, whose precise structure, imbrication, reciprocal interactions, relative density and specificity merit the attention of researchers.

Four circles which can be ordered into two groups, two major circles if you prefer: the circle of *endogenous social dialectics* – the struggle of classes and social groups within a single national socio-economic formation; and the circle of *exogenous social dialectics*, if one may so describe it – nations, cultural spheres, civilisations. The content of social dialectics within each of them is identical; it is a matter of exercising hegemony to assure the continuing status of the group concerned, and to project its continuity into the future.

Two great circles. Here, one can propose a first hypothesis: the endogenous circle and the exogenous circle of social dialectics constitute the two constituent poles of the diad which structures social dialectics in the contemporary era, and will continue to do so into the foreseeable future.

This social dialectic itself, infinitely richer and more complex than was conceived a century ago, when it was restricted to the class struggle alone, allows us to envisage a much wider range of possible actions, whether of the tactical order, and limited in space and time by virtue of the fact that they are the result of the interaction of a limited number of factors, or of the strategic kind, influencing the general course of historical evolution, because they are the result of the activation of a whole network of dialectical interactions between all the constituent elements of the two great circles.

On that basis, one can advance a second hypothesis, flowing directly from the first: the meeting or conjunction of the maximal effective presence of each of these two great circles – classes, social groups: nations, cultures, civilisations – in a given country or group of countries, during a given period of historical evolution, is capable of producing the great transformations in the general course of evolution of human societies.

On the other hand the failure to meet can only weaken the thrust forward and reduce its efficacy. Hence electoralism, the crisis of the civilisational project, despair and the negative idea.

Having situated the theoretical project at the heart of social dialectics, in which the *organic intellectuals* can take their full part by providing the background, the interpretation and the prospective vision, we can now distinguish two levels of theoretical work for the present and the future.

This social dialectics also allows a broad theoretical spectrum to be established, on the basis of the whole range of constituent factors of the two great circles at a world level, a world finally integrated in recent times as a result of the application of the innovations of the scientific and technological revolution to the planet as a whole, and of the great transformation of the relations of power on a world scale. The awareness of the real world, and the methodological rationality we have introduced into it, endows the theoretical work with an immense field of work – the world is its measure – a field of constructive activity, now that the very nature of the intelligentsia has been transformed under the influence and the constraints of praxis in contemporary societies.

The second stage is the reconstitution of the frame of theoretical coherence, that is the *restructuring* of the conceptual apparatus as a whole. We set out in 1970 what this process should be – the only process capable of laying the basis for the future of social theory. It has three phases: critique; marking out and typology; restructuration itself. It is at this stage that new scientific hypotheses, new notions and concepts, pre-theories and then theories of the totality can be elaborated; all of them shall be constitutive and formative elements of a new vision of the world, of the *Weltanschauung* of the future.

2
The Future of Social Theory

1. The double fact of difference and inadequacy

The course whose major outlines we shall present below starts from the fact that social theory is inadequate, an inadequacy of the conceptual apparatus of the social sciences which flows in its turn from the fact of difference. That is, the difference between the societies of the West that have furnished the essential analytical materials for the conceptual elaboration and location of theoretical systems in the different disciplines, and the non-Western societies of Asia, Africa and Latin America. It is only in the course of the last generation that this difference has come to be recognised. Clearly it is no longer possible to dismiss disdainfully its existence as a matter of principle; the concrete history of the societies of the real world in this second half of the twentieth century has raised an unanswerable objection to that. Yet it seems that the time has still not come for the consequences of that reality, of that double fact, to be accepted at the intellectual level; in this sense, there is still a long way to go.

The present stage is just that, a stage, a turning-point. Yet it is not at all clear that, having integrated that reality into the normal body of sociological and theoretical reflection, there is any automatic transition to a precise conception of the work to be undertaken as a result nor, *a fortiori*, any commitment to setting in motion the means necessary to realise the course thus defined. There are two major obstacles: on the one hand, the concentration in the West of the major scientific and cultural instruments, the fruit of empire and of a scientific and technological revolution which considerably emphasised the effects of that concentration; and on the other, the relative weakness of those same instruments in the countries of the tricontinental sphere, which accelerates the brain drain. The double fact of difference and inadequacy thus flows into a combination of other obstacles.

Nevertheless, we must go forward, along the critical road on which we began in 1960; the result of that work has been that we have isolated a series of elements whose validity now seems to us to be established. This chapter is part of that body of work.

2.   From universalism to reductionism

The universality of the conceptual apparatus of the social sciences is now in question; the double fact of difference and inadequacy has imposed itself, by way of the intrusion of a real world which imposes its own limits.

Universality – not universalism; for the later is a point of confluence, the confluence of two major exigencies. The first of these flows from a state of fact; the economic, political, cultural, scientific, technological and military hegemony of Europe, and thus of the West, through the crisis of the system of socialist states; the tricontinental movements of liberation and renaissance; the revolutionary Orient, but also the obstacles, the ossification, the US superpower. Hence the need to see the future of human societies in terms which would, so to speak, perpetuate the Enlightenment, humanist dream of a unified world, a world thrown this way and that by storms and tempests yet never relinquishing its reassuring, postulated oneness. The second exigency is a constituent element of all scientific thought, all theory, the characteristic of a concept being its simultaneously abstract and general character.

In sum; if one wishes to sustain a discourse that is at once logical and realistic, one must both recognise the relations of forces and understand the language of reason. Custom, the nature of things. At that point it becomes possible both to acknowledge the limitations of the Western-centrist conceptual apparatus and sustain the demand for universalism. More to the point, it will be possible to pass judgement on the insufficiently universal or universalising character of the conceptual apparatus now in crisis, on the basis and in the name of universalism itself.

2.1

The terminology reflects an ambiguity that leads to an attempt to achieve a structuration that restores cohesion without neglecting the diversity in movement. This is what we have referred to as the search for a *rationality with multiple variants*.

In the first place, the fact of difference must be accepted. This new flexibility, this widening of the perspective will be reflected first at the level of analysis, of the description of social phenomena, and then in the insertion of these analyses into theories that can account for them. A closer examination of this process shows that the inclusion of what is different, of difference, in the body of current theories meets vigorous resistance. In most cases, this can be overcome through increasingly precise, exhaustive, globalising measurement, by the elaboration of typologies (see Section 3.2 below). For there is a deep-seated reluctance to face up to the critical problem, that is the restructuration of the (universal) conceptual apparatus itself. As a result, notions and concepts remain as a rule outside the critical field – through critical activity must turn to them out of methodological need, rather than on the basis of a concrete programme of theoretical work.

In the course of this work, it is the very notions of differences and variables that have unwisely relegated the panoply of universalism to a secondary level. Must we then decide to accept that? The answer will be provided in the very field of different societies, for is the rise of liberation and revolutionary movements, of national and social revolutions, not rooted essentially in Marxist analysis? Can we not retain, in that case, the role of the economic infrastructure, given that even national liberation and class struggles make reference to it in insisting by turns on the peripheral circle and the endogenous facts? For if the non-Western societies have chosen the path of radical action to bring an end to their decline and marginalisation, can this process not be interpreted in economistic terms? For in that case, what would be at issue would be access to the normal, contemporary social system of the industrial societies. Do the revolutionaries not place the emphasis in the majority of cases on an imperialism conceived in economic and financial terms? And do they not regard imperialism as responsible for inhibiting the social and economic progress of the countries under its domination? It is as if the demand for independence and liberty could everywhere and in all cases be interpreted as the anger of men and societies prevented from industrialising, forced to renounce the promised land of a consumer, welfare society.

Such an interpretation allows universalism to bend to the contemporary reality, and grow a new skin. Rationality will be the key concept, making it possible to include at one and the same time the ideal-type of social

rationality, in the world view of industrial capitalism, and the march of
the oppressed, backward, dispossessed societies towards that ideal-type.
It goes without saying that, at this level, there are multiple variants. But
this state of fact, once recognised, is seen as an aberration, an undesirable
irrationality, a marginality which the interested parties themselves are at
pains to overcome. The struggles to transform societies are interpreted as
so many struggles to achieve rationality – which, of course, is what they
are in the long-term historical sense, and from a philosophical point of
view. However, the *content* of this rationality – and this is the source of
the distortion we have described – is reduced to the dimensions of the
hegemonic socio-economic formation as it is today; for this formation is
explicitly described as at once the most effective and the most open that
men could conceive, and it is understood that it is capable of reforming
and reshaping itself in many ways in a crisis.

What is real is rational; and this rational reality is that of the hegemonic
centre. Thus it is on the basis of the need for rationality – which in fact
lies at the heart of all societal maintenance, of all historical social
projects – that the non-Western societies are invited to develop in the
Western mould. From universalism to reductionism, the wheel thus
comes full circle.

2.2

We can now situate the second level, that of practical application. This is
achieved through *the assimilation of problems* – problems, not situa-
tions, for as we have noted the fact of difference is acknowledged from the
outset. In sum, it is a matter of rediscovering identity, and thus
universality, at the level of content, despite the double fact of difference
and inadequacy, which will be regarded as a scientific hypothesis and no
more.

Identity, the universality of contents and of the problematic. The
dimension of history will then be introduced, conceived of course in a
unilinear sense, so that the evolution of the range of problems – rather
than their specific content – will be simply diachronic. And by doing
this, furthermore, it becomes possible to present the assimilation of
problems as a process of advancement at all levels of social existence.

This is the inspiration behind the key notions that have been developed
in each of the major areas: 'new nations', 'national construction' on the political level; 'development' in the economic field; 'acculturation' in the
realm of culture. Among other things, it has become clear that some of the

so-called new nations (in the mould of the United States, which is the only new nation strictly speaking within the Western world) are the world's ancient nations, with a history stretching back centuries, and sometimes millenia; that the 'development' in question often referred to a growth without development, a development of underdevelopment; that the cultural grafts and imitations of the West were very different from the elaboration of a national culture, not to mention the process of renaissance.

From the learned societies, through scientific and political assemblies to mass communications, the record of recent years shows clearly how great is the confusion – often the will to confusion – and how often the growth of the one combined with destruction of the others serves to obscure our understanding of the real movement of contemporary societies.

Yet everything is there, if sociology and, in a more general sense, social theory gives evidence of its desire to insert itself and become effective at the point at which crises are lived out and rupture experienced – to be in tune with events.

Thus is established a dialectic, whose twin poles will be *specificity* and *universality* – which one finds in the preceding analysis in the form of a rationality with multiple variants and the assimilation of problems – which can provide the inspiration for a critical-historicist approach to the problems of the crisis of social theory and its future.

3. The three moments of the theoretical process

We have repeatedly referred to the crisis, in order to fill in the background that will allow us to emphasise the depth and gravity of that crisis. But the essential questions must be sought elsewhere, within the critical process itself, which is now under way in different countries, processes which are certainly hesitant, informal, sometimes confused, yet nevertheless directly linked to the double demand for concrete social and theoretical coherence. It can be seen that while, on the whole, the ground has been cleared to a relatively large extent, the second wing of the critical process – the initiation of theoretical renewal – is still beset by uncertainty.

That is why we believe it is necessary to focus our reflections on this latter area. How, on the basis of the double fact of difference and inadequacy, can we achieve the restructuration of the conceptual apparatus of the social sciences?

The general method which, in our view, is capable of realising the theoretical project is articulated as a development in three moments: critique, rejection, restructuration.

3.1   *Critical evaluation of the conceptual apparatus*

A critical evaluation, a study of the possibilities of the phenomena studied (in this case, the conceptual apparatus: notions, ideas, concepts and their ordering within given theories) – not a rejection. This will allow us to draw up an account of the two great stages of historical evolution, of the conceptual apparatus of the social sciences, the first of which – universalism, the universalism of the hegemonic sphere – has not yet ceded its place to the second stage.

This account can be developed in two stages.

(a)   A first distinction must be established between the *scientific* and the *operational* conceptual apparatus. Let us say immediately that, in our view, each of the two apparatuses has roots and extensions into the other, since each deals with human societies, with social dialectics, with the dynamics of social maintenance in all human groups in history.

As we have already shown, it is none the less possible to distinguish each category by singling out in each case its dominant characteristic. To take some examples, 'state' and 'bourgeoisie' are certainly scientific concepts, capable of a general, global definition and valid for all cases that relate to each category of phenomena (the organisation of power, of social violence, by one or several social groups or classes with the aim of maintaining and ensuring the evolution of a given type of national society, in the first case; the socio-economic formation characterised by the private ownership of the means of production in a system of production based on the market economy and wage labour, in the second). Both concepts obviously have roots and extensions in the domain of political action; but these roots, and above all their practical applications, do not structurally reduce the epistemological field covered by these concepts, whose scientific worth has thus successfully withstood the test of criticism. To take as an example the concept of the state; one can say that, whatever forms it takes or has taken in history, from slave society to socialism, from despotism to liberalism, from conservatism to radicalism, its definition as outlined above remains fundamentally viable.

The same is not true in the second group. The 'national democratic state', for example, seems to denote an advanced form of power structure developing principally in the confrontation with imperialism, whose class nature is considered secondary to the national political process. We can see how useful it can be in some ways and under certain circumstances. On the other hand a notion like 'national, independent state' seems more precise, less normative – a truly scientific notion within the general framework of the concept of 'the state'. Yet the operational notion of the 'national democratic state' indicates an orientation on the state's part to act in order to extend the participation of the mass of the people, or in their name. That is to say, it introduces a useful nuance in the appreciation of the political facts, a nuance which elsewhere could be expressed in a more objective way. But in fact it is no longer possible to consider this notion as coming within the general scientific domain. What is referred to here is a group of states which, in the framework of national struggles against imperialism, has opted for advanced forms of economic organisation and a foreign policy of dynamic independence ('positive neutrality'), from the end of the Second World War onwards. We are dealing with a recent phenomenon – even if it has been integrated into normal social and political analysis – covering different, temporary contents capable of surprising changes of direction. What is essential here is not the scientific character of the notion, but its operational usefulness.

The preceding examples do not, of course, constitute a model; the field of political sociology, and even more so the field that has come to be called the sociology of development, or the sociology of the new nations, is the favoured ground of this type of confusion and ambiguity.

(b) A second distinction of a more general kind bears upon the scientific character of the conceptual apparatus of the social sciences – that is, its *sectoral*, non-universal character.

In the first place, it must be said that this apparatus is not exclusively sectoral. A group of concepts, ideas and notions, borrowed it is true from the fundamental scientific disciplines – from biology to philosophy – furnished a framework for the specifically sociological: 'power', 'mode of production', 'ideology', 'structures of kinship', 'religious life', 'culture', 'organisation', 'superstructures' among many others. We must distinguish this first group from the specific contribution of sociology, a science mediating between the social sciences, and a method and a vision through which to consider the problems of society – for example: 'charisma', 'implicit ideology', 'messianism', 'organic solidarity', 'social control', etc. In fact, only a small group of terms seem to have arisen from sociological knowledge itself; that is why we have focused the analysis on the conceptual apparatus of the social sciences as a whole, and not of sociology alone.

The essence is otherwise, once these nuances have been introduced; the concrete materials, that is the social realities, historical experiences, the field of implantation of the phenomena under study at the moment when the human and social sciences take on their modern form (between the seventeenth and the twentieth centuries), arose in their totality in the European and Western world. In other words, the given facts that inform modern social theory at the moment of its constitution and development are not universal, but exclusively Western and European – the result of the fact of European and later North American hegemony, from the Renaissance to the nuclear age. There are some exotic notes, here and there, and even a 'terrain' reconstructed from bibliographies and card indexes . . . but Asia, Africa and Latin America are non-participants, in the period when the West is preoccupied with elaborating its vision of the real world, in the diversity of theories and political philosophies.

How can we imagine, then, that the conceptual apparatus of the social sciences, which has cut out the real world, could aspire to universality? Only by a pure and simple postulation – of Western-centrism.

It is the sectoral character of the given facts that inform social theory as a whole that gives that theory its sectoral – not universal – character.

But to say sectoral is not to say provincial, at least not solely or essentially provincial. For that sector of the world that has elaborated those given facts of the real world, which was reduced and subjected by it, is that sector that has exercised hegemony continuously over four centuries, in the course of which it has accumulated resources and knowledge – a cultural accumulation in the broad sense – without historical precedent. Through that process of accumulation the materials of the dependent countries and peoples were partially integrated – as objects, never as subjects; yet these materials have never been absent. Hence the distinction between according a sectoral character to this conceptual apparatus as a whole, and accusing it of a provincialism which would imply that it had totally ignored the rest of the world, rather than marginalising, mutilating and devaluing it – as it has in fact done.

A sectoral conceptual apparatus then – and thus not conceptual at all; a *pre-conceptual*, sectoral, Western-centred apparatus. Yet it is at the same time the only apparatus for the interpretation of human societies which aspires to generalisation. That is why, once the aspiration to universality has been set aside, its scientific, epistemological status must be situated. In our view that is the starting-point, the body of theory that can provide a *scientific hyphothesis* – the only one we have at our disposal at this time – with which to interpret the concrete exploration of human societies in the contemporary world. That is to say that we see the process of restructuring social theory as the specific content of the evolution of social theory itself – not as the rejection of the Western-centred conceptual apparatus.

One example will serve to illustrate the point. It is taken from the sector where the existence of other societies was most directly felt – that is, the national fact. Despite the diversity of schools of thought, the concept of 'nation' was defined as the mode of societal maintenance (the unity of territory, of settlement, of economic activity, of historical evolution, language and culture, of collective identity) which made its appearance in the period of an ascendant capitalism – of the rise of Europe on the basis of the maritime discoveries and the Renaissance. The formal criteria for this mode of societal maintenance appear more clearly in a group of nations anchored in a historical continuity dating from Antiquity – Egypt, China and Persia were, as we know, the most striking examples. Besides, this same mode of societal maintenance takes on different forms, and is situated at different phases of historical evolution. The rediscovery of the Orient, and thus of the colonial world, in recent research has marked out the path for the re-emergence of the non-Western worlds. How, then, can we retain this concept of 'nation' defined in nineteenth-century Europe, assured of itself and of its own pre-eminence? On the other hand, how else can we proceed other than by starting with the definition of this pre-concept, in so far as it is a scientific hypothesis, and restructuring it in a precise methodological process – for it is the only concept we have in the present state of knowledge? For the development of criticism is never a Manichaean process, here or at any other time.

3.2   Demarcation and organisation of the epistemological field: the constitution of typologies

'To analyse a nut you must break it'; from Hegel's definition of analysis, and having carried out just such an analysis, we must now move on to a second level and order the elements, giving coherence and form to their diversity. This will be a stage prior to synthesis, the restructuration of the conceptual apparatus.

Where, however, are we to find the ordering principle, the methodology if you prefer, which will allow us to bring together again the elements that the analysis has torn asunder? There are real difficulties here; for the diversity is at a world level. We can certainly imagine ways of reducing that variety – from the constitution of idealist typologies of Weberian inspiration, to the most contemporary structuralist-functionalist typologies. The fundamental critique we have directed at these two approaches was not concerned with their formal character, but with their fixist, non-genetic, non-dialectical nature – for all systematisation, all scientific development must necessarily have a formal aspect capable, in the last instance, of mathematical expression.

The constitution of typologies, the second stage of the theoretical process we have described, takes two directions.

(a) At a first stage, it is worthwhile applying the critical-historicist approach to the definition of the content of the specificity of the societies we are considering. Very briefly, it is a matter of isolating *the specific mode of societal maintenance* in that society on the basis of a critical study of the historical development of a given socio-economic formation. This specific mode of maintenance involves the specific means of ordering and the pattern of interaction of the four key factors which constitute all societal maintenance: the production of material life within a geographical and ecological framework (the mode of production); the reproduction of life (sexuality); the social order (power and the state); and relations with the passage of time (the finite quality of human life; religions and philosophies). Within that group of factors, it is the production of material life that occupies a decisive place in the ordering of the mode of maintenance – but only in the last analysis.

The application of this model to different societies will enable us to evolve a rough idea of the pattern as a whole, to add nuances and tones – using common notations – to the first analysis undertaken on the basis of socio-economic criteria.

(b) Thus clarified, the different national socio-economic formations present a profile which makes demarcation relatively simple. In fact, while many societies – the so-called 'hydraulic societies', for example – permit that demarcation on economic grounds, others ascribe more importance to the unifying bond of the state, ideological allegiance, internal communication, space and geo-politics, etc. What we are concerned with here is a preferential demarcation – not the analysis of specific content, whose model we have already set out (see *(a)* above).

Let us return to the pre-concept of 'nation'. Once the critical analysis is completed, the task is to draw up a systematic table of the major types of social organisations which fall within the epistemological field; the whole will then constitute a typology. The problem will arise in discerning which among the factors of this determined mode of societal maintenance (the 'nation') appears to be decisive. The starting-point is a careful analysis of the pre-concept, considered as a scientific working hypothesis; it is continuity within duration, that is to say what we have called the *depth of the historical field*, which gives each constituent factor (communal life, geographical space, economic unity, language, collective psychology) its role in the nation. For without this depth of historical field, each of the factors referred to could equally well define other social phenomena, themselves endowed with that depth (or otherwise) to a greater or lesser degree. A community can be created – the university campus, for example – without consituting part of the nation; a space can temporarily serve as the area of societal existence for a community other than the autochthonous community – like Alsace-Lorraine between 1870 and 1918, or Palestine after 1948 – without becoming constitutive of the nation; the same can be said for each of the constituent factors. It is essentially as a result of their simultaneous existence within a continuous historical duration – itself outstanding in various ways – that these factors become constitutive of the nation.

Thus the typology of the different kinds of nation, different 'national socio-economic formations' – on the basis of the notion of socio-economic formation – will employ the notion of the depth of historical field in a preferential way, given the specific nature of the concept of nation itself.

Elsewhere, the same need not necessarily apply; concepts and notions like 'social control', 'acculturation', 'development', 'industrialisation' can and should be used in the appropriate preferential model, that is that model which is in real accord with what constitutes the deep core of specificity of each of these processes.

We should emphasise this aspect of the *preferential* and non-exclusive *utilisation* of the deep core. In fact there are other analytical viewpoints, other models, which would rest on other aspects of the phenomena under study; for example, social solidarity, or identity, in place of the concept of nation. Preferential utilisation alone allows a typology to be established that is as non-arbitrary as possible, to the extent that it will be based on the concrete study of the deep core and the specificity of each phenomenon, each concept, each object of study and restructuration.

We can see how it has been possible in this first outline to establish a typology of national formations in non-Western societies: new states with a national vocation; new national states with a unitary vocation; nations and national states of European origin superimposed on a repressed and decimated alien foundation (in fact, an autochthonous one); renascent nations; and to ensure a universal normalisation, a fifth should be added to the list – that of the national states of Europe, precisely those whose experience has informed the structuration of the pre-concept of nation.

Within each of these major types, there will be ranged the societies that correspond to the fundamental criteria of each type. At a later stage of conceptual refinement, we will be able usefully to establish subgroups wherever it is possible to distinguish between contents – and this will allow us to go more deeply into and make more precise the scientific understanding of the phenomenon under consideration. Thus, for example, within type 4 – the renascent nations, principally Egypt, China and Persia – we can single out Egypt, which appears to be the only example of a national formation at once unified and endowed continuously over the last sixteen centuries with a centralising state.

The critical analysis has led us to pre-concepts, which, employed as scientific hypotheses for the purposes of research, have enabled us to draw up useful typologies within each epistemological field. Is a third stage now possible – the restructuration of concepts, restoring to them their universality?

3.3   Restructuration of the conceptual apparatus

Once the nut has been broken, the elements of which it was composed as well as those which can go to make up a more comprehensive nut – based on the real world – can, possibly, contribute to the restructuration of concepts, ideas, notions, theories, of which the conceptual apparatus is itself composed.

In the first phase, the operation seems easy enough; from this coexisting sum of constituent elements, one could derive, at no further cost, the constitution of the conceptual totality. The given facts of the real world, the concrete existence of concrete societies located in time and space, would in the same way become the constituent assembly of the new conceptual world. But an assembly, however constituent it may be, does not produce a constitution simply because it exists. It allows a process to get under way under the best possible conditions – but that is all.

The process of theoretical elaboration has been defined as involving the restructuration of the conceptual apparatus of the social sciences. That means that the problems and difficulties will certainly be the same as those that arise in any process of theoretical elaboration. A certain number of problems and difficulties, however, adopt a specific character. That is why we must now go on to consider certain key points.

(a)   This process of theoretical elaboration will be no more than a simple juxtaposition of a panoply of elements – phenomena and analyses – to which we can turn, once two operations that will be discussed below have been carried out. In other words, we are not talking here of symbiosis, of an ordering (or equation) of positivist measurements possible at this stage of the work. The positivist temptation would be all the greater if it seemed to take as its starting-point the very terrain that had, so to speak, been overturned by critical research: should one not, out of loyalty to its very complexity, attempt to provide a detailed and precise description of this world of differences, and of contradictory or antagonistic 'others'? But that would leave us at the stage of the constitution of typologies or, at best, of a synchronisation of typologies. One can see how far this desire for rigour, with a positivist emphasis, can serve as an alibi and as fertile ground for a positivist approach. Models, equations, structures and interpolations will allow this fixed tableau to be animated; positivism will lead to artificiality, once the real movement of the world has been distorted.

As in all theoretical elaboration (but here perhaps more than most) it is important to emphasise the *critical synthesis* that characterises all theory. The essential thing is the critical comparative study of those among the constituent factors of the different typologies which appear capable of generalisation, that is of integration as constitutive components into the restructured concept. The other, more limited, sectoral factors will remain outside the strict domain of this restructuration.

(b)   In the first instance, this critical synthesis will allow the traditional conceptual apparatus to be restructured. And this restructuration will be concerned above all with the concepts, ideas, notions and theories that will be found at the pivotal points of the social sciences. This concern must take precedence over all other work done in the domain of concepts, to the extent that the former constitutes the root and the framework of the edifice as a whole. Concepts such as 'power', 'nation', 'culture', 'ideology', 'social control', 'social movement', 'state', 'social classes',

'socio-economic formation', among others, should take priority.

At this level of generality in theoretical elaboration, we shall rejoin directly the parallel dimension of the *philosophical critique*. The contribution of a theory rooted in the concrete social terrain itself cannot but serve to clarify the theoretical process and the epistemological effort as a whole – a process and an effort which, if left within the sole dimension of the philosophical critique, would risk being wrecked on the rocks of formalism. And this, it will be acknowledged, is a far from negligible consequence of the process outlined here.

(c)   Does this mean that the restructuration has to do only with the conceptual apparatus that was its starting-point? In other words, is the process exclusively conservative, or can it also contribute to a renewal?

Here we return to the initial point (Section 3.1). What we have to restructure is the only conceptual apparatus that the history of human societies has endowed us with; to that extent one might imagine that the process of restructuration – the central object of social theory as a whole – will accomplish only a clarified conservation-restructuration. In these terms, the conceptual apparatus would be regarded as a scientific research hypothesis, the only body of scientific research hypotheses that we have at our disposal.

If that is the main characteristic of the work in progress, it is very important to recognise that the two major sources of renewal and creativity in our era – the emergence of the Three Continents into the contemporary world; and the scientific and technological revolution – make it possible to elaborate a growing number of ideas, notions and analyses. These will mark the limits of a new epistemological field, and enable us to construct new bodies of theory and new concepts, precisely on the basis of the great upheaval that has taken place in the world and in our knowledge of the many levels and facets of existence.

In this outline, we have placed considerable emphasis on the first of these two factors – the emergence of the tricontinental sphere – for its emergence into view after its long sojourn in the shadows has overturned the whole social and political chessboard in a spectacular way, providing up to this point the principal source of renewal in the field of the social sciences. Yet it must be recognised that the second factor has entered the fray in every area of human existence, in all its forms, though it is equally true that the acceleration is less visible here, where the habits of conservation and delaying mechanisms are so much more developed.

4.   Orientations

It is useless to try to enclose a theoretical process of such depth within a methodological mould whose progress and outcome can be foreseen from the beginning; here as elsewhere, the future has yet to be shaped.

On the other hand, it is worth trying to illuminate some of the different problems that will accompany the theoretical process now under way, and whose tendential effects we should attempt to enumerate.

4.1

The fundamental characteristic of the theoretical approach envisaged here is that it is a *scientific* rather than an ideological approach. Technically, the method set out above is critical-historicist in its deep nature and comparativist, of necessity, in the methods it adopts. This is the result of the extreme diversity of social phenomena and societal formations in their national-cultural and civilisational framework, as it unfolds through time. It proceeds to a critique, that is a study of the concrete possibilities of these phenomena and formations. The purpose here is to test what part of the conceptual apparatus, itself taken here as a research hypothesis, remains true. Its objective, like that of all science, is to attain a higher level of knowledge and comprehension of the totality that it studies – that of all human societies.

The ideological approach – much in vogue under its different labels – operates at two levels: first of all, a Manichaean distinction ('bourgeois' or 'proletarian' science; 'reformism' or 'revolution', etc.), which eliminates at the outset whatever is incompatible with the world view that it adopts, rather than whatever does not correspond to the facts of the real world as we know it (which is the core of the scientific approach); then, there is an orientation of the critical analysis whose aim is to find at the end of the process – the restructuration of the conceptual apparatus of the social sciences – the options which were present or implicit at the outset. The restructuration would then be a conservation of what was postulated, duly improved and relocated.

This caution imposes itself because the theoretical level possesses its own specificity, defined here as the specificity of scientific research itself. But this research takes place in a given socio-cultural framework and historical environment; it is evident that the ideological option in all possible social theory is an objective fact that must be borne clearly in mind – a necessary and often unifying framework. The essential task is to point to each of the stages, to analyse their relations in terms of dialectical interaction rather than in intangible structural terms.

4.2

The whole broad and complex process in turn affects the epistemological field and the scientific disciplines, on the one hand, and the national-cultural spheres in their civilisational framework, on the other, in a word, the unfolding of the whole course of the history of human societies.

What is involved here, then, is neither craftsmanship nor individual skill. The facts should be assessed through the most highly perfected methods of primary and secondary analysis. Theoretical elaboration should be seen in two moments: group work, contradictory and multidisciplinary, which will yield collective works that can usefully establish comparative and contradictory typologies and problematics; and then, at a second moment, *interpretative syntheses*, where the mediating and formative role of certain thinkers and theorists will continue to confirm their decisive role at the level of theoretical preparation and crystallisation.

4.3

The most serious problem arises at the stage that one could call the *theoretical no man's land*.

If we recognise the fact of crisis and then, at a second stage which will produce a more determined resistance, the futility of reductionist approaches, there is a great danger of seeing the whole conceptual edifice, once broken down, as incapable of restoration.

Certainly one can sense there the breakdown of a whole conservative tradition which is at the heart of Western-centrism. Is it not the case, in the end, that what has been gained has been the result of a long historical process? And the fact that this historical evolution had been marked by Western hegemony, which could not but accentuate the decline of the Orient, makes of what has been gained a very suspect heritage. In the end, what is done is done: the world is as it has been shaped by the West since the Renaissance, and it is and will remain so against all and any objections. Let the other societies try their luck; at best one can expect a hesitant progress – but chaos and impotence seem all the more assured.

These are the secondary obstacles, for the problem is a real one. It is true that the introduction of the hitherto marginalised worlds into the normality of science is provoking profound unease at the level of theory. It is equally true that those unusual facts that we have been obliged, willy nilly, to integrate into the analysis in progress have made it very difficult to envisage the critical syntheses of a truly univeral type to which we have referred (Sections 3.1 and 3.2). It is also true that our knowledge of non-Western societies, with a very few exceptions, and despite the progress that has been made in the present period, has scarcely reached the level of precision demanded in the transition from the stage of integration to the level of theoretical synthesis. And it has to be recognised that the rise to full movement of these worlds, the emergence of the national-cultural factor within the civilisational framework – the plurality and multifaceted nature of the world, which we are only now beginning to recognise, a heterogeneity which has only now begun to be visible – has created a whole new theoretical climate, very far from the flat and reassuring tranquility of other days.

Every possible theory that aspires to be scientific must acquire a rigour that is often expressed through a formalisation that can be expressed in mathematical terms; this means the definition of terms, the precise characterisation of relations of interaction, and a predictable and determined process of maintenance and evolution. Does this mean that what is clearly defined is equally clearly going to happen? To assume that would be to identify the demand for rigour, the possibility of grasping the deep content of the phenomena and the concepts studied, with the possibility of describing them in the current language, or if you wish through the optimal linguistic modes of the *hegemonic culture*. And this would convert the entirely formal question of the possibility of linguistic expression into the criterion of scientific intelligibility itself. Science would be reduced to common sense; dialectics would give way to formal analysis.

This is the objective convergence of intellectual influences which has led many researchers and social scientists to question the very possibility of working towards a profound renewal of social theory, that is, to challenge the possibility of building a new conceptual apparatus capable of accounting for the integration of the world. That is the constraining influence of the *dominant ideology*, in its classical and its pseudo-Marxist variants; it is a subtle domain, the intellectual ghetto of the experts in epistemological refinement and methodological sophistication united in a common disdain for the concrete history of the concrete societies of the real world.

The theoretical no man's land is not a conjunctural phenomenon. It gives the measure of the profound and sometimes radical – that is revolutionary – changes in progress and under way from one end of the earth on which we live to the other. Nothing lives easily through periods of rupture; for these are also the periods when the great forward thrusts of men and civilisations are set in motion. That is to say that the time of the great theoretical syntheses only points towards the horizon; the process under way is a critical evaluation of what is, rather than a reorganisation of the facts of the real world. So the present effort at conceptualisation is only the incomplete outline of a theory, a prospective marking out of the terrain – but a task as yet unfinished.

That is the difficult atmosphere in which, for a relatively long time to come, the effort to promote a future social theory must survive. If we are to refashion the theoretical pantheon – itself the product of a particular stage – in the image of the *social dialectics of the real world*, we must consent to live out the optimistic tragedy of the real world of our time. Then, the necessary distancing between the socio-political process and the level of science and of theory will no longer be a form of evasion, but a process of deepening. That is the orientation through which the future of social theory can be forged.

3

Meaningful Social Theory: the Cross-civilisational Perspective

Where there are three men walking together, one or other of them will certainly be able to teach me something.

Confucius

Perhaps the whole question reduces to the active practice of humility and brotherly love. We need a real conviction that all racialism, all self-satisfied beliefs of cultural superiority, are a denial of the world-community.

Joseph Needham

1.   The present status of theory in the social sciences

1.1

Never before have the human and social sciences, or the scientists, borne witness to such an explosion of theory, under its many labels: theory building, theoretical systems, theoretical essays, readers on theory, epistemological works on the theory of theory (a sort of 'Prolegomena to all possible theories'), theoretical manifestos, philosophy, sociology and psychology of theoretical processes, etc. In their wake, the concept of theory itself begins to waver; from the classical philosophical position to a highly fluctuating and ambiguous status in recent approaches.[1] By and large one can reasonably see this process of theorising as a response to the deeply felt need in the human and social sciences to find a new, universally valid, structured interpretation of societies in our contemporary world.

1.2

On the other hand, our world is now entering an historical phase of flux at all levels and in every field. The wind of change is felt primarily in the sphere of the new patterns of world power in the wake of Yalta, itself the peak of the historical moment of Western hegemony (between the Renaissance and 1945–9). A surging wave of societal processes, specifically the contemporary wave of national and social revolutions, of liberation and revolution, is clearly regarded as disruptive of the old stability, and often decried as marginal, abnormal, irrelevant and exceptional – the implicit assumption being that 'normality' can be defined as the legacy and manifestation of societal processes within Western hegemony.

How then can we relate the yearning for a universally valid theory on the one hand, and the disruption of the societal equilibrium on the other?

1.3

A tentative answer would be that there is a direct, organic relationship between the two. For it could be argued that the more our world tends towards a centrifugal pattern, the more the human spirit feels the need for that universally valid, highly structured interpretation of the societies of our time – what is called social theory. The theoretical explosion, then, can be seen as an heuristic process directed at the recovery of a lost unity. Equally, and perhaps more forcefully, it could be accounted for as the result of a widely felt need for emotional and deep psychological security in the face of the decline of that guarantee provided by the happy interlude of the 'one world' approach. In other words, theory appears here as a process of seeking security.

1.4

There are in the social sciences two main kinds of theorising:

1. The deepening of the epistemological approach, with an increasing stress on methodological refinement, conceptual sophistication, and an increasingly analytical, self-contained analysis. Security is sought in the perfection of the model. This model itself is more often than not derived from a formal critique of earlier concepts, that is in an analytical, deductive manner, rather than as a result of confronting the evolving

concrete reality of our concrete world. From this follows the increasing importance of linguistics and mathematics as the most formalised branches of knowledge. The divorce from reality leads directly to a negation of historicism, of historical dialectics, turning instead to neo-positivism in the guise of structuralist philosophy and its manifestation in the social sciences – functionalism.

2. From the mainstream of concrete societal processes there emerges another type of theory, which claims to echo the mood of the times. An examination of this second type, however, shows that it is in fact ideology disguised as social theory; that is, political visions and declarations of intent rather than a scientific, objective, critical interpretation of real societal processes. Clearly, the general framework here is Utopian, and the reality presented or negated in terms of that Utopian goal.

Thus both types of theory in the social sciences today belong to the same general type – neo-positivism or fideism, that is, structuralism in philosophy and functionalism in the social sciences – what we have proposed to call 'the negative idea',[2] the dominant ideology of the period of the decline of Western civilisational world hegemony.

2.   The rise of formal-reductionist comparativism

2.1

Comparativism is a very recent phenomenon across the whole range of human and social sciences. The formative classical period of modern times (the eighteenth and nineteenth centuries) rarely shows any interest in comparativism. From Montesquieu to Max Weber, the major figures busily derive social theory from case studies, with a very narrow comparative fringe, mainly as an additional reference to the case under study. Such works include Montesquieu's *L'Esprit des Lois*, Marx's *Capital*, Comte's *Cours de philosophie positiviste*, Maine's *Ancient Law*; others, which show the first signs of comparativism, include Morgan's *Ancient Society*, Engels's *Origin of the Family, Private Property and the State*, and the work of Herbert Spencer, J. S. Mill. W. Sombart and E. A. Westermarck, *inter alia*. Yet we then meet major figures – Durkheim, Tonnies, Simmel – who are intent on developing theory from the in-depth study of select cases or scientific sectors, in the first decade of the present century. It is certainly true, of course, that in earlier periods, key formative minds like Plato, Aristotle and particularly Ibn Khaldoun had been more at ease in evolving social theory from a comparative standpoint, though their frame of reference was necessarily limited in geographical terms (to Greece and the Hellenic world, for Plato and Aristotle; to North Africa, in the case of Ibn Khaldoun).

In what respect, if at all, can one speak of 'comparativism' at this early and indeed very recent stage in the constitution of the networks of the human and social sciences? It seems reasonable to assume that at this stage, comparativism is not regarded as a necessity. But it is worth adding that, paradoxically, the key formative minds of classical social and political thought in the Eastern Mediterranean were more advanced in this respect than the eighteenth- and nineteenth-century European founders of the human and social sciences and their theory. It is not really a paradox. For in ancient times, and precisely in the Mediterranean area, the range, intensity and continuity of the process of exchange – from commerce to metaphysics – were such as to demand explicitly the attention of the major thinkers, immersed as they were in their naturally historically and geographically conditioned environment. Yet Plato, Aristotle, Ibn Khaldoun are not alone. Seminal figures in the other centre of the Orient – Asia – such as Sun Tzu in China (*c.* 400–320 B.C.) and Nguyen Trai in Vietnam (A.D. 1380–1442), display a parallel range of comparative interests in the Asian-Chinese sphere proper. We can sense no such need in Europe, from the establishment of Church hegemony and the Renaissance, for it is a self-contained hegemonic centre, as yet secure and unchallenged. That is the reason for the lack of comparativism in the first, formative period of the human and social sciences in modern Europe – notwithstanding some notable exceptions.

2.2

The second stage in the development of the social and human sciences, of modern social and political theory proper, can be dated in the West from the last quarter of the nineteenth century onwards, from the Victorian age to Yalta. This was the stage of imperialism, of rising tension within the system between Western imperialist hegemony and the national liberation movements. These tensions can be classified under three main headings, on the basis of their emergence as societal waves through time:

(*a*)   tensions between constituent members of the Western hegemonic system (the intra-European wars, between two states and between coalitions of rival states, culminating in the 1914–18 intra-European war, usually referred to as the 'First World War');

(b) tensions between major constituent members of the Western hegemonic system on the one hand, and major constituent members of the then dominated world – principally the Orient: Asia and the Islamic-Arab areas – on the other (from the rise of the populist, revolutionary national movements of the early nineteenth century in Egypt, Algeria, Morocco, Persia, to the victory of the Chinese Revolution in 1949, and the war of victorious liberation in 1973);

(c) tensions between major constituent members of the Western hegemonic system, as from their division into two antagonistic blocs of states with diverging socio-economic and ideological systems (from the revolution of October 1917 to the 'Cold War', 'peaceful coexistence' and now 'constructive co-operation').

A survey of the field reveals that the major efforts, initiatives and achievements in the field of social theory from a comparativist standpoint occur in the first two areas listed above, and this precisely because of the rapid emergence and importance of the previously dominated areas of Asia, Africa and, later, Latin America. The same survey also confirms what was implicit in the 'peaceful coexistence' system – that the two socio-political-ideological blocs in the Western hegemonic sphere represent two component parts of a single civilisational sphere – the West – embracing two socio-political-ideological systems as well as several cultural areas (Europe, the United States, Eastern Europe) and nation-states. It is that which explains the current attempt to move from peaceful coexistence to constructive co-operation. Comparativism, however, remains at the level of politics and strategy: both blocs are involved in an advance, via productivism, towards the goal of all advanced industrialised societies; their divergences arise at the level of official value-systems, decision-making processes and patterns of power within each bloc.

In this area, there have been two key figures in our time: Max Weber and Joseph Needham. Hitherto, scant attention has been paid to Weber's transition from the level of comparative European studies to comparative East–West studies. Before and during the 1914–18 war Weber, in his capacity as the theoretician-ideologue of the German Empire, developed his *idealtypus* concept; its object was to enhance the validity of

Germany's struggle for hegemony over Europe. Later, he became immersed in the culture of such distant civilisations as China and India. For the first time in the field of social theory, there were minds in the West oriented towards the world as a whole, and taking it as the field for theoretical work; in this, they went far beyond the limits of the prevailing Western-centred approach. Yet it remains the privilege of the Master of Gonville and Caius to have produced the only major encyclopedic work of our time – *Science and Civilisation in China* – which has been growing since 1954 under the towering direction and inspiration of Joseph Needham. Here is a work that can be situated on the other side of the river, standing face to face with Diderot's *Encyclopédie* and the *Britannica*. Certainly the work is primarily devoted to China; yet key works both integral to the work and contained in accompanying volumes deal specifically with East–West comparisons in the attempt to answer basic questions at a theoretical level about science, technology, social organisation, culture, civilisation, philosophy and religion.[3] The very nature of Needham's work – in terms of sheer volume as well as its intricacy – has as yet prevented us from grasping the essential character of his contribution; and as yet there is no sign that it has been absorbed into the mainstream of comparative studies and social theory. Nevertheless, the whole process *is* beginning.

2.3

Parallel to this major development, there has also emerged another stream of comparative studies, which I propose to call 'formal-reductionist comparative studies'. The perception of the accelerated rate of societal change in our changing world has been increasing since 1917, and particularly since the world economic depression of 1929–32. The break-up of the Western hegemonic system from 1945 onwards, and the rapid ascent of the Orient, together with the wave of national and social revolutions, have encouraged a new crop of comparative studies, concerned with the development of social theory. Side by side with Parsons's 'grand theory' – the ideological platform of United States imperialism at its peak – dozens of PhDs, essays and symposia have concerned themselves with comparativism. And the instrument of that comparativism was to be quantification; the variables would be selected from among the postulated goals of the hegemonic world, and their frequency and range then tested in random surveys. This brought us comparisons of Turkey and Japan; of linguistic frequency in Peru, India and Canada and its relation to types of nation; of economic development in Bolivia and Egypt; of religions, or religious ideologies in Catholic France and Buddhist Vietnam, etc. Any societal totality, any nation, could, it seemed, be compared with any other such unit; they would be labelled according to pre-established goals, and sometimes considered merely out of curiosity or para-culture. Comparativism, as a result, has become fashionable, respectable and much sought after. At the political level, its object was as we have described it above; its scientific object was to process 'other' contemporary societies, and nations, into the pattern(s) of the Western hegemonic centres.

Reductionism, in a word, disguised as 'comparativism-leading-to-universalism'; and a reductionism still rooted in quantitative techniques, that is, formalism and formalisation, renamed 'methodology'.

Yet at the same time a deep dissatisfaction has begun to be expressed, particularly in the most recent period (1948–73). Comparative studies of the prevailing type do very little comparing; and even when they do, they do not add to our explanations, interpretation or understanding of a changing world. Yet it is precisely now, when the world has been finally brought together through imperialism and socialism, oppression and revolution, science and technology (particularly via the mass media), geo-politics and ideology, that the need is most urgently felt for a vision capable of unifying different societies, of combining dialectically the one and the many. How, then, could this challenge be met?

3. Positions

3.1 The framework of comparativism

The preliminary step, before embarking on the path we have been advocating, is to introduce some form of coherent typology of the societal units to be compared. In other words, before comparing, we should really know what we are comparing.

The framework of comparativism consists of three major, interwoven types of circle:

a) Civilisations This is the outer, more general circle, defined on the basis of Needham's approach: (i) the circle of Indo-Aryan civilisation; (ii) the circle of Chinese civilisation. This leaves Latin America unaccounted for at this level of analysis; we shall deal with that question under (*b*).

(b) Cultural areas   The mediating circle, often confused with the civilisational circle (as in Toynbee's work, whose successive attempts at establishing typologies can usefully be followed). Broadly, the following cultural areas can be defined:

1. within the Indo-Aryan civilisational circle:
   Egyptian, Persian and Mesopotamian Antiquity;
   Graeco-Roman Antiquity;
   the European cultural area;
   the North American cultural area;
   major parts of the Indo-European cultural area in Latin America;
   the sub-Saharan African cultural area;
   the Islamic cultural area, in part, that is, the Arab-Islamic and Persian-Islamic cultural areas (excluding the Asian-Islamic cultural area, which falls within the Chinese civilisational circle).

2. within the Chinese civilisational circle:
   China proper;
   Japan;
   Mongolia-Central Asia;
   Vietnam and South-east Asia;
   the Indian subcontinent;
   Oceania (with the exception of Australia and New Zealand);
   the Asian-Islamic cultural area (from Persia to the Philippines).

These two major outer circles should be interpreted on the basis of the introduction of the fundamental historical differences between the worlds of mankind: the West and the Orient.

In fact, the 'Orient' can be seen to consist of the following constituents:

1. the circle of Chinese civilisation and its cultural areas;
2. the civilisational-cultural circle of Islam, the one major link between the circle of Indo-Aryan civilisation and the circle of Chinese civilisation; both a mediation and an area of maximal tensions;[4]
3. parts of the Indo-European cultural area of Latin America, directly linked to Africa (specifically Brazil, but also the Caribbean);
4. the sub-Saharan cultural area.

The 'West' is therefore composed of the major sectors of Indo-Aryan civilisation.

(c) Nations (or 'national formations') The units basic to the very existence, continuity, unfolding and evolution of macro-societal processes. We have suggested a typology based on five categories:

1. the fundamental nations, also described as *renascent nations* (Egypt, China, Persia, as well as Turkey, Vietnam, Mexico and Morocco);
2. the European, hence Western type of nation-state;
3. the new nation-state moving towards unification. Both the new nation-states strictly speaking (Ethiopia, Ghana, Mali, Burma, Thailand) and the national formations within the framework of multinational groups (Armenia, Georgia, Uzbekistan, etc.);
4. the dualistic Indian, later European nation-state, mainly in Latin America;
5. the new states with a national vocation (mainly in different parts of sub-Saharan Africa, as well as a minor sector of Central and South America).

The key distinction between the three circles can only be dealt with here in very broad outline.

Civilisational areas would be defined on the basis of the general conception of the relations between cultures, nations, societal formations on the one hand, the time-dimension on the other. More than a world view strictly speaking, it is this philosophical relationship with 'time, the field of human development' and its consequences, that can be said to distinguish the Orient from the West. Cultural areas can then be seen as societal groupings sharing a common *Weltanschauung*, more in terms of historical-geographical determinism through history (both ecological and geo-political) than of philosophy proper, a conception of the world often expressed in a limited set of main languages, and sometimes in one only (Arabic, Chinese, English, Persian, Japanese, in each of the cultural areas concerned). Nations, or national formations, are more easily demarcated, once agreement is reached on the necessary structuring typology.

And yet, having posited as the framework of comparativism these three major, interwoven types of circles, we have done no more than provide a topographical description (anatomy) of the field of comparativism. We must now go on to relate dialectically the different units within each of the three circles to the surrounding two circles. This, precisely, is the object of our introduction of the concept of specificity.[5]

4.   On the feasibility of comparativism and its prerequisites

From the outlines we have given, it becomes clear that comparativism is not a matter of techniques or methodology – although techniques and methodology will need to be developed considerably if they are to meet the needs of comparativism within the cross-civilisational perspective.

The various stages in the history of comparativism in the human and social sciences, as well as in social theory proper, as described above (Sections 1 and 2), can be related to precise stages in the evolution of patterns of power in the world. Therefore, comparativism within the framework of a cross-civilisational perspective can only be proposed as the foundation of meaningful social theory on the basis of a combination of the following factors:

1. The emerging new patterns of power in the world after Yalta; the emergence of the Orient, in renaissance and revolution; the wave of national and social revolutions in the world; the impact of the new levels of science and technology on industrial change.

2. The clear perception that the rules obtaining say from a century ago until Yalta no longer apply. Social scientists and social theoreticians alike should understand clearly that the interactional-dialectical process in the concrete world can and must be reflected in a parallel process in the realms of science and theory. It is no longer possible for a select, self-appointed group of social scientists and theoreticians belonging to one, hitherto privileged sector of the world (Western Europe and North America) to contain such a movement; the more so since this movement by its very nature, content, objective, means the end of this sector's political and cultural-ideological hegemony over the whole planet. Only teams of genuinely representative national-cultural areas, representing as it were the different schools of thought in each of these areas – and not the all-too-willing 'yes-men' – can undertake such a vast task in a meaningful and effective way. The field is open to all; but the voices that will be listened to, and their ideas acted upon, will necessarily be fewer in number, for the reasons we have already suggested.

3. The capacity jointly to organise such projects, bringing to bear political resources (the states and parties concerned), cultural resources (both academic and research, as well as broadly cultural factors) will depend largely upon the institutional facilities and political philosophies of all the major partners concerned. To that effect, the opening up of new

fields on the basis of the vision outlined here can have a catalysing influence upon the whole process, which is now in a formative period.

Meaningful social theory, therefore, can and should play an important role as a mediating influence throughout the very complex and conflictive process of the restructuration of the pattern of world power in our times. It could also quite validly provide a broad and noble field for dedicated scientists and theoreticians with a vision of history. And in our view, they would benefit from that new standpoint, the cross-civilisational perspective, where they will join hands with vast and powerful human, societal and cultural-scientific potentials.

That would be the promise of the 'sociological imagination', coming together in common activity at the level and in the framework we are here proposing to all concerned.

4

Sociology and Economic History: an Essay on Mediation

Economic historians working on the Middle East – and particularly on its modern period – have been subject for a generation or a little more to the impact of a complexity of factors of change; these factors have reshaped fields of study hitherto as remote from one another as social science (including economic history) and regional studies (that is, the study of the underdeveloped Three Continents, including the Middle East). From the point of view of methodology – which must be scientific and generally valid, rather than limited to one region – we should question the uses and limits of economic history, not *per se* but within the framework of the social sciences. This analysis must be concerned with the field under study, with its specific features – the modern Middle East, with special reference to Egypt – yet at the same time be located within the broader framework of Asia, Africa and Latin America.

The limited vision of modern Orientalism has its principal source in the inadequate training and preparation of specialists in the 'modern' disciplines.[1] I would suggest that the central problem is the narrow way in which the problem is posed. For methodology is but the prospecting head of different social philosophies applied to the concrete reality.

1. Economic history and national development

The science of economics, or political economy as we know it today, retains few of the features attributed to it by the classical writers, like Plato and Aristotle or a founding father like Ibn Khaldoun. Today it is acknowledged that it was born in the transition from feudalism to capitalism in Europe, from scholasticism to *The Wealth of Nations*. Mercantile and later industrial capitalism had to resolve a number of problems: the (apparent) nature of the economic obstacles to progress; the role of the different factors of economic activity; the objectives of that activity; the search for moral and political justifications for that activity; and so on. Adam Smith's work of 1776 contrasts sharply with the happy pastoral interlude of the Physiocrats. By then, a new socio-economic formation – capitalism – was coming into being; a new class – the bourgeoisie, and later the industrial sector of the bourgeoisie – was emerging, which would finally come to power with the victory of the French Revolution.

Economic analysis or economic history? The question posed by *The Wealth of Nations* was raised again in *Capital* (1867–94). The specialists in the various fields of political economy and the emerging social sciences were compelled to revise their approaches in the face of these two towering works, which combined economic history, economic analysis, social analysis and philosophy.[2] They had set out not to describe but to interpret what Smith had called *homo economicus*, social causation, and the dynamics of human history as Marx had understood it – and not just as a collection of facts, nor merely by rearranging the order of their presentation. Meanwhile, positivism was beginning to emerge in the wake of empiricism and of the dominant ideology of the nineteenth century. Thus in modern times, and in the domain of the economy itself, these two thinkers confirmed Oscar Lange's thesis that 'the existence of a scientific knowledge of economics depends on the existence of a social class that seeks to discover in reality the economic relations, the laws that govern them, a class whose aspirations express themselves in progressive ideology, and an ideology that unveils reality'.[3]

The rise of the historical school (W. Roscher, B. Hildebrand, K. Knies, etc.) from 1843 onwards, and the work of Richard Jones, more or less coincide with the beginnings of economic history, conceived at that point as the history of economic ideas.[4] A brief survey of the work of that century in the field of 'economic history' shows that the definition embraces three different fields: (i) the history of economic ideas and systems; (ii) the history of the economic development or evolution of a single country or group of countries; (iii) the history of specific areas of economic activity (industry, transport, etc.).

The economic history of the Three Continents, including the Middle East, recent as it is, falls within the second field and leads on to the third. There has rarely been any serious effort to analyse the movement of economic ideas, or to relate them to the general stream of the history of ideas. It was assumed that colonial countries could not evolve an autonomous body of theoretical ideas, let alone of economic theory.

Broadly speaking, and for obvious reasons, this continued to be the situation in the main ex-colonial countries until the 1930s. That is why it is so important to clarify the nature of the work done by the classical European and North American economic historians as a whole; this will enable us to bring into perspective the work of their colleagues in the ex-colonial countries, and more particularly in the Middle East.

The basic postulate of economic history, and indeed of all the social sciences, is that the patterns and concepts evolved in the advanced capitalist countries of Europe and North America have a universal validity. Obviously, the world was not made up of like units, but it was assumed that the differences could be minimised in defining the rational principles which would ensure their 'normal' development in conformity with the model offered by those countries that were in the forefront of progress. It will be clear that this basic postulate has its origins in general humanist philosophy, or even perhaps in the evolutionary philosophy which permeated the field of social studies towards the end of the nineteenth century. It was reinforced by the tacit assumption that what was good for the West could not but be a guideline for the rest of the world, for example the colonial countries. Thus Euro-centrism gradually came to take the place of evolutionary humanism, as the colonial countries struggling for national liberation came into the limelight. Naturally, this tendency was reinforced as the nineteenth century drew to its end by the concentration in the West of academic life and institutions. Centres of specialised scientific education; libraries; publishing and the press; the leading scholars and teachers, provided the major sources of support in thought and action for the universal postulate in this field. The whole conceptual framework of the social sciences was, and remains broadly to this day, Western in its origins and orientations. In the field of economics this tendency was considerably reinforced by the leading economic role of the major capitalist countries in world politics, by the creation of a world economic market and the forced integration into it of the colonial and dependent countries, and by the hegemony of the West over that market. The traditional cultures and religions of the non-European type continued to dominate the greater part of the world; only in the field of economic activity were most peoples and countries compelled, as it were, to follow the Western road.

Asa Briggs has recently pointed to the fact that 'it is primarily through the development of ''sub-histories'' that theory has been injected into history. Economic history provides one of the best examples.' The main influence is Marx, followed by Max Weber. 'The theories will rest on "concepts", "frameworks" and "techniques of thinking"; when the historian begins to study a particular problem he will start with these as data.'[5] This 'two-way traffic between history and economics' has been developing with growing intensity in (normal) works of economic history and theory; and specialists have found it necessary to collaborate with anthropologists, sociologists, psychologists and other social scientists.

Gradually, the problems to be studied appeared as complex totalities, rather than as separate phenomena. That is the origin of social history as a discipline, which soon superseded traditional historiography, notably in France with Marc Bloch's *Annales* school.

Economic changes, their rate and scale; economic growth and stagnation; prosperity, economic development and social values; what did these economic notions and concepts reveal when economic historians applied them to the Three Continents?

Let us now consider the kind of problems that present themselves. They seem to lie within two areas:

(a)   The type of economic milieu. Everything points to the fact that we are dealing here with heterogeneous units – and this at several levels. We know of the 'two sectors' in underdeveloped or developing economies, that is, the traditional and the modern, the archaic and the developed, forward-looking sectors.[6] We can now see how 'economic development' can be combined with 'economic backwardness', though much still remains to be explored if we are to attain a meaningful level of analysis.[7] The contrast between the old nation-states (Egypt, China, Persia, Turkey, etc.) and other types of 'national formation' – including the so-called 'new nations' – and the problem of artificial colonial frontiers has brought into question the operational concept applied to the 'Third World'.[8] The image of broad devastated areas beset with famine and death looms large in the manifestos, the directives and the minds of the *guerrilleros*; in fact, it has come to be accepted as an aspect of our contemporary human condition.

This points to heterogeneity, and not merely to a dichotomy; not a combination of old and new, but the consequence of complex, divergent factors at work throughout the social fabric of these countries – a basic incompleteness, a fundamental imbalance, unease and disorder. In such a human realm one can no longer search for *homo economicus*.

(b)   And yet, despite this basic structure, chaos has been consistently and decisively averted in the old nation-states, and the will to do the same

exists in the other categories too. How, then, can we explain this tendency to cohesion amid heterogeneity?

In the West, specialists and public opinion alike have gradually come to realise that beyond these economic disparities and this incoherence there lies a whole, deeply entrenched stratum of beliefs, customs, ways of life, ideas and systems of thought, a will-to-be, a collective, even a national will. The source of this national will must be sought in an implicit ideology[9] which is, so to speak, the nerve-centre of its deep structure; this ideology represents the largest part of the iceberg, the hidden part beyond statistics, surveys, polls and the like. It is something global, a submerged, specifically national, socio-historical structure which no social analyst can afford to ignore or underestimate. This, then, is my working hypothesis, and this chapter will seek to prove it correct.

That said, and the problems defined, we can now go on to consider the work of economic historians in the field that concerns us.

1. A first set of books and studies provide factual surveys – mainly descriptive, sometimes analytical. In the latter case, the analysis is usually set against a sketchy 'historical background', except when its starting-point is a general assumption about Oriental religion in its relations to economic activity. Under the influence of Colin Clark, a whole trend of economic thinking has tried and is still trying to evaluate the economic development of the ex-colonial countries through a unified set of statistical, mathematical criteria, particularly international 'comparisons' of national income;[10] accountancy and econometrics have pushed historicism firmly to one side, ignoring the problem of specific national characteristics.[11]

2. Studies set against a 'historical background' usually start from general postulates about the interrelation between Oriental religions and modern economic activity. Underdevelopment, and the prospects for the future, are explained in terms of permanent structural units, and learned disquisitions on *homo islamicus* are propounded to fill the inevitable gaps left by the work described in the preceding paragraph.

3. There is, however, a third group of studies, of more recent appearance, which sets out to combine the use of modern analytical tools with a social analysis set in an historical perspective. The main issues posed in this body of work are discontinuity, heterogeneity and the specific character of economic development in different countries of the Three Continents; the interrelation between past history and present

development, between ideology and socio-economic structure; the reasons for the uneven evolution of different countries; the role of voluntarism and political activism, etc.

The hypotheses formulated have provoked considerable theoretical discussions concerning the direction of future practical activity. In both fields – theory and practice – the work of this newly constituted group aims to establish precise historical relations between the universal and the particular, between science and national development, which are both significant and effective.

2. The uses of sociology

It has recently been forcefully argued by Raymond Aron that the dividing line between the two sociologies – Western and Soviet, bourgeois-liberal and Marxist – is now in process of being replaced by a new division, between empiricist-experimental and theoretical currents.[12] And although it seems that Marxist sociological writing still stands within the realm of theoretical sociology, major works by prominent Western liberal sociologists (Aron himself is at the forefront) suggest that the two intersect in many sectors and instances.

Clearly, if classical economic history, in its application to the Three Continents, invites severe criticism for its lack of theoretical insight into the *nationalitarian* process, then the help we require at this time from sociology will not come from its empirical-experimental sector. In fact, the sociological theory which we are now turning to is not a philosophical digression on society, but the very precise conceptual elaboration of sociological findings within the framework of history.

Marx and Weber, albeit in different ways, are in the forefront. Our generation, so different from theirs in having witnessed the appearance and growth of socialist states, the resurgence of national movements and the awakening of the ex-colonial world, has evolved a sociology which is gradually coming to be recognised as more adequate than the previously dominant schools of thought. This is perhaps especially true in our specific field, so rich in new, non-classical phenomena which undermine the received ideas.

For its scope and vision, its passion and its insight, let alone its merits in classical scientific terms, C. Wright Mills's *The Sociological Imagination* (1959) has impressed a great many social scientists and non-specialists alike as a turning-point in the intellectual history of our times, as well as an inspiration and a guide to method for those whose work is concerned with the new problems raised by the profound transformations taking place in the contemporary world. Three points require some brief consideration:

(a)   Currently, sociology is considered to be two things at once: a vision of things, and a specialised discipline concerned with social institutions, both material and spiritual. As a vision of things, it is only now beginning to take shape. 'The sociological imagination' enables us to grasp history and biography, and the relation between them within society,

by asking three types of question:

1) What is the structure of the particular society as a whole? What are its essential components, and how are they related to one another? How does it differ from other varieties of social order? Within it, what is the meaning of any particular feature for its continuance and for its change?

2) Where does this society stand in human history? What are the mechanics by which it is changing? What is its place within and its meaning for the development of humanity as a whole? How does any particular feature we are examining affect, and how is it affected by, the historical period in which it moves? And this period – what are its essential features? How does it differ from other periods? What are its characteristic ways of history-making?

3) What varieties of men and women now prevail in this society and in this period? And what varieties are coming to prevail? In what ways are they selected and formed, liberated and repressed, made sensitive and blunted? What kinds of 'human nature' are revealed in the conduct and character we observe in this society in this period? And what is the meaning for 'human nature' of each and every feature of the society we are examining?

Whether the point of interest is a great power state or a minor literary mood, a family, a prison, a creed – these are the kinds of questions the best social analysts have asked. They are the intellectual pivots of classic studies of man in society – and they are the questions inevitably raised by any mind possessing the sociological imagination. For that imagination is the capacity to shift from one perspective to another – from the political to the psychological; from examination of a single family to comparative assessment of the national budgets of the world; from the theological school to the military establishment; from considerations of an oil industry to studies of contemporary poetry. It is the capacity to range from the most impersonal and remote transformations to the most intimate features of the human self – and to see the relations between the two.[13]

I have quoted at length from this first work on the 'sociological imagination' because it draws together all the problems raised in Section 1, and clearly shows the spirit in which it is proposed to use sociology to overcome the difficulties which classical economic history now faces.

(b)   The main issue – once we have reached agreement on the relations between the different social sciences and their respective subdivisions – is how to integrate the historical dimension into social studies.

We are all familiar with Ferdinand Braudel's distinction between the three levels of history: short-range micro-history at one extreme and long-range, structural history at the other; between them stands an intermediate, medium-range 'conjunctural' history. In his view it is the second level that unites history with sociology.[14] And the middle-range history that is our central concern cannot fail to show traces of this earlier symbiosis. Hence the broad acceptance of Wright Mills's thesis that 'history is the shank of social study', and of his conception that 'all sociology worthy of the name is "historical sociology" '.[15] Several reasons can be put forward to explain this intimate connection between history and sociology, and its applicability to all societies.

In our statement of what-is-to-be-explained, we need the fuller range that can be provided only by knowledge of the historical varieties of human society . . . . A-historical studies usually tend to be static or very short-term studies of limited milieux . . . . Knowing that what we are studying is subject to change, on the simplest of descriptive levels we must ask: What are the salient trends? To answer that question we must make a statement of at least 'from what' and 'to what' . . . . Longer-term trends are usually needed, if only in order to overcome historical provincialism: the assumption that the present is a sort of autonomous creation.[16]

A second thesis follows: if 'historical change *is* change of social relations, of the relations among their component parts', it follows that the social scientist 'when he compares, becomes aware of the historical as intrinsic to what he wants to understand and not merely as "general background" '.[17]

The third thesis is based on Marx's famous 'principle of historical specificity'. Does it imply that the past dominates and shapes both the present and the future? T. B. Bottomore has recently stressed the fact that the whole range of national phenomena (as well as the bureaucratic rationalisation of society) remained unrecognised until Weber.[18] Marx's principle, therefore, would refer 'first, to a guide-line: any given society is to be understood in terms of the specific period in which it exists', and second 'that within this historical type various mechanisms of change come to some specific kind of intersection'. Wright Mills, however, goes further in exposing Marx's ignorance of the scope and significance of the national process.

> It is, of course, quite clear that to understand a slow-moving society, trapped for centuries in a cycle of poverty and tradition and disease and ignorance, requires that we study the historical ground, and the persistent historical mechanisms of its terrible entrapment in its own history. Explanation of that cycle, and of the mechanics of each of its phases, requires a very deep-going historical analysis.[19]

The reference here is to Asia, Africa and Latin America, but also in some ways to North America.

> It is only by comparative studies that we can become aware of the *absence* of certain historical phases from a society, which is often quite essential to understanding its contemporary shape . . . . A retreat from history makes it impossible – and I choose the word with care – to understand precisely the most contemporary features of this one society which is a historical structure that we cannot hope to understand unless we are guided by the sociological principle of historical specificity.[20]

(c)　Historical specificity should not lead to immobility and stagnation. 'We must often study history in order to get rid of it . . . . Rather than "explain" something as a "persistence from the past", we ought to ask "why has it persisted?" ' Hence 'it is very often a good rule first to attempt to explain its contemporary features in terms of their contemporary function'.[21] For history, conceived as a non-revokable condemna-

tion, can block the way to evolution and render 'the present as history', in Paul Sweezy's excellent phrase, simply non-existent, as the present would be but a contemporary image of the historical past. 'The national mould of historical composition encourages the use of stereotypes, including stereotypes about national character'; herein, as Asa Briggs forcefully points out,[22] lies the danger of Weber's 'ideal-types'.

Typology in its application to the whole ex-colonial world is a veiled racism. In place of and in contrast to this static approach, the principle of historical specificity, precisely because it introduces the notion of history, leads on directly to the concepts of evolution and change, and these in their turn demand the introduction of critical tools. The central question as far as the present is concerned becomes 'why?', and with regard to the future 'how?'

How are we to conceive the principle of historical specificity in the light of the sociological imagination as it applies to our specific concern, that is, economic history?

1. Since we are dealing with a part of the world with a very long historical tradition of ethnic existence, and in some cases of national cohesion, our first aim should be to study in depth the long history of these countries; not as a record of events but as a sequence of socio-economic formations. We should then try to isolate those features which appear consistently, carefully distinguish their shape and the degree of their impact in different historical periods, and reach thus towards what would appear to be the central core, the kernel of any particular historical tradition – the historical specificity of a given society.

2. This kernel should be conceived as a factor both of continuity and of change. Its influence on continuity is far greater and more direct; in the final analysis, this kernel is the very texture of national continuity. When it comes to change, however, the interrelations are more complex; that kernel, which guarantees persistent stability, can only be seen here as providing the basic framework within which a certain limited range of patterns of change can occur.

3. Change, transformation, evolution – these are the key concepts that should provide the basis of modern, scientific historical studies. Such changes as do take place within the framework of any given historical specificity cannot but leave their mark on the basic framework itself. This means that by acting in a conscious, persistent and forceful manner upon the nodal elements of change (such as technology, institutions, the

structure of social relations and, perhaps especially so, ideology), those elements which appear most open to modifications that will be broadly acceptable to public opinion, one can reasonably hope that the basic framework itself, the kernel of historical specificity of a given society, can in its turn be gradually modified.

It is neither a matter of change, any change at all of the uniform, cosmopolitan kind – the hegemonic dream of the leading industrial societies – nor of the immutable stagnation to which ethno-racial typologies inevitably lead, but rather of a specific range of possibilities and possible modes of transformation.

3. Egypt's past towards present and future

Let us now consider how these two series of considerations can be brought to bear on certain concrete and reputedly complex problems in the modern economic history of Egypt. I shall refer to a select number of studies to illustrate this analysis and to point up the central questions.

The first problem concerns the transition from feudalism to capitalism. It is noteworthy that this problem, which belongs to the classical tradition of economic history, has only recently been raised under the impact of ideological discussions about the nature of the Egyptian revolution – and not as a result of academic study. Social thinkers and political cadres alike were obliged to consider the nature of Egyptian society during the Second World War, in order to frame the vision of the future which the national movement so urgently demanded. Was Egypt predominantly a 'feudal' society, such that the objective should be a national-capitalist, bourgeois-democratic revolution? Or was feudalism simply a relic of the past, and the immediate objective to press on towards more radical advances, perhaps even towards socialism?

The economic system before 1952 was heavily based on agriculture. The ruling classes and groups, with a few exceptions, belonged to different sectors of the landed aristocracy. Culture and traditions, the role of religion, the quality of interpersonal relations, the condition of women, all tended to confirm this backward, 'agrarian' picture. Political denunciations of the overt or tacit alliance between the Egyptian ruling groups and imperialism centred on the notion of the *iqta'iyyin*, a term designating those who were, or could at first sight be considered the big landowners or 'feudal' landlords, with the ex-royal family at their head. Several radical groups, despite their different outlooks and programmes, adopted this definition of Egypt's economic and social system, among them the MDLN, one of the main Communist organisations, and the Free Officers. By and large, public opinion and the press did the same, and there were several instances when the theme was taken up by universities and scholarly circles. After the 1952 *coup d'état* the agrarian reform came to be understood, one could say, as the liquidation of feudalism and the launching of a new, modern phase of Egypt's economic and social history. The industrialists, for their part, seized on this thesis to claim their share in the control and management of the economy and the state, pointing out that both the bourgeois-democratic and socialist revolutions could be averted once the important objective was achieved, that is, the destruction of 'feudalism' and the shift towards industrialisation. Economic history, mainly in the form of popular essays and articles, took on a curious appearance of total discontinuity: the period between Muhammad Ali and 23 July 1952 remained unexplored.

The discussion of 'feudalism' did not begin until around 1944–6, some years after the publication of A. E. Crouchley's pioneer work on *The Economic Development of Modern Egypt* (1938). In 1944, two economic histories of Egypt – one by Muhammad Fahmi Lahita, the other by Rashid al-Barawi and Muhammad Hamza Ulaysh – were published. By then, a serious discussion was under way in the Marxist politico-cultural centres of Cairo and Alexandria. The application to Egypt of what was then the classic periodisation of socio-economic formations[23] could not fail to reveal that, at least since the institution of private landed property under Said, and particularly since Egypt's integration into the world economic market under British rule after 1882, the whole socio-economic structure had moved on to a new level, namely capitalism, with its two (Marxist) characteristics of production for the market and wage-labour. 'Feudalism' could no longer be said to be the prevailing system in Egypt; al-Barawi's formulation, under the influence of the contemporary Left, can be considered the first academic expression of this trend of thought[24] which gained official (national) recognition with Husayn Khallaf's analysis of modernisation in 1962.[25] The most important work, however, was carried out between 1956 and 1958 as greater attention was given to the forms of transition from Oriental feudalism to capitalism under Muhammad Ali by a group of Marxist historians and theorists, the most important of whom, for our present purposes, was Ibrahim Amir.[26] A more sophisticated and less stilted study of the same problems was undertaken independently by Issawi and Baer, though its conclusions were basically similar.[27]

'Feudalism', then, is not the issue; but if it is capitalism, what kind of capitalism is it? The current formulation to describe the still considerable hangover from the era of the great decadence was 'relics of feudalism'. The aftermath of Suez stimulated research in two directions.

1. On the nature of Egyptian capitalism. Clearly, in Egypt as in other colonial countries slowly emerging from underdevelopment and foreign domination, monoculture and an 'export-oriented economy' (Issawi) contributed to shaping a distorted version of Western capitalism. The agrarian sector at the time could not be called 'feudal', yet it was so predominant that other sectors – industrial, commercial and financial – lagged behind. Thus the economic system prevalent in modern Egypt (from Ismail to 1952) could be broadly described as 'backward capitalism of the colonial type with a predominant agrarian sector'.[28] This definition could help us to interpret the course of development from the 1930s onwards, that is, during the period when the industrial and financial sectors of Egyptian capitalism fought to gain access to the power of decision in economic matters, with the ultimate aim of reshaping the whole power structure from the top. It could also help us to understand the economic history of Egypt under the new regime – from the agrarian reform to the massive nationalisation of the modern sectors.

2. The second topic required a more penetrating analysis, this time in the domain of sociology. How could a society so tightly integrated into the world market since the 1860s present such a vast panoply of 'relics of feudalism' in the mid-twentieth century? It could be explained by the persistence of ideological factors over material factors (the 'infrastructure'). In the specific case of Egypt another explanation was suggested by one of its specific historical features. The persistent central hegemonic role of state religion as ideology meant that one could expect its effects to be felt in the secondary fields of ideology and culture, in the sociology of everyday life to which reference has already been made. This greater persistence was in turn reinforced by the exceptionally intense ethnic and national unity that has characterised Egyptian society. When interested economic historians and observers seek out the diverse ways in which the universal relates to specific individual cases, they can and must recognise the clear differences between Egypt and, say, India, as far as their integration into the world market and their level of ethnic and national unity is concerned.

The second main problem is socialism. The history of the creation and growth of the public sector from 1957 to 1963 and beyond is impressive. The mass media have tried to obscure the figures issued by government sources; the estimates for the 1962–3 budget put the private sector's contribution at 65.8 per cent, leaving only 34.2 per cent to the public sector. The targets for the 1964–5 Plan indicate that the expected value added was £1538 million from the private as opposed to £375.7 million from the public sector. Meanwhile, between 1963 and today, nearly 80 per cent of industry, transport and commerce have been brought into the public sector, and by 1970 the bulk of agricultural output will be produced within the framework of the producers' co-operatives.[29]

In 1964, summing up twelve years of economic development, I wrote the following:

> The Egyptian economy emerges as a mixed economy. It is still in many ways capitalistic; the land remains almost untouched by nationalisation; the public sector, though under the direction of managers (technocrats), is still ruled by the market and the (public) profit motive. Planning, and foreign aid in particular, tends to reinforce this pattern, at least in the short run. It is a relatively fast-growing economy with a central State-capitalist sector (the public sector) of unusual proportions; yet every new wave of nationalisations, while it weakens the power of private capital, only serves to provide more entrenched positions and more power for the technocrats.[30]

A more critical assessment had just been offered by Hassan Riad,[31] while Patrick O'Brien's careful study, despite its subtitle, chose 'the term centralised market economy [as] more revealing than vaguer adjectives like ''planned'' and ''socialist'' '.[32]

These three assessments, as well as the recently published work of several specialists, all revolve around the key notion of centralisation. I have tried to show that seventy centuries of centralisation have not been limited to the economic sphere in this most compact of all 'hydraulic societies'. The state controlled the Nile and, until the second half of the last century, owned the land; Egypt's geo-political situation required it to concentrate a powerful apparatus in its hands; and there was a clear ideological homogeneity, which often became theocracy, from the Pharaohs through the Coptic era to Sunni Islam. Here, in this symbiosis, lies the kernel of Egypt's historical specificity. Any analysis of its economic history must take that as its starting-point if it is to arrive at a rational, concrete interpretation which can point ahead towards the future. The central, hegemonic role of the state does not itself indicate a collectivist socio-economic formation, nor yet a free market economy.

The approach to these two central problems of modern economic history has centred on the relationship between ideology and the economic structure, and the analysis of short-term change in its relation to the millenial historical specificity of Egyptian society. Ideology and historical specificity thus appear, in the case of this exceptionally old nation-state, as factors of the first magnitude – what Louis Althusser in another context calls *overdetermination*[33] – and these two factors themselves in the final analysis appear to be shaped by the geographical and economic conditions which have put this indelible stamp on Egyptian history from its beginnings until today.

This very sociological approach to economic problems, moreover, can throw light on the possibilities of a non-Utopian future. The future role of this overcentralisation in all spheres of social life suggests at least two possible courses:

1. The first would entail using that tradition to accelerate the building of an even more powerful leading economic sector as the spearhead of development. It would be interesting to study in detail the impact of the world economic crisis (1929–32) on the Egyptian economy and society; the shift to the Right and the imposition of the dictatorial rule of Ismail Sidqi against the Wafdist masses was coupled with protective tariffs for the nascent industry and a whole policy designed to favour national capital, especially its industrial and financial sectors. But it could reasonably be argued that Egypt's present regime has already gone a very long way in this latter direction, and that the main obstacles to further economic development lie in the deeply entrenched 'new classes' and the veiled, bureaucratic sabotage by a wide array of government organs of the social dynamics – objective and not ideological – of the current radical-national policy. And it would be highly unrealistic to imagine that any change in the nature of the state itself could decisively enhance the role of the peasantry, the working class or the radical intellectuals.

2. The second course belongs to medium-range history. The nodal point would be the very texture of Egyptian society itself, with its majority of *fallahs*. Here, as elsewhere in the Three Continents, is the crux of the matter. Underdevelopment, poverty and illiteracy are still much greater

in the countryside than in the cities, though notable progress has been made since 1952. But the formidable effort required to develop Egypt is not limited to the levels of technology and the state; it requires the mass mobilisation of the people, and if this mobilisation is not to take an undesirable turn, it can only be brought about in a rational, humane manner by institutions and organisations emanating from the peasantry itself. Such appears to be the true significance of the Kamshish affair (April 1966) and its aftermath.

3. Finally, attention should be drawn to the profound transformation of the socio-economic terrain itself, both at the level of the infrastructure (economic institutions, the living conditions of the working people) and of ideology (the profound impact of the adoption of socialism as a national programme and ideology, for all its vagueness and distortions). The intermediate level of the sociological pyramid, that is the state apparatus and the 'new class', on the other hand, appears far too static; willy nilly, action reflects intent – for we have reached the very heart of the problem of power.

To apply the 'principle of historical specificity' to the cases we are considering is a delicate matter, it is true; but the difficulties in applying it are not insurmountable, and analysis shows that its elements are dynamically cohesive. And although the range of potential variables of change with regard to future history – including economic history – may be limited as far as the near future is concerned, the dialectics of Egyptian society have never lain dormant, and have been intensively at work since the 1939–46 period.

History, from curse to promise? That could be the role assigned to the sociological imagination.

Part II

Dialectics of Civilisations

5

Orientalism in Crisis

It is indispensable to see Europe from the outside, to see the history of Europe, its failures as well as its successes through the eyes of that vast part of humanity formed by the peoples of Asia and Africa.

Joseph Needham

If we are to draw back what Claude Roy called the 'iron curtain of false enigmas', we must urgently set in motion a critical revision and re-evaluation of the general conception, the methods and the instruments which have given the West its knowledge of the Orient, at all levels and in every area – a process begun in the early years of the last century.

Any rigorous science that aspires to understanding must subject itself to such revision. Yet it is the resurgence of the nations and peoples of Asia, Africa and Latin America in the last two generations that has produced this belated and still reluctant crisis of conscience. A principled demand has become an unavoidable practical necessity, the result of the (decisive) influence of the political factor – that is, the victories of the various national liberation movements on a world scale.

For the moment, it is Orientalism that has experienced the greatest impact; since 1945 it is not only the 'terrain' that has slipped from its hands but also the 'men', those who yesterday were still the 'object' of study, and who today are its sovereign 'subject'.

The human and social sciences have also begun to recognise the need to recast, extend and transform themselves, and not simply their field of application. Nevertheless, there is as yet no crisis as such. What has happened is that different factors, and in particular the increasing importance of a universalist and historicising Marxist methodology, together with the methods of modern science and modern rationalism which connect with it at certain points, have made possible a greater flexibility, a new syncretism – although these remain deeply inadequate.

In considering the question in more detail, our study will naturally concentrate on the Arab world, and on Egypt in particular, though China and South-east Asia will also be considered in this connection.

On the history of traditional Orientalism – from the decision of the Council of Vienna, in 1245, to found the first chairs in Oriental Languages at the *Universitas magistrorum et scolarium parisiensium*, to the 1939–45 war – researchers will find a number of works available. It is a disparate collection, suggestive but rarely rigorous.[1]

It is interesting to note, however, that Oriental studies in the two key sectors – the Arab world and the Far East – effectively took off in the period of colonial intervention, and above all at the point at which the European imperialisms began to dominate the 'forgotten continents' (from the middle to the last third of the nineteenth century). The first wave is marked by the establishment of Orientalist societies (Batavia, 1781; *Royal Asiatic Society*, London, 1834; *Société Asiatique*, Paris, 1822; American Oriental Society, 1842; and so on). The second phase saw the organisation of Orientalist Congresses, the first of which was held in Paris in 1873. Sixteen Congresses were to take place prior to the First World War (the last in Vienna in 1912); since then, there have been only four.

But what kind of study is it that we are discussing?

The Orientalist, 'a scholar versed in knowledge of the Orient, its languages, literatures etc.'[2] – what kind of man, of scholar is he? What are his motivations and concerns? What objects does he set out to achieve?

Michelangelo Guidi (1886–1946) stands within a history of philosophy perspective opposed to the *hellenocentrism* of Werner Jäger in particular:[3]

I understand Orientalists to be those concerned with the Near East; for Indian and Chinese thought are certainly of great interest in understanding the ways of the spirit, but they have no vital contact *with us*. . . . We others, we Orientalists, look in fact towards those cultures where the Oriental element appears in its most complete form – the pure national cultures, Islam for example. Our object here is not only to recreate a strange world (though it is a great culture worthy of scientific interest) but also because it is the only way in which we can come to understand fully the nature of the elements of the admirable and fruitful fusion that has come about *in the cultural sphere of Hel-*

lenism.[4]. . . The complete Orientalist must start with the Classical world; but it would be anti-historical to turn his glance away from a whole period that stands between us and the Classic period as such. At a certain point, *homo classicus* and *homo islamicus* become for us no more than a memory or a pure abstraction.

The *homo novus* of Hellenism alone is a 'living' product of 'living movements, rather than of movements created artificially by scholars; all have been created by an original historical force'. Thus

> we do not study those worlds in order to draw up a new series of phenomena destined for a glass case in the museum of humanity, to describe marvellous and exotic forms, to know the *bartaron sofia*; rather do we study these worlds in order to relive in their fullness the phases of intimate union between two different cultures, and seeking to distinguish the modes and functions of one of them. For our vision has become sharper as a result of considering the manifestations of Oriental culture in its most complete expression; and it is possible that we may thus make a more precise assessment, and become far more sensitive.[5]

Is it an exaggeration, here, to speak of a 'Euro-centrist' romanticism,[6] bearing in mind that Raymond Schwab speaks in identical terms[7] and A. J. Arberry's recent seven portraits of English Orientalists[8] (S. Ockley, W. Jones, E. H. Palmer, E. G. Browne, R. A. Nicholson, Arberry himself, etc.) take essentially the same direction? It is important to recognise, however, that we are, historically speaking, in the age of European hegemony – any retrospective critique must take this into account.

The key works of the main schools of Orientalism in the West (France, Great Britain, Germany, Holland, Spain, Italy, Russia, the United States) stand within this current of thought, this vision of Orientalism. Their contribution has been fruitful and diverse: the Lebanese bibliographer Youssef Asad Dagher distinguishes several positive elements in Arab and Islamic studies: the study of ancient civilisations; the gathering of Arab manuscripts into European libraries; the compilation of catalogues of manuscripts; the publication of a number of important works; the lessons in method thus given to Oriental scholars; the editing of studies, often deficient and erroneous from the linguistic point of view, yet rigorous in their method; and finally, 'this movement has contributed to awakening national consciousness in various countries of the Orient, giving impetus to the movement towards scientific renaissance and the unfolding of the ideal'.[9] We shall return to this point later.

This was not the dominant vision of traditional Orientalism, however; or rather, it represents the essential direction of the work done in universities and learned societies while not covering the whole gamut of work carried out there and elsewhere. On the other hand, that work was itself deeply imbued with postulates, methodological habits and historico-philosophical concepts which often compromised the results and the scientific value of difficult work; *objectively* it led a number of authentic Orientalist scholars towards the politico-philosophical positions of the other group of scholars working in the field.

This second group comprised an amalgam of academics, businessmen, military men and colonial functionaries, missionaries, publicists and adventurers. Their only objective was to reconnoitre the ground they were to occupy, and to penetrate the consciousness of the peoples, the better to ensure their subjection by the European powers. 'The vision of the Arab Bureau', as Jacques Berque has rightly pointed out, ensured that 'supported and both nourished and limited by action, the study of the societies of North Africa has since the beginning moved in a particular direction';[10] it is not difficult to guess what direction that was. The phenomenon is a general one, a constituent element of all social science in the European countries in the period of imperialist penetration and colonisation: Italian Orientalism under Mussolini; the psycho-political penetration exemplified by Lawrence and his school, and before that the relations between missionary circles, the military and the Orientalists (notably at the time of the Third Provincial Congress of Orientalists in Lyons, 1878), etc. The examples abound, and repeat themselves, for we are still in the epoch of humiliation, of occupation – before the great liberating revolutions.[11]

Despite these very real differences, however, is it still possible to speak of a certain similarity in the general conception, the methods and the instruments brought to bear by these two groups within traditional Orientalism?

Our reply is that one can; the community of interest (and not only of interests) is fundamental in the face of that other world which would later be called 'third' in its relation to history in the making.

1. Traditional Orientalism

1.1 General conception

That is, traditional Orientalism's vision of the Orient and the Orientals:

(a) On the level of the *position of the problem*, the *problematic*, both groups consider the Orient, and the Orientals, as an 'object' of study marked by its otherness (like everything that is other, be it 'subject' or 'object') – but here a constituent, essential otherness, as we shall see in a moment. Here the 'object' of study is considered to be, as it should be, passive, non-participant, endowed with an 'historical' subjectivity that is above all non-active, non-autonomous, with no sovereignty over itself. The only Orient, or Oriental, or 'subject' that can be marginally acknowledged is the philosophically alienated being, other in relation to himself, defined – and moved to action – by someone else.

(b) On the *thematic* level, both groups adopt an essentialist conception of the countries, nations and peoples of the Orient, a conception that translates itself into a characteristic ethnist typology; the second group would soon convert that into racism.

According to traditional Orientalists, there is an essence – sometimes described in straightforward metaphysical terms – which constitutes the inalienable, common root of all the beings under consideration. This essence is at once 'historical', since it reaches back into the depths of history, and fundamentally a-historical, since it fixes the being, the 'object' of study, in its inalienable and non-evolutionary specificity, rather than making it, like all other beings – be they states, nations, peoples or cultures – the product and result of a combination of the forces at work throughout historical evolution.

Thus we arrive at a typology based on a real specificity but detached from history, and thus conceived as intangible and essential. It converts the 'object' studied into an other, in relation to whom the studying subject is transcendent; we shall have *homo Sinicus, homo Africanus, homo Arabicus* (and why not *homo Aegypticus?*),[12] while man – 'normal' man – is the European man of the historical epoch dating from Greek Antiquity. We can thus see clearly how, between the eighteenth and the twentieth centuries, the hegemonism of the possessing minorities exposed by Marx and Engels, and the anthropocentrism dismantled by Freud, go hand in hand with Euro-centrism in the human and social sciences, particularly those which have a direct relation to the non-European peoples.

Among the masters of traditional Orientalism, none had developed this theme better than the great scholar Louis Massignon (1883–1962), when speaking of the Arabs, so dear to his mystic's heart. In one of his last essays, written shortly before his death, he wrote as follows:

> I believe that the problem of the future of the Arabs has to be linked to the question of Semitism. For at the root of the difficulties of the Arabs lies the dramatic problem of the fratricidal hatred between Israel and Ismael. I believe that it must be overcome; but can it be done? The issue is not to be resolved at the level of the mechanical incidence of contemporary technology, where Israel leads that whole world, but in its superiority of thought and its way of posing problems. Israel has never ceased to pose problems for itself; that is its force of hope, intellectual speculation in the pure form. Thus the Arabs have found themselves robbed of their claim to Semitic exclusivity, to be the Semites by right and by privilege. On the contrary, they are the out-laws, the pariahs; for many reasons they proved to be inferior to the task that Israel did know how to confront; but it seems to me that there should be reconciliation between brothers, for Israel, like the Arabs, can offer internal evidence; the evidence of its language, which is a sacred language as well as an instrument of abstract scientific research. The Jewish elite thought and wrote in Arabic throughout the Middle Ages. That is the essential problem.[13]

The generosity of the sentiment cannot conceal the deeply misguided nature of this thematic approach, so open to pernicious historical projections. It would be more or less like looking at the history of Europe through the deforming prism of Aryanism.

1.2   Methods of study and research

Inevitably these will be determined by the general underlying conception:

(a)   The past of the Oriental nations and cultures will, naturally, be the privileged field of study.[14] By 'implicitly admitting that the most brilliant periods of the Oriental countries belong to the past', one is recognising by the same token that 'their decline was inevitable'. Jean Chesneaux has rightly pointed out that 'the course of Graeco-Roman studies from the

mid-19th century onwards, their reemergence as studies of "dead" civilisations completely divorced from their contemporary inheritors, provided Orientalists with an eminent model'.[15]

(b) That past would be studied in its cultural (linguistic and religious) aspects, detached from questions of its social evolution. It is the general offensive of irrationalism in Europe before and after Hegel that explains the stress laid on the study of the religious phenomenon and its para-psychic, esoteric *aura*. In the same way, it was the revival of Classical studies in the light of historical method, and more precisely of historical philology, at the end of the last century, that explains the priority given to linguistic and philological studies by traditional Orientalists. But the study of very much *living* Oriental languages, like Arabic, as if they were dead languages, necessarily produced a large number of errors, contradictions and inconsistencies; it is as if one set out to write a commentary on the French language (the language of Martin du Gard, Sartre, Aragon) on the basis of a reading of the *Chansons de geste*, the English of Shaw or Russell by reference to Anglo-Saxon, or the Italian of Croce, Gramsci or Moravia through a reading of ecclesiastical Latin.[16]

(c) History studied as 'structure' will, at best, shed light on the recent past. That resurgent history will appear as the continuation of a great but limited past. History will cease to be historicist, and become exotic.

(d) The scientific work of scholars in the different Oriental countries will be received in silence, but most of the time totally ignored, save only those rare works that share the same orientation as metropolitan Orientalism. The rest will be deemed to have no value, denigrated, and the backwardness attributable to historical conditions, and in particular to colonialism, will be converted into a specific constituent characteristic of the Oriental mentality.

1.3 Instruments of study and research

(a) These are essentially composed of the wealth of materials from Asia, Africa and Latin America which have been accumulated and concentrated within the great European metropolises: the history of the Guimet and Cernuschi museums in Paris, and of the great collections in

the British Museum follows the same course as the (voluntary or enforced) emigration of the treasures and scientific minds of Europe to the United States after 1919. As far as Arab studies are concerned, the situation is particularly serious; tens of thousands of manuscripts (the figure of 140,000 has been quoted) are now outside the Arab world, and so in practical terms beyond the reach of Arab scholars. For the most part, therefore, they are obliged to approach the very core of their own national and cultural history using indirect sources only. The Arab League, as well as a number of individual states, including Egypt, have set in motion a number of projects, publications and organisms, with the object of restoring these irreplaceable sources[17] to the Arab world.

(b) As far as modern and contemporary history are concerned, the major and essential part of the material concerned with the colonial and dependent countries (notably India, Egypt and the Arab Near East, the Maghreb, black Africa, etc.) are collected in the state archives of the great ex-colonial powers. More often than not, these sources are inaccessible, hemmed in by prohibitions of one kind or another (the least serious of them being the famous 'fifty-year rule'). The approximative knowledge of the past thus becomes a search for self – a quest littered with dangerous pitfalls.

(c) The secondary sources used by the traditional Orientalists of the West – reports of colonial administrators,[18] of religious missions, both Catholic and Protestant,[19] the accounts and reports of the managing boards of societies, travel documents, etc. – are profoundly tainted with ethnism and racism in all its variants; the least extreme are exoticist and paternalistic. It is clear, then, that such secondary sources, while providing some elements of research, conceal many others and cannot, in any case, sustain valid scientific research.

   These are the principal characteristics of the most traditional Orientalism, which represented Orientalism as a whole until the end of the 1939–45 war and which today still occupies a disproportionately important place. Yet the renaissance of the peoples of Africa, Asia and Latin America since the end of the nineteenth century; the rapid acceleration of this process as a result of the victories of the national liberation movements in the ex-colonial world; and the appearance of a group of socialist states together with the subsequent separation of the 'two Europes'[20] have shaken the edifice of traditional Orientalism to its very foundations. Suddenly, specialists and public alike have become aware of the gulf between Orientalist science and its object of study, but also – and this is decisive – between the conceptions, instruments and methods of work of the social sciences, and those of Orientalism.

Rejected by history and by the national renaissance of the Orient, traditional Orientalism has found itself out of phase with the progress of scientific research. Clearly, the whole body of thought now needs to be reconsidered.

2. Two faces of neo-Orientalism

'Two Europes' are reconsidering this body of thought: the Europe (and European America) of the colonial powers; and the Europe of the socialist states and movements, soon joined by the revolutions of the three 'forgotten continents' – People's China and Cuba. The gulf between them is very deep, particularly as far as general conceptions are concerned.

2.1   The neo-Orientalism of Western Europe

Two essential documents – the inaugural class given by Jacques Berque at the Collège de France in December 1956, and the 1961 Hayter Report – as well as a number of methodological works, will permit us to analyse this renewal of traditional Orientalism among the Western colonial powers.

(a)   General conception   Berque notes that

the personality of the world of Islam appears barely communicable . . . to anyone who approaches it, it awakens the just images of the 'cavern' and the 'daedalus' . . . it defends itself against the outside, aberrant world. Evasive, threatening or charming, it exposes itself little by little through mystery, insult or seduction. It fights to hide its true point of entry; it hides its truth. Many step back in the face of this first obstacle, whether because they have been seduced by the picturesque, caught in doubt or repelled by the gesture of combativity. But research must continue to go forward . . . We must grow more and more sensitive to the *other, Arab face* of things.

The work undertaken, the first account of which he gives here, leads him to think that 'the Arab countries are born into their modern history after the first world war, and especially after the second'; the result, in his vew, is 'years of tragic revision'. And yet, he says, 'we must learn to recognise the evidence (to use a term dear to Louis Massignon) beneath the gesture'. There is disorder everywhere.

> Tension deforms them. Their structures become fleeting, their deter-
> minations ambiguous. For them the concrete is constantly over-
> whelmed by the affective, the act by the symbol. For them all
> phenomena break down into multiple stages, all behaviour has to be
> understood in more than one register. Hence the extreme difficulties of
> expression which they experience, and the problems of interpretation
> that affect us.

Of course, 'the structures are indecipherable if they are isolated from their historical context and a whole social psychology'. But the verdict is no less decisive.[21] 'The vast ebb and flow of ideas which then began . . . in a confused way associated structure with existence, causalities (true or false) with the needs of the heart and the extension of an epic thrust'. All these attempts 'seem to me to respond above all to the search for solidity. The research is often awkward, summary and distorting – sometimes even insincere, if a friend may be allowed to say it from a distance – inexpert and hasty in most cases. The analysis of the current political forms in the Orient does not go very far either.' In many respects recalling Renan,[22] he goes on:

> This history is not autonomous . . . . Until now, this humanity has
> rejected what has been called the 'prejudice of things', for history takes
> from it the taste and the rigour of things . . . . Harassed by what an
> Egyptian essayist has called 'their weighty history', they will be
> tempted to seek affirmation outside continuity, outside logic, and
> perhaps even outside history . . . but can one fight facts with symbols,
> even symbols as august as liberty?

Having thus established the fact of non-autonomy, of the impotence of the Arab and Islamic peoples to think for themselves and to forge the instruments of knowledge which alone can lay the basis in depth for action and progress, Berque naturally goes on to fill that vacuum, notably in *Les Arabes d' hier à demain*, published in 1960:

> Today, the Arab soul maintains or restores a reference to self, an

autonomy of sensation and of expression which no external system, however enriching it may have been, should ever have taken away from it. Would that be a sufficient motive for the foreign researcher, because he is suspected at first, and held back by a thousand precautions for fear of wounding the living sensibilities of others, to abstain from putting his theory forward? On the contrary, his contribution could develop the spontaneity of the Arabs. If I then dare to offer them a system to explain their contemporary history, it is in the hope that they will judge it. The more criticism it evokes from within, the more it will have helped those to whose progress it seeks to contribute. It is of course at a disadvantage simply because it comes from a foreigner; it may, on the other hand, have a secondary advantage. For its success or failure will be those of a new Orientalism, both disinterested and committed.[23]

The reactions provoked by this view of the work to be done moved Berque, two years later, to bring his ideas up to date: 'An Egyptian essayist suggested in relation to my last book that I was directing myself at the Oriental as well as the Western reader; as if that were something new! Is it too ambitious? A study conceived in this way thus demands of its object that it become a critical and participant interlocutor.'[24] The instrument of this investigation will be French culture, 'for I dare to assert that the French have taken Hellenism from the Arab peoples'.[25]

The author's two works – one on the Arabs, the other on the Maghreb – establish the framework of this new typology. We are concerned here with methodology, so we shall not examine its postulates, its theses, or its conclusions. However it should be noted that the new typology, while remaining essentialist at heart, adopts new nuances by taking the economic factor into account.[26]

The approach to the problem is different in the Anglo-Saxon world. In 1946, the Middle East Institute was founded in Washington, followed in 1949 by the Council for Middle Eastern Affairs, in New York. It was in 1947 that the Scarborough Commission, advised by A. J. Arberry, set in motion the renewal of Orientalism in Great Britain. The end of the war demanded that 'we take up the responsibilities which we must still assume in the colonies, our relations with the dominions, near neighbours of the peoples of Asia and Africa, and our new relations with India, Burma and Ceylon'. The report formulated an overt critique of 'Euro-centrism', and pointed out that the backwardness of Oriental studies in Great Britain, as compared with France, Germany, Italy,

Holland, the Soviet Union and the United States (in that order) 'ill befits our situation as a great power, and fails to match up with our imperial responsibilities'. What was required was the organisation of modern studies in order specifically to assist the scientists, doctors, engineers and economists who wish to make a career in the Orient and enable them to find a valid place there.[27]

Four years later, the Hayter Commission reacted in vigorous political terms to a situation that remained weak. The world centre of gravity having moved away from Europe, it was not a time for linguists but rather for a 'surplus of historians, jurists, economists and other specialists in the social sciences'. The objectives envisaged there were the following: 'to provide the nation with a greater and more balanced reserve of research and published material on those countries'; 'to contribute to the formation of an informed body of opinion on those countries'; 'indirectly to stimulate interest in Oriental languages'; and finally 'to increase the proportion of modern studies, and the study of modern languages in relation to classical studies'.[28] The Commission analysed the efforts of the United States, albeit well after the Scarborough Commission's findings; it noted the strong impression made upon it by the 'growing effort being undertaken, the type of organisation on which it was founded and the emphasis given to modern studies'. And it drew the British government's attention to the following points:

> The powerful support given by the US government to Oriental and Slavonic Studies, in view of their national importance; the attention given, through the centres for area studies, to breaking down the barriers between the different disciplines in order to promote a balanced study of these areas; the stimulating effect of the emphasis on modern studies; the role of grants given to graduate students with the object of directing them towards new fields of work; the value of the intensive language courses and the development of mechanical aids designed to overcome the problem of learning languages that are not taught in schools, and to reduce the learning period.

Does this mean that one should follow the example of the United States? 'The traditions of Classical, Hellenistic and Oriental scholarship are less deeply-rooted than in Europe . . . . British research within this field, and particularly in Oriental studies, falls within the strict Classical and linguistic traditions of Western Europe, while the most modernist developments, with the emphasis on the social sciences, are taking place in America.'[29] Dialogue, and the interests of state, should be ensured by extending and bringing up to date such work as has been done and by improving the qualifications of researchers, rather than by 'penetrating' the object to be studied – an object without autonomy – by European Orientalism.

No one will deny that this fundamental postulate, which is at the heart of all European Orientalism, whether traditional or renewed, continues to underlie the work of all non-socialist Western scholars. Thus Sir Hamilton A. R. Gibb, reviewing the history of Islam from its origins to our time, bases himself on nineteen European authors; only one Oriental – A.-E. Afifi – figures among them.[30] The recent Colloquium on Moslem sociology (Brussels, 11–14 September 1961) heard twenty speakers, not one of whom was from the Orient. It is precisely this that Jacques Berque denounces.[31] The essential question is the evolution of Arab and Moslem societies in the twentieth century. The Egyptian historian Hussein Mones is well placed to show how deeply out of phase with the history that is in the making are many of the writings.[32] G. E. von Grunebaum's recent writings share the same perspective; moreover, their author's serious philosophical background allows him to present structured analyses that reveal an effort to go beyond old habits.[33] Vincent Monteil's recent thesis on *The Modern Arab* is replete with inaccuracies – unlike Hans Wehr's work – the fruit of a will to theorise without knowing the terrain from within.[34]

(b) Methods of study and research   The past continues to occupy the forefront of Oriental studies; but it is no longer alone there. The demands of politics, the displacement of the centre of gravity beyond the European shore, the emotions evoked by the thrust of those people of the Orient who had until so recently been to various degrees submissive and malleable, the need to bring habits of work up to date, or if nothing else the need to bring themselves into line with the other social sciences – all these factors have contributed in a decisive way to leading the new Orientalism into the modern, contemporary era.

The present, finally acknowledged as an object of study (often at great cost) cannot avoid the demand for typologies appropriate to the different peoples of the Orient. It is structuralist philosophy that will mediate between the socio-political demand for these typologies and modernism; and that philosophy, as we know, sees its task as examining the sectors of reality as such, as 'structures', and not, or no longer, as the product, the sum or the meeting-point of a process of historical evolution. Thus conceived, structuralism in the human sciences appears as the most acceptable, the most 'objectified' expression of phenomenology, the dominant form of irrationalist philosophy in our times. In the field of Orientalism, the structuralist method moves on familiar territory, so to speak, given that it takes as its starting-point the linguistics of Saussure's *Cours de linguistique générale* (1906–11, published in 1916). Traditional Orientalists, the majority of them linguists or specialists in religions, are used to structuralism and are at their ease with their modernist, neo-Orientalist colleagues for whom the structuralist method provides the surest – as well as the most 'modern' – means to develop their typologies in the context of renewal.

It will continue to be the case that the scientific work carried out in the Oriental countries will be deprecated, whether through ignorance (for it will become more and more difficult, if not impossible, to theorise about a whole sector – be it Arab, Chinese, Asiatic, Latin American or Islamic – on the basis of necessarily limited documentation, and while indigenous production grows daily), or in order to maintain a (theoretical) primacy of knowledge.[35]

The method based on participation and penetration, suggested and set in motion by Berque, appears by far the most interesting: 'In a subject as alive, as contentious, as full of suffering as this, the habitual instruments of science do have an immense value, but they are not themselves enough. One must live in contact with the people, look into their daily life, practically share that life with them. And is it possible to do that in a dispassionate way?' Referring to this 'increasingly participatory search' he was, quite correctly, to note: 'Impressionism is not my forte. Our role is to understand. But if the analysis is to be effective, and go deeply enough, it must not dissociate the facts from their emotive context, nor from the sense that lived experience gives them.'[36]

For W. Cantwell Smith, whose Canadian background is 'non-imperialist', the value of that participation depends upon the judgement of the indigenous peoples: 'The work will fail if intelligent and honest Moslems are unable to recognise its observations as precise, or perceive in its interpretations and analyses a contribution and a real desire for clarification.'[37]

(c) *Instruments of study and research*   The Western powers, and notably the United States, aspire to add to their already existing stocks new centres of accumulation of cultural wealth and materials. Their means are disproportionately greater than anything that the Orient, its scholarly institutions and its researchers have at their disposal.[38]

Collaboration with the scholars and researchers of the countries of the Orient is recognised as an objective necessity. It will be noted, however, that the United States has at its disposal university chairs and quite substantial means of dissemination,[39] while in Europe this collaboration is regarded as very secondary.[40]

The realism of an H. A. R. Gibb, however, leads him, at the end of an account of the failures of historical studies of the modern Orient, to argue for a division of labour: 'The first task of the Western academic is to research, coordinate and critically evaluate the Western sources. The particular domain of the indigenous academic will be to research and organise the local archives and documentary materials.' It will be noted that, in the latter case, there is no question of 'critically evaluating' the materials collected. At the same time 'it must be established, with no room for any possible misunderstanding, that the Western academic will not carry out any work on the academic level in his own domain unless he has an adequate knowledge of Arabic, Persian or Turkish, according to the case, and of the historical and cultural background'. This means, of course, that 'the adult student of Middle Eastern history should be, in a sense, an Orientalist'; but that is only 'if a historian has technical qualifications in a wider field than he would need simply to be a good Middle Eastern historian'.[41] The priority, therefore, is to be a specialised scientific education, to which is added an adequate linguistic, ethno-cultural preparation.

Up to now we have, quite properly, looked at neo-Orientalist scholarship in the West. At the same time, however, the persistence of 'Euro-centrism' in the post-Second World War manifestations of modernism, together with the accentuation of the direct struggle between the colonised countries (the Orient) and the imperial powers (the West), favoured the formation of a new sub-group of publicists and journalists specialising in Asian and African affairs – and occasionally reaching into the universities. Ignorance of the language of the Oriental peoples is very often coupled with a patchy scientific education; the rhetorical and stylistic tricks and the talent of the great journalist may well serve as a guarantee and a rationale for specious publications, which will present themselves as sources of direct and 'specialised' information to the intellectuals of the Orient and the Western public.[42]

2.2   *Neo-Orientalism in the socialist sector*

We are principally concerned here with the socialist sector (movements and states) of Europe. For, despite their common sphere, the work emanating from China seems to have more in common with the conceptions of the independent, non-socialist states and the socialist movements of Asia, Africa and Latin America.

It was in the aftermath of the Second World War that research in the socialist sector began to concern itself with a deeper study of the countries of the Orient. We have already referred to the pioneering role, in the Arab and Islamic sphere, of the work of Jacques Berque, whose great overview is marked out in *Dépossession du monde* (1964), *L'Egypte, impérialisme et révolution* (1967) and *L'Orient Second* (1970), with its supporting interdisciplinary studies. From 1950 onwards, Maxine Rodinson began her reflections on traditional Orientalism, in response to the thrust of the national liberation movements in the Arab and Islamic countries.[43] Simultaneously, Jean Chesneaux began to develop his ideas in *Le mouvement ouvrier chinois de 1919 à 1927*.[44] The eminent Cambridge biologist Joseph Needham, after twenty-five years of preparation, began in 1954 to publish his monumental encyclopedic work *Science and Civilisation in China*, with the intention of restoring to the civilisation and culture of our time its second, Chinese dimension, which had fallen into oblivion from the (European) eighteenth century onwards: it is a model of erudition, scientific rigour and theoretical depth and has rightly been described as 'the greatest act of historical synthesis and intercultural communication that any human being has ever undertaken' (L. Picken).[45]

In the socialist countries, it was a matter of taking up again an ancient tradition, now infused with new concerns by Marxist methodology and the political resurgence of the Orient.[46]

The Bandung Conference for the Solidarity of the Afro-Asian peoples (April 1955) gave a decisive impetus to cultural renewal – notably in the fields of history, social science and literature, on both continents. It was soon to be followed by the twentieth Congress of the CPSU (1956) which determined the 'new course' of Soviet Orientalism. The first Congress of Soviet Orientalists, held at Tashkent in 1957, dealt with general themes: (i) rolling back the imperialist system; (ii) the tasks of Soviet Orientalism after the twentieth Congress; (iii) the world significance of Bandung. The twenty-first Congress of the CPSU laid still greater stress on this orientation which was to reach fruition at the twenty-fifth International Congress of Orientalists held in Moscow in August 1960.

This short historical introduction will allow us to situate the analysis of neo-Orientalism in the socialist sector.

(a)   General conception   On the level of the *problematic*, the end of European political hegemony – witness the Bandung Conference, Unesco, the Hayter Report and the ideological positions of the Chinese leaders – must be accompanied by a fundamental critique of 'Eurocentrism', and its definitive rejection in principled terms. 'Western civilisation continues to suffer an unjustified cultural pride which falsifies its contacts with the other peoples of the world; this can validly be described as "spiritual scorn from above" and also *ta preunatika tes poneriasen tois epouraniois* – "the spirit of evil in divine matters"'. Or as Needham says, having denounced 'the ideology of domination permanently present',

> The realisation that the peoples of Asia could also participate in all the benefits of modern science, that they could study the world of nature in a new way; note, read, study and internally assimilate the *Journal of Biophysics* (for example) and regain their self-respect, reaching a standard of living as high as any other part of the world while preserving all that is best in their religions and cultural traditions – that comes much more slowly.[47]

'The fundamental error of Eurocentrism is the tacit postulate that modern science and technology, which in fact took root in Renaissance Europe, is universal – and that it follows that all that is European is equally universal.' He shows that this is wrong both in science and in history, and emphasises the role of religion as an instrument of penetration and integration into Europe.[48]

It was a very different tone that A. I. Mikoyan, first Vice-President of the Council of Ministers of the USSR, adopted in his important speech to the opening session of the twenty-fifth Congress of Orientalists:

> It goes without saying that the revolutionary upheaval in the life of the peoples of Asia and Africa has radically altered the character and the content of Orientalism. We can say that the particular new theoretical aspect of principle in Orientalism is that now the peoples of the Orient are themselves creating their own science, elaborating their own history, culture and economy. Thus the peoples of the Orient have been promoted from the object of culture to the rank of creators. That is what distinguishes this Congress from all previous ones.

This statement of principle, which links with the *fundamental core* of the thought of the peoples of Asia, Africa and Latin America and their intelligentsia, has a corresponding political vision – the world front of anti-imperialist struggle:

> The duty of Orientalists in their work [Mikoyan went on] is to reflect effectively the most important processes in the countries of Asia and Africa, to involve themselves in a creative way in the elaboration of the fundamental problems of the Oriental peoples for their national and social liberation and to bring an end to their economic backwardness. We have the right to say that it is only then that Orientalism will be able to be taken seriously, and be able to count on success, from the moment in which it serves the interests of the peoples of the Orient.[49]

These were the ideas expressed by Academician B. G. Gafurov, director of the Moscow Institute of Oriental Studies, in his speech closing the Congress:

> We others, Soviet Orientalists, consider it to be our duty, our scientific duty, as well as the dictate of our own conscience, to help the peoples of the Orient unceasingly, in their struggle for a better future; we are convinced that our scientific discoveries and results, our deep scientific method, the Marxist–Leninist method which reality has proved to be correct, as well as the experience of our countries in the building of socialism – an experience based on a progressive scientific theory – we are convinced that all this will help the people of Asia and Africa to find the best and most effective way to achieve progress.[50]

It will be noted that Orientalism is evaluated scientifically in terms of its objectivity and the contribution it may make to the work of national liberation and construction; it is in the latter sense, above all, that it should participate with the subject, the 'creators'.

On the *thematic* level, however, several European socialist Orientalists continue to believe, like Chesneaux, that

> purely and simply to base the scientific study of the countries of Asia and Africa on the generality of historical or linguistic science would be, at the present level of world development, to fall back into Eurocentrism. Not only does the linguistic barrier justify a special organisation of work, but we cannot ignore the many features that are

still common today to all these Asian and African countries, and which clearly distinguish them from Europe. Orientalism is an old and out-moded concept, but Asian and African studies continue to come up with their own problems: underdevelopment, the history of imperialist ex-pansion and national movements, their own medieval traditions etc.[51]

The author points, quite correctly, to the enrichment of the 'general Marxist theory of world history' by the following elements, which have emerged from studies of the specific national peculiarities of Asia and Africa: the importance of the 'Oriental mode of production', in the general framework of the periodisation of human history into five fundamental modes of production;[52] an account of colonial imperialism 'which describes its internal contradictions', whose 'principal feature is its brutal domination and the repression and stagnation that go with it', yet without 'ignoring its secondary but equally real feature, namely the emergence of "new elements in society" ' to which Marx referred when speaking of 'the double character of British imperialism in India';[53] the emergence of national liberation movements in the colonies as more advanced movements, objectively speaking, than the workers' move-ment in the European countries; the importance of the so-called 'national psyche';[54] the emergence of a third type of nation (beyond the two defined by Stalin) within the Afro-Asian group, according to their degree of cohesion through history; the 'universalisation of Marxist thought';[55] the different role of the working class, which tends to become the central element of the popular forces, of the people, and not of the single hegemonic class.[56]

The official Soviet formulation after the twenty-first Congress of the CPSU was more traditional: 'The multitude of new problems and phenomena emerging as the great countries of the Orient embark on the road to sovereign development, in particular the struggle of the working class to raise its living standards; the role of that class in the process of industrialisation in countries underdeveloped from the economic point of view, and its participation in social life and the State as a whole'; the study of problems relating to class differentiation within the peasantry, and to the accelerated capitalist evolution of agriculture and its consequences; 'the problems of the struggles of the working class for hegemony at the heart of the peasant movement . . . all these are particularly interesting and important . . . [and] the incisive research in the field of the creation and development of the national literatures of the countries of Africa and Asia, will deal a fatal blow to Euro-centrist theories; to that end the study of the problems of interaction between the writings of Orient and West are of paramount importance.'[57]

(b)   Methods of study and research   First of all, we must define a 'new attitude towards the problem of the relations between Orientalism and each of the human sciences, each conceived within its planetary and universal character... whether it is history, economics, sociology, literature or linguistics, the perspective must be to "de-orientalise" studies of Asia ... to lead those studies to what we might call the "common law" of each discipline.' Chesneaux continues:

> We cannot evade the obstacle of language nor of the social heritage of custom ... but once these two difficulties have been overcome, we should be able to approach with a single method and a shared problematic the Italian or the Indonesian bourgeoisie, the analysis of the *Aufklärung* or the Chinese literary renaissance of 1920, the examination of the British economy in the continental context or of the Indian economy since Independence. This orientation will not only benefit Asian studies; it will also allow us to give a truly universal foundation to each of our human sciences, whose conceptual apparatus and basic elements have hitherto derived exclusively from the study of Western Europe – with very rare exceptions.

Yet the idea of a certain general specificity attributable to the whole Afro-Asian sphere does persist.

> This perspective for the universalisation, the normalisation of Asian studies does now, however, exclude the possibility that there persist today closer actual relations and objective links between the different countries of Asia.[58] The name of Bandung is enough to make the point. We must constantly bear in mind, and take great care to remember, the similarities that still present themselves in the contemporary evolution of the countries of Asia [and Africa], similarities which still today clearly distinguish them from the West. That, however, is a very different thing, from the methodological point of view, from preserving the traditional notions of Orientalism. For it is perfectly compatible with a methodological unity in the study of the societies of East and West.[59]

Western ignorance of the Orient has frequently been denounced, particularly by Needham and Etiemble.[60] The philosophy studied in the universities of Europe and America up to graduate and doctoral level is essentially European philosophy. Yet Chinese philosophy represents nearly 3000 years of continuous development;[61] Greek philosophy was deeply permeated by the religious philosophy and the myths of Egypt and the Orient; Oriental philosophy in the Middle Ages was very different from the simple 'transmission of the Greek inheritance';[62] and the idealism of Indian thought has nourished a broad, diverse and iridescent civilisation. One can say the same about the history of science, notably mathematics; biology, medicine and astronomy. Europe is only now beginning to discover the traditional literatures of Asia and Africa, thanks in particular to the work of the different national commissions of Unesco; the modern period, however, is still almost totally unknown.

The emphasis would then be put on the priority of studying the present, the processes of evolution of Oriental societies in the modern and contemporary era.[63] 'A more profound consideration of the current problems of the contemporary period should become central and fundamental'; the Soviet author immediately adds that 'this will help to find creative solutions in the future to the problems of Soviet foreign policy in relation to the countries of the Orient, which should be a question of honour for Orientalists'.[64] The twenty-fifth Congress of Orientalists in Moscow marks the rapid proportional growth of modern studies even among traditional Orientalists; and the flowering of national sections is an irrefutable sign of the emergence of nations and states which can no longer be grouped under 'typological' headings.[65]

However, this decisive and inexorable change in the respective weight of 'classical' and 'modern' sectors in Oriental studies cannot be carried through at the expense of the past.

I have no intention [writes Needham] of minimising in any way the extraordinary improvement brought about by the present Chinese government, under the leadership of the Communist Party in their condition as the 'hundred ancient names'. On the other hand, the present work will be hard for the West to understand if they lose sight of certain ancestral characteristics of Chinese culture, of which they stand in lamentable ignorance. In fact, contemporary writers themselves, in their desire to emphasise the profound renewal and renaissance that their country is experiencing, sometimes tend to denigrate their own past, either by stressing its more sombre aspects – like the subjection of women or the rapacity of the landlords – or by overestimating the philosophy or the art of preceding periods. This is like sawing off the branch on which they are sitting. It is a fact that the rest of the world needs to learn, in all humility, not only about contemporary China but also about China in all its ages; for in Chinese wisdom and experience are to be found physicians for many diseases of the spirit, as well as indispensable elements for the future philosophy of mankind.[66]

Naturally enough, it is the Marxist conception of history and its accompanying methodology that inspire the bulk of these works. It is clear, however, that the scholars of the socialist sector also understand the eminent non-Marxists – like Needham – who stand within the broader current of philosophical rationalism.

Sometimes, however, the demands of practical action, and in particular of regroupment, have invited the neo-Orientalists of the socialist sector, notably in the countries of Western Europe, to accommodate themselves to irrationalist methods. They have been drawn especially towards a certain phenomenology, expressed through an emphasis on typology, directly akin to the currently fashionable structuralism; and this has compromised the scientific rigour and the common direction of the fundamental work which we must seek out among the intelligentsia of the countries of the Orient in the struggle for their liberation and for progress.[67]

(c)   Instruments of study and research   The socialist states, principally the Soviet Union, have not had the same material sources at their disposal – direct or mediated – as the colonial powers. On the other hand, the increasingly close relations between the USSR and the Afro-Asian movements and states since the Bandung Conference in particular have led it to embark on a truly colossal effort in the field of modern Orientalism. The 'Institute of the Asian Peoples' is, next to the Academy of Sciences, the largest in the world; all the universities include studies of Asia, Africa and Latin America in their work; new and important scientific journals have been established;[68] and all the academies of sciences in the separate republics include sections or groups devoted to these studies. Today (in 1962) the personnel working in the field (including lecturers, researchers, technical assistants, translators, librarians, etc.) number between 18,000 and 20,000 people; a single publishing house specialising in Oriental studies produces a new title every two to three days; modern studies run in parallel with the

classical Orientalism honoured in yesterday's Russia; and in 1959, the 'African Institute' was finally created under the direction of Academician I. Potehkin.[69] In a matter of a few years, the scientific status of studies concerned with the modern and contemporary Orient have rapidly changed; thus, it is no longer possible to become deeply involved in them without a knowledge of Russian as well as the traditional European languages and one of several Oriental ones.

The scientific work of researchers and scholars in the different countries of the Orient is not only known, appreciated and studied – which should go without saying – but also accorded, as is its due, a privileged place. Chesneaux, among others, refers to 'the problem of the foreigner's aptitude for studying the contemporary social facts with the same chance of success as nationals'; in fact, 'the latter are obviously privileged by reason of their knowledge of the language and their familiarity with the whole range of customs, with the heritage of these Asian peoples'. 'Taking this reasoning to its extreme, one might ask whether it is not reasonable to consider the study of contemporary problems to be legitimately the province of nationals, while the further the theme of study reaches back into the past, the easier it will be for non-Asiatics to make a contribution.' In this conclusion he seems to concur with H. A. R. Gibb's view, cited earlier:

> If one can speak here of a national privilege, one cannot speak of a national monopoly as far as studies of the contemporary world are concerned. Strangers from far away, with a very different social and cultural background, can often penetrate quickly and with an original clarity into the life of other peoples. Among the best works on political life during the last five years, for example, are studies by Anglo-Saxons.[70]

The cultural policy of today's China is less open to foreign researchers: 'The first thing to note is that academic research [by foreigners] is extremely rare', for it is 'difficult to distinguish from espionage'. The central thesis is that 'foreigners are not capable of understanding us; Chinese studies belong to the Chinese'; However, 'if the study can be carried out through the use of materials, of official documents and with the aid of close examination, then it may be possible to look at more delicate subjects. But if the study involves direct observation in the field, with no clear plan, and requires free and open access to people and independent work', then obstacles will arise 'for anyone other than the most secure foreigners'.

It might at first appear, for example, that archaeology is not a delicate political area; yet on the other hand it is one reserved exclusively to all intents and purposes to the Chinese, as part of the study of their own national treasures and involving as it does the authoritative interpretation of their own history. Here the Japanese specialist will recall the very delicate nature of archaeology in pre-war Japan.

However the American author of this study[71] points to the massive and intelligent aid given to Needham and, rather more reluctantly, to J. Chesneaux; and R. Dumont, Geddes, C. P. Fitzgerald (from New Zealand) and S. Chandrasekhar (India) enjoyed open access. Here the attitude of the Communist leaders and the People's Republic of China was more akin to the attitudes of the independent national states of Asia and Africa than the socialist countries and movements of Europe.

The very nature of the scientific researcher must change radically. The study of the medieval classical Arab or of the mystique of Islam does not usually have to confront the question of the differentiation of sectors of the bourgeoisie in this or that Arab country, the problems of Arab realist literature since 1945, or the ideology of the different components of the national and democratic movement.[72]

The 'normalisation' of modern Oriental studies brings to the fore the question of the solidity and depth of a specialist education in one or other sector of the social sciences (economics, law, history, sociology, political science, philosophy, aesthetics, etc.). This should be combined with a rapid but reasonably adequate study of the language of the country or sector under consideration, as it is in the modern era in both its spoken and written forms. The aim of this linguistic study is on the one hand to make possible direct access to primary materials, and on the other to facilitate a psychological and sociological understanding of the daily life of the country. In the Soviet Union, this 'double formation' takes eight years, while in the United States 'intensive' linguistic instruction is provided when specialised studies are completed.[73] On this point the official concerns of the Anglo-Saxon countries parallel those of the European socialist sector and, in essence, the vision of the countries of the Orient themselves too.

The time for a necessary reorientation has come. And we can see that, objectively, the various sectors of contemporary Orientalism have in recent years themselves begun to recognise that imperative.

6

Marxism and the Sociology of Civilisations

1. On the Odyssey of the marginalised sociological concept of 'civilisation'

The 150th anniversary of Karl Marx's birth occurs in a fundamentally different setting from that in which his critical theses were developed. Those theses, from his 'youthful' work to *Capital* (which is celebrating its own centenary) and the foundation of the International, have changed the destiny of the world, of its peoples, states and nations. Obviously we are aware of the modifications that have occurred in historical, economic and political conditions, under the onslaught of revolutions and confrontation. Yet it is only with difficulty that the specialists, whether of theory or practice, take account of the other dimensions of this difference – a difference that we consider *fundamental* to, and constitutive of, the very formulation of the theoretical problem which is the object of this essay. None the less, the nationalitarian phenomenon increasingly asserts itself, with each day that passes, as objectively the central factor in the multifaceted dialectics of revolution and evolution, of counter-revolution and apparent stagnation. A geographical thread is added to the historical; yet it is not, as some would have it, a matter of topography. The object of this geographical dimension, or rather, of historical geography, is not to accommodate the geo-political analysis of the contemporary world, but on the contrary to provide a framework for the emergence on to the sociological level of the key factor of civilisation, and the key concept of specificity. This concept seems to us indispensable in determining the general theoretical pattern of the evolutionary process of human societies in this second half of the twentieth century.

Seen from the 'periphery', from the Three Continents which today embrace more than three-quarters of the human race, Marxism appears as a world view (*Weltanschauung*), a theory – philosophy, ideology and methodology in one – which represents the most advanced critical synthesis of Western civilisation and Western cultures, and more particularly of Enlightenment Europe and the great political, social and economic revolutions. This vision of Marxism, the vision of Marx, Engels and Lenin, locates it in terms of civilisation; and it allows us to define its characteristics as well as its relations with the body of conceptual and practical problems that arise in the non-European, non-Western world.

What was the central problem facing European and Western civilisation in the mid-nineteenth century? There existed a complex of national states, each very different from the other, which had already been 'assured' for several centuries, or which were then entering into a decisive phase of national unity; economic systems based on the industrial revolution and the technology of modern science; social regimes emerging from the long apprenticeship of a feudalism dismantled by the bourgeoisies who were at that time the bearers of a message of liberty and social rationality; a whole spectrum of national cultures, and a shared stock of accumulated culture and a homogeneous conceptual apparatus; political hegemony over the peripheral world – the great colonial empires – the result of this unique concentration of the means of power, sustained through a network of finance, the mastery of the seas, and the operation of powerful military means deployed according to a strategy formulated by Napoleon and Clausewitz in the era of the industrial revolution. Nothing, it seemed, could either then or in the foreseeable future challenge that hegemonic civilisation. That, at least, is how it appeared from the outside.

Yet at the heart of the system, the contradictions, conflicts and incoherences abounded, and gave rise to bitter class struggles between the wealthy and the dispossessed – principally the proletariat, the bearers of the future; these struggles, in their turn (from the Peasant Wars, through the Paris Commune to March 1917), led to insurrections and armed revolutions against the hegemony of the bourgeoisie on the internal front. The very 'rationality' of a system that claimed to be rationalist and humanist was thus challenged by the peoples of the West themselves, through that same 'critique of arms' which is today under way throughout the Three Continents.

An agonising, an unthinkable revision became necessary. Did one dare to call into question so striking an achievement as Napoleon's, Hegel's and Victoria's Europe? In the name of what? To whose benefit? To what end? The irrefutable and irreversible merit of Karl Marx and Friedrich Engels on the theoretical and historical planes is that they clearly perceived the necessity of this critique on the basis of the most advanced elements of Europe's very civilisation and culture (German philosophy, English political economy and French socialism). It was they who conceived and defined the central role of praxis, they who understood the revolutionary role of that social group which was at once the best prepared and the most impoverished – optimally so by comparison with the peasantry and the petit bourgeoisie of Europe. They proclaimed that the message and the object of socialism and the classless Communist society was to restore man to himself, his alienation overcome, to become master of his own destiny – not, let it be remembered, in Utopian terms, but on a warm, human and concrete basis. The only way to resolve the crisis of a distinguished civilisation, or 'civilisation' itself, as it was then, was to strike at the heart of the dehumanising socio-economic system. That was, indeed, the central theoretical problem of the Marxism of Marx; that, indeed, was the root of its very nature – that is to say, an *endogenous* militant and theoretical critique based on the ideological and political leadership of the equally endogenous process of the struggle between the social classes.

However, although the fundamental theoretical problem of Marxism is indeed endogenous, it will be seen that it cannot be called centripetal. For this Marxist humanism which Europe, having insisted for so long on 'universalism' alone, has discovered and marvelled at, has always been the very object of the socialist revolution described by Marx and Engels. And this objective has never failed to illuminate with a warm glow socio-economic analysis in those countries of Asia, Africa and Latin America, where men have known the need to survive in physical terms in the most urgent way, and thus could only conceive the satisfaction of their needs, so to speak, in humanist terms.[1] For there, bread takes on the colour of independence, of liberty, of dignity and of fraternity – of *happiness*, that ever-new idea.

The beginnings of ethnology, and later of anthropology, coincide with the work of the founders of scientific socialism. In a first phase, the question is how to describe the uncivilised peoples. Exoticism seeks to become measurable, a descriptive inventory to which the human atmosphere is restored. The perspicacious irony of Montesquieu's 'How can anyone be a Persian?' leads quite naturally to research into *differences*, into the division and categorisation of realities. But according to what criteria?

At first, historical evolution.[2] Then *historicism*, with E. B. Tylor (1871) and L. H. Morgan (1877); the latter's work was taken up by the original Marxist anthropologists, and retained by the contemporaries (Engels, V. Gordon Childe, R. and L. Makarius).[3] The model is 'civilisation' – that is, Europe and North America in the age of empire and imperialism. In Tylor, we find a civilising proselytism which extends into our own day in the form of American social ideology. All in all, this approach remains an *ethical* one. It came to an end with the introduction of a notion of *coherence* or of *internal efficiency*, notably in the work of V. Gordon Childe (1951), who defined the specific characteristics of civilisation in terms at once sociological and Marxist:

> The aggregation of vast populations in the cities; the primary producers (fishermen, cultivators etc.), the full-time specialised craftsmen, the merchants, the officials, the priests and the rulers; an effective concentration of economic and political power; the utilisation of conventional symbols to register and transmit information (writing), and equally that of conventional criteria for weights and measures, for space and time, leading to a certain mathematical and calendar science.[4]

The ethical – or moral – dimension properly speaking dominates the work of A. L. Kroeber (1949) and R. Redfield (1953) in particular. The classical approach is effectively summarised by J. H. Robinson in the article 'Civilization' in the *Encyclopedia Britannica* of 1928.[5] The process of differentiation reaches its climax on the conceptual level with Alfred Weber's well-known distinction between 'social structure', 'civilisation' and 'culture':

> Civilisation represents the human effort to conquer the world of nature and of culture by means of intelligence in the spheres of science, technology and planning. . . . Culture, as distinct from civilisation, is based on the realisation of the mind, of the philosophical and emotional self.[6]

Naturally, this effort is made by a 'vital aggregate', a European and Western *Lebensaggregierung*.

The turning-point of the century from the point of view of the relations between Europe and the West. and the colonial world, is not, or at least not yet, characterised as a crisis. Europe and North America remain supreme and hegemonic; but the 'other' world has entered the arena. The revolts and wars against colonialism and imperialism (India, Egypt, Algeria, China and Iran, in particular) receive a surprising and unexpected *viaticum* with Japan's victory over Tsarist Russia in 1905.[7] The 'other' asserts itself, and in the latter case, proves itself by force of arms – therefore it exists.

The field of sociological study concerned essentially with the sociology of knowledge, historical sociology and social philosophy was at that time a discipline in its formative stages which, quite naturally, looked at non-traditional phenomena in a new light – while historiography remained, at best, positivist. The link is made through a study of inferior societies (E. Durkheim, M. Mauss in particular) in conjunction with the social and cultural anthropology which was making its appearance at about that time. And exactly in 1922, a new sector of sociology emerges under the name of 'colonial sociology' (R. Maunier).

Can one therefore speak of a new theoretical contribution, a new problematic? The principal works of this period, none of them either Marxist or inspired by Marxism, are very poor in theoretical content. In 1880, however, a new concept – 'acculturation'[8] – arose in the United States and enjoyed a measure of success, in so far as it expressed the kernel of deep Western thought, explicit at that time and now always implicit, as Malinowski's critique of the concept clearly indicates (though it was in fact only presented in 1940):

> The term 'acculturation' is an ethnocentric term with a moral significance . . . [It] implies, by the preposition *ad* which begins it, the concept of *terminus ad quem*. The uncultured man must receive the benefits of our culture; it is he who must change, and be converted into one of us.[9]

It could not be better put.

There is no trace of Marxism. In Lenin's works on imperialism and the national question, the superstructural dimension remains secondary. Austro-Marxism pays more attention to it, on the basis of the German tradition of cultural history and philosophy; but it is always the problem of nationalities in Europe that concerns it.[10] The generous socialist humanism of Jaures goes unnoticed. In a recently unified Italy, the Southern question gave rise to an intense but incomplete theoretical elaboration by Gramsci.[11] It was through the medium of Italian cultural dualism that European Marxism came to glimpse the problem of the dialectics of civilisations, the incompatibility of the industrialised and cultivated North with a South whose roots lay in the human landscape of the non-European Mediterranean. Only the theorists and the sociologists of the imperial countries who are directly concerned seem to recognise that the problem exists, albeit only in the restricted sense mentioned above. The 'other' is certainly perceived – but as literally 'barbaric' and 'uncivilised'; the point is to 'reduce' them at both the real and the theoretical level.

The central problematic of Marxism provides the instruments of analysis and the appropriate means of action by which to face up to and resolve what we have defined as the central problem – the crisis – of Western civilisation at this stage in its historical evolution. The key was to be the development of Marxism within the body of the social sciences and of sociology, while the state born of the October Revolution of 1917 shook the world – and not only the 'civilised' world.

2.   The era of world revolutions: sociology and civilisations

After October 1917, the history of the world – both the 'civilised' and the 'peripheral' world – unfolds under the aegis of the revolutionary phenomenon. There are socialist revolutions and revolutions of national liberation (we cannot offer here even the outline of a typology), but also, of course, counter-revolutions, wars of extermination and genocide. The world is rediscovering its unity, and at the same time its diversity. It could be argued, of course, that every age has known violence. In the twentieth century, violence presents itself as an instrument with which to realise an aim that is human, millenarian, Utopian, voluntaristic, revolutionary-romantic, or more simply concretely and historically inevitable, given the existing reality. And the very elaboration of this objective, and of its essential problematic, as well as the global counter-objective of imperialism and reaction, takes as its starting-point an ideology – Marxism – which it seeks either to realise or to hold back. It must be understood, of course, that we are not concerned here only with the influence of the first great socialist revolution, but with the impact of all those national and social revolutions, from the Paris Commune to Vietnam, which have been moved and inspired by Marxism.

At the level of the content of sociology itself and its relations with the dialectics of civilisations – the level which concerns us here – there are a number of factors of change that merit our attention.

First of all, the differentiation of sociology into different sectors affects both research and theory, as well as teaching programmes. The current rift between theoretical and operational sociology is not the result of their use of different methodological instruments (mathematics, history, field research or ideological postulates, etc.), but of the different objectives which these two major trends in modern sociology set themselves. There are major differences in the way in which the nature of the work is defined, and their sociological aims described by the epigones of either side. In our opinion, that rift can be dated back to the years of the great world economic crisis of 1929–32.

At that time, European positivism has fulfilled its role in the field of the human and social sciences, and the deep-rooted ideology of pragmatism and empiricism of the state, and the culture most directly affected by this crisis – namely the United States – enters the fray. It was to adopt two main forms. On the one hand, sociologists educated within the European schools of philosophy and history, and in terms of its a- or anti-historicist structuralism, would devote themselves to enumerating 'types', 'models', 'schemes' and 'structures', disentangling relationships that are inextricably interwoven, and refining descriptions and analyses that will then be employed in reinforcing rigid criteria justified in terms of the exigencies of 'methodology'. For that methodology is devoted to describing and quantifying what is, in the belief that historicism can only lead to causal interpretations and to praxis. This tendency, of course, has its leading exponent in Talcott Parsons; his many emulators, however, often lack his inspiration.

The second form, on the other hand, consists of a social science which grows out of the vulgar scientism of the late nineteenth century, and is not to be confused with the other, structuralist, sociology. We enter here the fertile field of social surveys and statistical aggregates of all kinds, whose resolutely anti-historicist and anti-theoretical character gives rise to tables, typologies and calculations whose interpretative value is practically nil. It is to these professional sociologists that we owe the commercial evaluation of[12] and the reluctance to adopt a scientific attitude towards sociology today.

It is true that the crisis sent a number of rising sociologists in the wrong direction. The culminating point seems to have been reached between 1930 and 1952, when the Second World War and later the war in Korea seemed to prove that the centre of Western hegemony had overcome the internal threat; the 'Great Society'[13] established during the Cold War affirmed its ascendancy, while productivist ethics and the productivist way of life appeared to become the model for everyone. Theoretical sociology travels its own road under the shadow of its great founders, among whom Marx and Weber stand out. The quality of Weber's disciples and the number of works inspired by him are well known, although his own writings are now being strongly challenged. Raymond Aron called him 'our contemporary', a thinker 'who makes the rejection of dogmatism itself dogmatic, who lends definitive truth to the contradiction of values, and who ultimately recognises only a partial science and a strictly arbitrary choice', a tortured thinker rather than the philosopher of industrial society; as E. Fleischmann called him, a 'Marx of the bourgeoisie'.[14] His idealist philosophy of history leads him to assign to culture a central role in the dialectics that is set in motion with the establishment of the state. His approach is strongly marked by the formalism of his age, the formalism of the German Expressionists – hence his influence on American structuralist sociology.

Weber takes Marx as his starting-point, as indeed do *all* thought and all the human and social sciences of the twentieth century. Marx's influence expresses itself in a number of ways: directly, in the thought and research of avowedly Marxist sociologists, some of whom are directly engaged in revolutionary political activity; and indirectly, in the work of those who explicitly recognise the contribution of Marx's theses without calling themselves Marxists. Implicitly, that influence is present in the work of the great majority of sociologists – particularly the theorists, but also a significant number of operational sociologists. For the central theses of Marxism are everywhere, so to speak, taken for granted, whether in works concerned with the importance of the socio-economic infrastructure, in theoretical approaches to the relations between infrastructure and superstructure, or in a more complex way, in those that deal with the dialectics of classes and social groups or the historical evolution of societies. In all of them, however, the role of praxis is underplayed.

At this point, we should draw attention to a fourth group – of sociologists in the Three Continents; there the majority view is explicitly Marxist, and Marxism has inspired theoretical and empirical research in a number of countries (Brazil, Mexico, Egypt, Tunisia, India, etc.)[15] which has led in its turn to new and highly original theoretical formulations.

These considerations should illustrate the problems resulting from the division of the discipline of sociology into different sectors, as well as the difficulties associated with a sociology of civilisations. As the Second World War ended, four types of classification remained worthy of attention: first of all, the Durkheim school in its critical and socialist development by G. Gurvitch; the Anglo-American classifications, recently brought up to date under the aegis of Unesco; the classification put forward by the neo-Marxist sociologist T. B. Bottomore; and finally, in the wake of its seventh Congress at Evian, 1966, the list of research commissions issued by the International Sociological Association.[16] Two factors are worth noting: first, that the number of disciplines and branches concerned with the sociology of the superstructure is markedly greater in categories 1, 2 and 4, than in the – essentially American – Anglo-American classifications; secondly, despite the increasing importance of superstructural sociology, there is a marked unease at the level of elaboration about the possibility of a sociology of civilisations. Already in 1950, a useful sociological manual inspired by Durkheim isolated the 'sociology of civilisation' within the framework of a discipline called 'political sociology' ('the state, the nation, the civilisation'); here the problems were considered in the light of the dialectics of the non-Western civilisations with 'the' civilisation within a humanist perspective on progress.[17]

The publication in 1960, under the direction of G. Gurvitch, of the *Traité de sociologie*, marked the consecration of the sociological concept of civilisation (it merits two sections of the ten that comprise the two volumes); its real concern, however, was with the various problems posed by the 'sociology of the works of civilisation' (religions, knowledge, morals, law, criminality, childhood, language, art, music, literature); it did include, however, a study by R. Bastide of 'the problem of the interrelations between civilisations and their works'.[18] The comparative approach is also to be found in Section Ten, which deals with the 'problems of the relationship between so-called "archaic" and "historic" societies' (three chapters), as well as in the chapter on 'the sociology of the underdeveloped regions'. What is basically under consideration here is the modern civilisation of Europe and North America; the 'others' are called 'societies' or 'regions', and are the objects of a nascent political anthropology. The problem of the dialectics of civilisations is thus posed. In 1966, eight (plus political sociology) out of the thirteen main disciplines officially recognised by the International Sociological Association belong to the sociology of the *superstructure*, notably the new disciplines of mass communications; education, leisure and popular culture; the sociology of medicine; psychiatry and the sociology of science. Shortly afterwards, a committee was created for research into the 'sociology of the new nations' which would concentrate on research into national formations (among them some of the oldest in the world) and contemporary underdeveloped societies. So the sociology of civilisations was still not internationally recognised.

T. B. Bottomore's manual brings us to the heart of the problem; for it is the *first*, and until now the only manual of general sociology which studies every aspect of the discipline in terms of the *double problematic* of Western sociology (the sociology of countries with capitalist and socialist socio-economic regimes) and of the underdeveloped world, represented in this case by India.[19] It is not only that the work includes a chapter on 'social structures, societies and civilisations' (chap. 3, p. 7); it also looks at the classical problems on the basis of the dialectical problematic in sociology. Thus the ex-colonial world serves as a case study, as an index, against which to measure the truly scientific (that is to say universal) coefficient of the two major tendencies in traditional sociology. And it is significant that the author is both a subject of one of the great ex-colonial powers (Great Britain), and the advocate of a Marxism that is coming to grips with the problems of the Three Continents.

These problems are not problems of development but essentially of civilisation. But before broaching what is the kernel of this essay, it would be appropriate to consider the historiography of this process of conceptualisation. Taking his lead from the insights of Durkheim and Mauss,[20] Arnold Toynbee elaborated from 1934 onwards a typology of civilisations (he numbers twenty-one and rather vaguely calls them 'societies'), one of whose principal notions he was to retain: that different societies maintain relations with each other to the extent that they share a common culture and cultural tradition.[21] In this way, the superstructural factor becomes, for the historian and the sociologist alike, the key to an understanding of a different world, of other civilisations formerly regarded as peripheral, barbaric or colonial. But there was still a need for something more than a methodological hypothesis; and once more, a case study in depth was to produce a theoretical renewal. For the object of Joseph Needham's monumental encyclopedia *Science and Civilisation in China*, which began to appear in 1954,[22] was precisely to explore the other, the major civilisation of the contemporary Orient, with its millenarian tradition – China. If its aim is indeed to erect a new universalism – 'To dissipate the shadows, to break down the ignorance, to bring together the divergent streams of human enterprise – to discover perhaps that they are not so divergent as is sometimes thought' – its method is sociological and Marxist: 'Only an analysis of the social and economic structures of Eastern and Western cultures, not forgetting the great role of systems of ideas, will in the end suggest an explanation of both these things.'

No work of this magnitude on the non-Western world, combining as it does the most extreme scientific rigour with insight, the voice of reason and feeling, has ever been undertaken before. In volume after volume, that 'other' world rises in all its grandeur, specific and universal; a civilisation unfolds with its own conception of man and scale of values, its own philosophy and ideology. The whole is interpreted on the basis of the specific history of that country in which economic and social structures underpin the analysis, and thus both make the Chinese phenomenon intelligible and at the same time considerably clarify the great debate of our time. This work is clearly of central importance; yet another civilisation – Islam – has also been the object of comprehensive studies by C. Cahen and M. Rodinson within a Marxist framework.[23] Other, often very original works (by J. Berque, N. Berkes, etc.) have shed new light on aspects of that civilisation and on the question of the relations between the classical legacy and the contemporary Arab and Islamic world,[24] though it does not lead them to furnish an interpretation of that world within the general framework of the sociology of civilisations. The great domains of India, Japan, Vietnam, Persia, Turkey; the relations between the great civilisations of Andean America and modern Latin America; and the corresponding relationships in black Africa, have been partially explored, but we still do not have an exhaustive and significant interpretation of them.

These works, whether historical or written from a sociological point of view, have helped us to arrive at definitions which will be valuable in the future. 'By *culture*, we understand the ideal aspects of social life as distinct from the relationships and the forms of association existing in reality between individuals; and by *a culture*, the ideal aspects of a particular society.' In this sense, culture belongs to the domain of the sociology of knowledge and of culture in its widest sense – that is, to the sociology of superstructures.

In that case, how are we to study 'a culture'? By what principles or criteria can one distinguish one culture from another? The same writer, in defining civilisation, provides the outline of an answer: 'By a *civilisation* we mean a cultural complex made up of the main identical characteristics of a certain number of individual societies.'[25] But the author resolutely abjures the 'culturalist' approach and insists on the organic relationship within each society between the 'material and non-material elements of culture'.

This, then, is the turning-point. Consider the dates – they are all *after* 1950, that is to say after the victory of the socialist revolution in China (the largest country in the Three Continents, and specifically of the Orient) and in the midst of mighty national liberation movements, and national and social revolutions which broke the essential hegemony of the traditional imperialisms and triumphantly defied the neo-imperialism of the United States. For historically speaking, sociology is the last-born of the human and social sciences; usually in an implicit way, it claims to be the *mediating* discipline between the different sciences; its theorists wrestle with non-traditional problems. It could not, therefore, escape the profound problems posed by the concrete practice of human societies. For that practice was not concerned with 'development', in the technological sense, or with 'cultural lag' (a relic of a proselytising paternalism), or yet with 'modernisation' (which is the expression of the technocratic ideology in the 'colonial' field). Their concern is the dialectics of different civilisations which clash on the political level now, yet which at root all pose the problem of man, of his new face, of the values that should be brought to life in the present, values for which he wishes to live and is willing to die – the problem of happiness on a planetary scale.

We have pointed to the necessity for this sociology of civilisations; what then is its fundamental problematic, and how should Marxists see their role in and contribution to its elaboration?

3.   The dialectics of the specific and the universal

There is no better illustration of the failure of the pseudo-universalist approach to the phenomena of civilisation – which is really a cosmopolitan and hegemonic phenomenon – than the collapse of W. W. Rostow's stillborn 'theory' of the so-called 'stages of development'.[26] The White House's chief adviser on Far Eastern politics is carried by the very logic of the social thought he expresses into the tragic impasse where the greatest power in history now flounders. For imperialist assimilationism, and the structures that must inexorably follow one upon the other (that is, 'development'), find themselves face to face with the peoples, the nationalitarian phenomenon, and the ideology of Marxism – in a word, civilisations.

3.1   Position of the theoretical problem

(*a*)   What one might call the technicist, or developmentalist approach, is founded on one central postulate: that there is no civilisation other than

Western (mainly European) civilisation, though its axis of power has now been displaced towards North America. The peoples, countries, regions, cultures and states that are not part of this civilisation must conform, if it is within their power, to 'the' civilisation – the Western way of life in its American variant. At best, in dealing with the more coherent and more restive totalities, it might be possible to recognise the existence of 'cultural areas'. But at all costs the spectre of the existence of different civilisations must be kept out. For it is there that the central challenge of history is to be found, when national and social revolutions arm themselves with scientific thought and modern technology.

(b)   Modernity has allowed the *depth of historical field*, the civilisational factor, to realise its potentiality – whether latent, or extinguished, or set in motion and then robbed of its nature during the period of decline of the non-Western civilisations, between the (European) Renaissance and the mid-nineteenth century.

It is impossible to deny the coexistence in time of different civilisations. The resurgence, or renascence of these civilisations in contemporary terms is a process whose irresistible force might, for the moment, be hidden by the immediate hazards and difficulties.

Once independence has been achieved, it becomes clear that the historical objective of the nationalitarian phenomenon is to make it possible for nations, and national-cultural units (cultures and civilisations) to sustain a dialectical interaction with the hegemonic civilisation, and to make their own specific contribution to it. And the instrument for this collective assumption of the destiny of man is none other than the independent national state, the effectiveness of whose action and vision of the future depends on its popular political content. It is precisely these factors that condition the full emergence of 'marginal' civilisations into contemporary life – and not their condition as members of a 'Third' world which is rich in numbers but impotent in action and without influence in the field of civilisation.

(c)   The principal problem, therefore, is the dialectics of the *specific* (the nationalitarian, cultural and civilisational factors) and the *universal* (the future syncretic civilisation that will embrace all men through the mediation of science and technology). In the first instance, the danger lies not in an excessive emphasis on the nationalitarian phenomenon, but in the imposition of hegemonic, so-called 'universal' moulds. For now more than ever, these will ensure the denaturing of the civilisations of the

non-Western world, reducing them to the status of by-products of technicism and productivism, of economic, demographic and ethnological reserve armies, in the shadows of an alienated world.

This is the point of coincidence between the revolutions of (national and social) liberation and the unavoidable restatement of the role of Western civilisation in dialectical terms; the aim is to create an authentically humanist civilisation in which the great national-cultural units, the principal civilisations will act through confrontation and through historical time to restore to all men their fullness and the sovereignty over their own lives.

(d) It follows that the fundamental categories, the general tone of the sociology of civilisations will be dynamic and dialectical: 'revolution', 'change', 'flux', 'transformation', 'mutations', 'evolution', 'liberation', 'industrialisation', 'national culture', 'the reconquest of identity', 'national rebirth', 'modernity', etc. Gross or net national income, productivity, development aid (bilateral, multilateral or whatever), the formation of technicians are all important elements − but they are never decisive. One must seek a foundation in oneself, and in the national popular collectivity, where the essential resources for renaissance are to be found.

The concrete-historicist formulation of the problem now allows us to move to the critical level.

3.2   Critique of the different non-Marxist approaches

These approaches can be divided into two major groups − although they could be categorised in a more differentiated way:

(a)   *Idealist* philosophies and methodologies, embracing in their turn the following subgroups:

1. Philosophies of history: Hegelianism continues to inspire many works, particularly those which seek to account for the superstructural factors which for some time had been hidden by the deeply wrong interpretation of Marxism as economic materialism. The notion of the dialectical cycle, of the analysis–synthesis diad are not unrelated to Toynbee's ambitious project. The same themes recur in a number of doctrinal works on the national 'mission' or national resurgence set within a spiritualist framework, both in the Orient and in the West.

This view of the problem has its value; I have already pointed to the positive contribution, in some areas, of Toynbee's work. Others, if less distinguished, can offer insights into those elements of the social and national psychology which survive a study in depth. Nevertheless, the interpretative value of such works remains limited. In fact the philosophies of history postulate, in a general though still highly diversified sense, the concrete history of the societies which they are examining on the basis of real principles presented as if they were so many distinct entities. The resulting *exceptionalism* in fact borders on an ethno-racial typology and a structuralist stasis; it is recognised that history evolves, but only within this structure rooted in an abstraction.

2. Spiritual philosophies essentially religious in inspiration: Their source is different, yet their character is similar to the preceding type. The civilising mission of Christianity denotes a similar conception in fundamentalist Islam and contentious Judaism. Here, however, the philosophical framework is explicitly universalist – and perhaps more so in Islam than in the other two major monotheistic religions, because of the very conditions of their emergence. Their interpretation of civilisations and their evolution is rooted in the civilisational milieu in which they originated. Their universalist aspiration implies the integration of elements, environments, cultures and societies – all of them reducible, to the extent that they belong to the same, or similar civilisations – into the model which is regarded as predominant or most authentically representative, whether it be the Christian West (despite its attempts to come up to date) or Arab Islam (despite the Afro-Asian sphere).[27] The mediation towards modernity, towards the evolution of civilisations, cannot be analysed in their terms; at best it provides a means of moderation. For it is impossible that theological doctrines founded on intemporality should now focus on the changing face of the contemporary world, most of which is concerned with the problem of physical survival in its most literal and immediate sense.

(b) *Positivist* philosophies and methodologies, including the following subdivisions:

1. The phenomenological approach (phenomenology, existentialism, etc.). It is ambiguous in nature since it seems to have its roots both in realist philosophy and in subjective idealism. Realist in the sense – to follow A. Lalande's customary definition – that it is 'the descriptive

study of a complex of phenomena as they manifest themselves in time or space, as opposed to either the abstract and fixed laws of these phenomena; or to transcendent realities of which they are manifestations; or to the normative critique of their legitimacy'. Subjective idealism, in Husserl's version, in which the objectivity of the world appears as a 'transcendental intersubjectivity' (G. Berger), and particularly in existentialist philosophies from Kierkegaard to the present day.[28] Without entering here into the philosophical controversy, phenomenology at all events provides no principle for interpreting the evolutionary process or continuity, nor does it provide a method for relating the specific and the universal. While it is true that it offers a description whose richness and depth considerably enhance our perception of 'the moment of being' and its resonances within the individual subject, it offers little to causal interpretation. Ultimately, the nature of the philosophical project does not differ greatly from the positivist, though the phenomenologists would vehemently deny it. No catalogue, however subtle it is, can provide the insights or the causal keys to movement in time.

2. The structuralist approach sets out to steal the limelight from Marxism. I have no intention of offering a general critique of this school at this point; recent work by H. Lefebvre, E. Hobsbawm and L. Goldmann, among others, provides an adequate scientific foundation for such a critique. What I do wish to do here is to define the structuralist approach to the sociology of civilisations, and to assess its contribution.

It seems that the main objective is simply to refute, at all costs, historicity itself, to dehistoricise the world. Thus its research was undertaken in the marginal societies, the societies 'without a history', and its method implicitly or explicitly generalised for the whole field of sociology. It remains to be seen whether there are any human groups without a history. What is certain is that the (historical) marginalisation of human groups, of societies from the great flux of change and movement in the world is itself a historical phenomenon; for only history can enable us to understand its causes. Toynbee's recently published conclusions,[29] which echo those of Wright Mills, E. Gellner and G. Balandier,[30] make the point in what appears to be a decisive way; the very choice of so-called a-historical groups and societies is itself an ideological choice dictated by the desire to fix the 'present moment of being' as structure. The structuralists themselves, of course, will refute this description of them. But then the very fact that they pay exclusive attention to marginal societies reputedly without a history means that they cannot offer their methodology for use in a domain ruled by the dialectical movement of history. By avowedly limiting itself to the study of marginal human groups, structuralism marginalises itself from 'the great thrust of history'.

3.3   Critique of the Marxist approach

(a)   For our purposes, the central Marxist concept is that of 'historical specificity', a concept taken up by a number of authors including Wright Mills, F. Braudel and others; today it has been adopted by the majority of sociologists and theorists in the Three Continents. Let me begin with Wright Mills's development of the concept:

> What Marx called the 'principle of historical specificity' refers, first, to a guide-line; any given society is to be understood in terms of the specific period in which it exists . . . in work on a contemporary society, I think it is very often a good rule first to attempt to explain its contemporary features in terms of their contemporary function. This means to locate them, to see them as parts of and even as due to other features of their contemporary setting. If only to define them, to delimit them clearly, to make their components more specific, it is best to begin with a more or less narrow – although still of course historical – span.[31]

(b)   This principle means, in the second place, that 'in the framework of this historical type, different mechanisms of change intersect in a specific way'. But, why 'specific', if all science is general?

(c)   In the first place, why 'necessarily historical'? Because 'history is the nerve-centre of social science'; because 'every social science – or better, every well-thought social study – requires a historical scope of conception and a full use of historical materials'. It is in fact the case that 'a-historical studies usually tend to be static or very short-term studies of limited milieux. That is only to be expected, for we more readily become aware of larger structures when they are changing, and we are likely to become aware of such changes only when we broaden our view to include a suitable historical span.'

It is true that 'in our time the problems of Western societies are almost inevitably problems of the world'. But the historical dimension is an important factor of interpretation in the non-Western world: 'That knowledge of the history of a society is often indispensable to its understanding becomes quite clear to any economist or political scientist or sociologist once he leaves his advanced industrial nation to examine the institutions in some different social structure – in the Middle East, in Asia, in Africa.' For the *coefficient of causal interpretative value* of the historical factor is not everywhere and always the same.

> I believe that periods and societies differ in respect to whether or not understanding them requires direct reference to 'historical factors' .... It is, of course, quite clear that to understand a slow-moving society, trapped for centuries in a cycle of poverty and tradition and disease and ignorance, requires that we study the historical ground, and the persistent historical mechanisms of its terrible entrapment in its own history. Explanation of that cycle, and of the mechanics of each of its phases, require a very deep-going historical analysis. What is to be explained, first of all, is the mechanism of the full cycle.[32]

It thus becomes clear how the historical factor leads into specificity, in the first instance. And the 'sociological principle of historical specificity' is as valid in studying America as it is in the non-Western societies: 'It is only by comparative studies that we can become aware of the *absence* of certain historical phases from a society, which is often quite essential to understanding its contemporary shape.' Comparative studies of what phenomena?

> As the history-making unit, the dynamic nation-state is also the unit within which the variety of men and women are selected and formed, liberated and repressed – it is the man-making unit. That is one reason why struggles between nations and between blocs of nations are also struggles over the types of human beings that will eventually prevail in the Middle East, in India, in China, in the United States; that is why culture and politics are now so intimately related; and that is why there is such need and such demand for the sociological imagination.[33]

The use of the principle of historical specificity leads directly to the concept of 'civilisation' as defined below.

(d)   Is it then possible to conceive of the dialectics of the specific and the universal? There can be no universal without a comparative framework; there can be no universal in the framework of Euro-centrism. 'In our very statement of what-is-to-be-explained, we need the fuller range that can be

provided only by knowledge of the historical varieties of human society.'
Thus 'when [the economist or political scientist or sociologist] takes up a
fuller range, when he compares, he becomes more aware of the historical
as intrinsic to what he wants to understand and not merely as "general
background" '. That is also why 'some of the very best sociology being
done today is work on world areas and regions'. From these insights flow
the fundamental principles of method: 'Comparative study and historical
study are very deeply involved with each other . . . the mind cannot even
formulate the historical and sociological problems of this one [national]
social structure without understanding them in contrast and in comparison with other societies.'[34]

Therein lies the significance of a long-term history that is not
structuralist, but structural (Braudel): 'The long-term view is always
necessary, if only to overcome historical provincialism and the postulation that the present is some sort of autonomous creation.' 'For historical
change *is* change of social structures, the changing relations between
their constituent parts.' And he adds, 'Just as there is a variety of social
structures, so there is a variety of principles of historical change.' Does
this call into question the universality of scientific criteria themselves?

(e)   The question merits deeper consideration. If we were to take the
phrase literally, we could find there echoes of Weber's ideal-type; for, as
Asa Briggs shows, 'the national mould of the constitution of history
encourages the use of stereotypes, including those that deal with national
character'.[35]

3.4   Factors of interpretation

One should distinguish two groups of factors of interpretation within this
field:

1. The traditional factors, and in particular the 'infrastructure–
superstructure' diad which the majority of contemporary research still
employs. These two factors become more obviously significant in periods
of revolution, of profound changes, and in the course of periods (or
structures) of a more even, regular, 'normal' kind.

2. Within this general social and historical dialectic (which I take to be
the central core of historical materialism) there is room for *far more
attention* to be paid both to superstructural factors, and to the new dialectics located at the very heart of the traditional diad, and leading to the

synthesis called 'the principle of historical specificity'. This reconsideration is imposed by the very civilisational framework in which Marxism emerged and developed up to 1930–49.

The superstructural factors which appear as 'overdetermined' and 'overdetermining' (Althusser) are national ideologies, both explicit and implicit (M. Rodinson, V. Lanternari), national social psychology, particularly in the framework of the old nations or national formations (Egypt, China, Persia, Mexico, etc.).[36] They are *over*determining, because they are often apparently more powerful than infrastructural economic or sociological factors.

We must recognise, however (and this is the second part of our answer), that the effective nature and power of these factors are the *result* of the depth of the historical field of the national community itself. Hence, as I have shown, this astonishing symbiosis of economics (the mastery or control of water and earth), politics (a highly centralised autocratic power under the army) and ideology (be it political or religious) which has dominated the history of Egypt through seven millenia. This 'principle of historical specificity' is Egyptian in terms of its specific context, yet also universal (and thus intelligible in Marxist terms) in terms of the dialectics that explain it, that is to say the socio-geography of Egypt. For it is the 'most compact of the hydraulic societies' (Wittfogel), located as it is at the crossroads of the Orient and the West, surrounded by deserts, squadrons, and the networks of commerce and of civilisation that struggle and compete.

It now becomes possible to 'study history in order to get rid of it', rationally, patiently and deliberately to modify the operation of specific factors and their long-term dialectics – although always within the general framework of that historical specificity itself. In the case of Egypt, for example, we must selectively place the ideological and the political in their dialectical relation through a concerted pluralism. The aim would be to draw together the most radical, and as yet neglected, transformation factor – the mass action (in a literal sense) of the people of the country and the city – and the whole (pluralist) existing or potential spectrum of ideological and political factors. Only thus can the curse of centralisation, with its weight of static and reactionary bureaucratism, be broken. This action is itself impossible, however, if we lose sight of the general framework, if we deny the role of the state and of the sociological symbiosis in Egypt.

To make historical specificity dialectical is not to turn one's back on it – quite the contrary; here, as elsewhere, 'liberty is the recognition of necessity'. It is a harsh necessity; a hard school. But that is the future.

*   *   *

Is it simply coincidence that the intelligentsia of the Three Continents find their fundamental theoretical support in Marxism, which has repudiated Euro-centrism in depth and in principle? Is it by chance that it is sociological works and political action inspired by Marxism that strike the observer in their acuteness and originality?[37]

The Marxism in question is a *general sociological conception and method – historical materialism*. The application of this method to the advanced industrial societies will not yield up any lasting contribution to the non-Western societies in their hour of renaissance. Yet the same truly scientific vision and method applied to other factors, on the basis of historical specificity, make Marxism in our day the most perceptive instrument of analytical research into civilisations as well as the privileged mediator between them. For it is understood that 'Man must prove the truth, that is, the reality and power, the this-sidedness of his thinking, in practice'.[38]

There is no doubt that for the Marx of 1845, whose great human stature we salute today from one end of the globe to the other, the 'this-sidedness' in question was not in the Three Continents, but elsewhere. Yet today, 150 years later, the ideas and the spirit that inspire Marxism are the essential factors which make revolution the privileged instrument in the rebirth of civilisations. It is that, more than anything else, which testifies to the effective and theoretical truth of work which is only now embarking on its *universal* historical course.

7

Charles de Gaulle and the Dialectics of Civilisations

Inevitable though it may be whenever one is dealing with someone outside the mediocre, it is time we put aside hagiography and polemic, and studied the thought and action of Charles de Gaulle in critical terms. We must try to assess its limits and its possibilities, and not merely its immediate effects or its tactical validity.

One must begin with a well established fact; here is a man from a social class, a spiritual family, a milieu that has traditionally been at the service of the bourgeois, Catholic, military order, the order of that state maintaining the French nation throughout its post-revolutionary phase. Three times already that class has turned its back on the interests of the nation – in order to break Napoleon, shoot down the Communards, and submit to Hitler – and we know that on the last two occasions at least the motive was fear and hatred of the working people. Here a critical, comparativist appraisal would note that this continuity of behaviour on the basis of the primacy of class imperatives is not repeated among other European bourgeoisies in power. If the conservative and royalist political leadership had not chosen the battle of London and the burning of Coventry rather than their own form of Petainism, the European will to independence and democracy would have crumbled in the face of Hitler's Fascism ten years before Stalingrad.

Charles de Gaulle, born into the class and that milieu, rejected that tradition. He placed loyalty to the nation, love of country, and the will to maintain national honour – which is also the honour of the people – above and beyond his class position.

Everything else is a consequence of this fundamental position, in particular that aspect of the dialectical dimension of international relations which de Gaulle had the lucidity, the merit and the courage to define and structure.

It is not our intention here to consider the internal course of that policy or its better known international aspects – like his attitude to the polarised world that emerged from Yalta, or to atomic weapons, which no doubt others will discuss. Our purpose here is to bring to the fore a reality based on his fundamental positions as defined with great flourish on 18 June 1940 – that reality is de Gaulle's understanding of the dialectics of Orient and West, or rather between the various Orients and the different Wests.

Nothing, in fact, had prepared the man of 18 June to go beyond the Brazzaville Charter. At the time, it was a great step forward – in comparison with traditional colonialist positions. Yet the content of the Brazzaville theses is very limited: encouraging the autochthonous development of the colonial territories of Africa, evolving towards autonomy within the framework of union with the ex-colonial and still hegemonic power; yet giving primacy to the major options defined by the centre, whose culture was wilfully defined as the culture of the whole. It was a rearrangement of the colonial empire, rather than a real move towards 'self-government'. The date, nevertheless, is significant and justifies our interest in this first approach to the problem.

From the Brazzaville Charter to the speech at Phnom-Penh, scarcely a quarter of a century elapses; yet it traces an immense curve from liberal paternalism to a denunciation of imperialism and support for the great revolutionary national liberation struggles in the Orient. How and why did this happen?

Between 1940 and 1968, despite Nazism, despite the world power balance agreed at Yalta, one fundamental truth imposed itself; the great social and political movements of our time are deployed along a matrix of nations. This is the case of the national resistance fronts against Nazi occupation, and of the national liberation fronts against imperialism. It is the case in the newly structured powers, whether within the capitalist variant or as part of the socialism under the banner of Marxism whose progress after the 1939–45 war was so marked. This reality, so obstinately denied by an important layer of intellectuals in the West (though not by the political class, which was in touch with the real world), provided a resounding proof, if such were needed, of the stupidity, the inadequacy and the pernicious character of the calculations and perspectives emerging from the hegemonic centres alone. The division of the world among the two Great Powers was to face increasing and unexpected difficulties throughout the world. Charles de Gaulle saw there a powerful ally, whose role he had foreseen in relation to occupied

Europe from the French point of view. At the same time, others began to recognise the inexorable character of what was then called 'decolonisation' (instead of national liberation, independence, the reconquest of identity, etc.).

But this time, the nationalitarian phenomenon was to strike Europe at its very heart. With China, Egypt, India, Indonesia, Malaysia, Iran, Cuba, Vietnam, Algeria and the Maghreb, and the whole of the Arab world, the problem began to take on the dimensions of revolution. And in their very diversity, these movements revealed in the most brutal way the root of the problem; the existence of nations, forming part of different cultures, themselves organised into two great civilisations whose struggles and clashes formed the framework of that dialectic of cultures and civilisations which was thought to have dissipated, to have disappeared under the joint impact of the industrial revolution and the universalism postulated in the encyclopedic rationalism of the hegemonic West.

For Charles de Gaulle, that was the time of his retreat into the wilderness. What was at issue now was not state power, but how to respond to the position of the problem of state power, of all possible state power in our time; to what ends did one seek power? Was it a state whose task is to maintain and remodel a nation endowed with a sufficient depth of historical field?

At the time (1940–68) there was only one possible reply, with a number of variations; the object of the state is to maintain a given social order at the service of a specific political project. Hence the primacy at this level of 'international relations', of 'foreign affairs'; hence the Brazzaville Charter.

Yet de Gaulle, because of his roots and education as well as his experience as an eminent leader of the French nation, was able to go further. For the crisis of which he was one of the principal protagonists was the crisis of the West, of the Wests. It reached into the classical European colonialism and imperialism (of Great Britain, France, Holland, Belgium, etc.) and into American imperialism and neo-imperialism, from Hiroshima to Vietnam. The content of this crisis was the confrontation between the hitherto hegemonic Wests, and the various Orients; for in our time, the Orient as a whole has reached the level of national renaissance and social revolution through vast and complex struggles against imperialism.

Left to themselves, these struggles could not but deepen even further the gulf between the developed and the poor nations, between the hegemonic states and the dependent nations struggling for their liberation – between the Orient and the West. Unless, of course, there arose a mediator, or an instrument of mediation; de Gaulle, from a Western and specifically European standpoint, presented himself as the first among men of intelligence and reason. He turned first to the two great spheres of movement: China and the Asian sphere, and Egypt and the Arab world.

Why did he make that decision? It was because de Gaulle, the statesman, could also call upon de Gaulle the historian and political philosopher. A broad historical, political and military culture, an understanding of the realities of religion and ideology, and an exceptional sensitivity to the relations between politics and culture, enabled him to understand that the Orient was in fact structured around two great spheres of movement (and not merely 'cultural' spheres) inspired by Chinese civilisation, and by an Arab culture nourished by Islam. Thus the only possible authentic mediation must address itself to the main poles of attraction at the heart of each of these two spheres. A historical consciousness led to an understanding of the political movement of our time and of the future, beyond a simple political realism.

This is the source of the major overtures. The first genuine embassy sent by the European West to China came from France. The first Western European state prepared to make an effort to overcome the emotional and cultural heritage of the Crusades in the Arab and Islamic world was also France – by accepting Algerian independence, and by recognising the positive character of Nasser's Egypt. The texts abound, though they are little known. Paul Balta refers to one, for example, in which de Gaulle comments thus on French policy towards the Arabs:

> Trade, economics, culture, are all very important. We must look at what is happening, for it is there that the future is being made; and we must look well ahead. You see, on the other side of the Mediterranean there are developing countries. But they also have a civilisation, a culture, a humanism, of their own; they have a sense of human relations which we tend to lose in our industrialised societies, and which one day we shall be glad to rediscover through them. We and they, each at his own pace, according to our own possibilities and our own capacity, are moving forwards towards industrial civilisation. However, if we want to build an industrial civilisation around the Mediterranean – that midwife of great civilisations – that is not built along American lines, and in which man will be an end not a means,

then our cultures must be more open to one another. ('Le monde arabe et la France' in *Le Monde*, 20 July 1972, pp. 1 and 4)

It needed the genocide in Vietnam to make certain people fully realise (far too late) the import of de Gaulle's 1966 speech at Phnom-Penh. How much time and how many proofs will it take for Western public opinion to become aware of the rising dangers in the Arab and Islamic world – from Morocco to Central and Southern Asia – dangers that will affect them directly if they go on combining against their renaissance?

In the Orient, in the era of its renaissance and its revolutions, in the footsteps of Mao and Nasser, it is the popular masses even more than the political class who have recognised in de Gaulle an eminent mediator between East and West in the tradition of Alexander and Napoleon Bonaparte. It is their fervent hope that his example will open Western eyes and lay the paths of our common future.

8

Joseph Needham: Encyclopedist of Civilisations

The time has come at last when the West must begin to realise that the Orient of the Orientalists is no more, that it must overcome the reticence and the prejudice, the ignorance born of non-recognition. Today, the West must listen to the voices and recognise the new ways arising in that great arc of civilisations and cultures that is the renascent, revolutionary Orient – from Morocco to the China Sea. There has long been a marked reluctance to take this step, but this time the development of ideas has opened the way, in advance of any political overtures. And that development is set in motion by the work of Arnold Toynbee and Jacques Berque, but above all of Joseph Needham, the outstanding encyclopedist of the dialectics of civilisations in our time.

The trajectory of both the man and his work has been a curious one; and the full recognition of the scientific and cultural contribution represented by that great *summa*, *Science and Civilisation in China*, with its accompanying volumes of essays, has taken an equally strange course. Needham was born at the beginning of the century; his father was a doctor, and his mother a musician. He read medicine at Caius College, Cambridge, and became passionately interested in historicism through his studies in the history of science, as well as in philosophy, the comparative study of religions, and mysticism. His bedside books – Lancelot Andrewes, Jeremy Taylor, Angelus Silesius, Herbert of Cherbourg, Miguel de Molinos and the *Fioretti* of St Francis of Assisi – the influence of Edward Browne's exposition of Arab and Persian medicine, of F. C. Burkitt's treatment of Manichaean religion in the sands of the Gobi desert; 'these were the scholars', according to his lifelong friend Henry Holorenshaw, 'who inspired him with a sense of the excitement and romance of humanist scholarship, especially when combined with the history of the natural sciences'.[1]

124 *Dialectics of Civilisations*

These were the sources of a truly encyclopedic vocation, not limited merely to calculation, inventory-making or formal analysis, but committed to a syncretic, global approach, a vision in which reason and emotion are tightly interwoven. Having completed his medical studies in 1921, Needham undertook research in biochemistry at Cambridge and in 1924, having received his doctorate, he became a Fellow of his own college (he was to be elected its Master in 1966) and married Dorothy May Moyle, a talented biochemist in her own right who would later be elected together with her husband to a Fellowship of the Royal Academy. This was the beginning of a period of intense intellectual liberation, with R. G. Collingwood, Vaihinger, and above all Rudolf Otto, whose 'Idea of the Holy' would bring Needham closer to an understanding of the aesthetic, miraculous value of liturgical symbolism; the writings of William Blake, D. H. Lawrence, Edward Carpenter and Havelock Ellis were pointing the way to sexual liberation. A number of Needham's essays, sometimes side by side with those of prestigious colleagues like Dean Inge, Malinowski and Eddington, were collected in several volumes: *Science, Religion and Reality*; *The Sceptical Biologist*; *The Great Amphibium*; and above all *Time, the Refreshing River*, with its autobiographical introduction. Encouraged by F. G. Hopkins, the father of British biochemistry, he established himself at the Cambridge Biochemical Laboratory where, between 1929 and 1942, he gave ample evidence of his capacity in the scientific field: the three volumes of *Chemical Embryology*; *Biochemistry and Morphogenesis*; *History of Embryology*; and later the Yale lectures, *Order and Life*, in which he put forward a pioneering conception of the role of micro-structures within the living cell – before the age of the electron microscope. He was Visiting Professor at the Universities of Yale, Standford, Cornell, London, Oxford, Warsaw, Cracow, Lyons and Kyoto. He undertook a number of study trips and lecturing tours, culminating in the award of a number of distinctions including, in 1968, the George Sarton Gold Medal at the Paris International Congress of Scientific History.

The threads would be drawn together at the community of Thaxted Church, in Essex, under its vicar, Conrad Noel, where a socialism inspired by Christianity was combined with a great musical tradition and a search for liturgical beauty.

This doctrine of the Kingdom of God [wrote Holorenshaw] was of particular importance. Joseph Needham formed at that time the conviction, never afterwards abandoned, that it should be regarded as a realm of justice and comradeship on earth, to be brought about by the efforts of men throughout the centuries not primarily as some mystical body existing already, or some spiritual state to be expected sometime in the future. Gradually this became linked up in his mind with a conviction of the essential unity of cosmological, organic and social evolution, in which the idea of human progress, with all due reservations, would find its place. Parallel with this was the conviction that the Christian must take Marxism extremely seriously, such doctrines as historical materialism and class struggle being perhaps recognition of the ways in which God has worked during the evolution of society.[2]

Thus *History on Our Side* (1945) is subtitled 'Essays in Political Religion and Scientific Faith'. This was to be the fruit of his post-war meeting with Teilhard de Chardin, at a time when Needham was well into the second, Chinese stage of his work; to some extent it represented the culmination of the development towards an ideal on which he had embarked with Charles Raven and John Lewis, in 1935, with *Christianity and the Social Revolution*. In 1925, at the Marine Biology Station at Roscoff, Louis Rapkine had introduced him to the works of Spinoza and to Marxism. Thus, on the eve of the Second World War of 1939–45, Needham's whole life history pointed towards the development of an encyclopedic vision.

Then – China. Various Chinese scholars had come to Cambridge before 1938; Wang Ying-Lei, who later became Director of the Shanghai National Institute of Biochemistry; Shen Shih-Chang; particularly Lu Gei-Djen, who was to introduce him to the language and civilisation of China and became an intimate friend to the Needhams, 'the commentator, the antithesis, the proof, and the assurance of a relationship which no separation could undermine'.[3] Towards 1938, Needham 'evolved a plan to write a systematic, rigorous and objective treatise on the history of science, scientific thought and technology within the Chinese cultural sphere'. War dispersed the companions; yet it also provided the stepping-stone which would enable this historic project to come into being. In 1942, Needham left for China, first as director of the British Scientific Mission, later as scientific adviser to the British Embassy at Chungking. He directed the Sino-British Science Co-operation Office, with the stated objective of establishing relations between Chinese and Western scientists; he became Adviser to the Medical Administration of the Chinese Army and to the Chinese National Commission for Natural

Resources. He travelled tirelessly around China by camel, on horseback or by raft and thus gained a knowledge of the deep country, of the men, the scientists, the immemorial history, the regions and the ecology of the country which remains unequalled to this day. The diaries and notebooks covering this period are reproduced in *Chinese Science* (1945) and *Science Outpost* (1947). He was elected a foreign member of the Chinese National Academy – now the Academia Sinica – and was awarded the Order of the Brilliant Star. In 1958 he undertook another similar long mission for the government of Ceylon. In 1944, Needham began to advocate the establishment of an International Scientific Co-operation Agency; as a result of this campaign, UNECO added science to its existing areas of concern – education and culture – and became UNESCO, whose Natural Sciences division was directed by Needham between 1946 and 1948.

Meanwhile, the 1938 project was beginning to take shape, and revealing hitherto unsuspected dimensions. The first volume of *Science and Civilisation in China*, published in 1954, made it clear that the project could not be held within limits; a vast collective of a dozen or more scholars and researchers under Lu Gei-Djen, Wang Lung, Ho Ping-Yu, Lo Jung-Pang, K. Robinson, D. de Solla Price, J. H. Combridge and N. Sivin has ensured the publication of four parts, in six volumes, up to the present; each volume numbers some 2000 to 3000 pages in an encyclopedia format. The completed work will number seven parts in eleven volumes, plus a cumulative index.[4] Needham himself assumed responsibility for the presentation and synthesis, for formulating the theses and the problematic for each volume and each subject. He was to publish simultaneously a series of volumes that amount to a sort of reflection, as well as including more detailed studies into some of the fields referred to in the encyclopedic work itself: these include *Heavenly Clockwork, The Development of Iron and Steel Technology in China*, and in particular the three volumes of 1970: *Clerks and Craftsmen in China and the West, The Grand Titration*, and *Science and Society in East and West*; the latest work is *La Tradition Scientifique Chinoise*.[5]

The specifically scientific contribution of this encyclopedic work arises in two major areas of achievement: it has made it possible to understand the national-cultural and civilisational foundation of the Chinese renaissance under the leadership of Chairman Mao Tse-Tung and the Chinese Communist Party; and it has convinced the historians of science and, more recently and with more reservations, the historians of cultures and civilisations that it is no longer possible to treat the history of the world in any of its domains in the terms that have been applied hitherto – that is, on the basis of Western-centred reductionist postulates imbued with cultural racism. It is true, of course, that the traditional works continue to postulate 'universalism' on the basis and as a function of the traditions of a West whose hegemony was established between the sixteenth century and Yalta. Undoubtedly we are still a long way from the time when the scientific and ideal knowledge gathered in Joseph Needham's encyclopedic work will by fully integrated into the general body of human knowledge. Was not the same thing true of the Encyclopédie of Diderot, d'Alembert and their companions which accompanied the French Revolution and the triumph of the bourgeoisies in Europe?

It is thus well worth taking stock of the experience and the lessons of the work already completed or still in progress, mainly by examining the volumes of essays that accompany the encyclopedia itself.

One must begin with the source of such a great vocation, of the orientation of an entire life. Needham's insistence that his complete integration into his own tradition, and into the religion of his own civilisation – Christianity – made him particularly sensitive in his attempts to understand Confucianism, Buddhism and Taoism as well as Islam. The influence of the community of Thaxted Church, to which we have already referred, is summarised by Holorenshaw in a striking phrase: 'The first essential here was the realisation that the numinous must be dissociated from the theology of a creator God.'[6] Hence the recognition of the teachings of

the Sage, the Master of a Hundred Thousand Generations, Confucius (552– 479 B.C.), the supreme moral model of Chinese civilisation, an uncrowned emperor whose influence is very much alive today in the houses of Singapore as well as in the communes of Shangdong, the ineluctable foundation of the Chinese spirit, be it traditional, technical, or Marxist; his life has been at least as historic as that of Jesus . . . . The Tao of the Sage was not put into practice in his own epoch; but he ensured that men and women could and should live in peace and harmony wherever and whenever it was practised. Its beliefs, less concerned with the other world than Christianity . . . were associated with the revolutionary ideas implicit in the origins of Taoism, in the radically apocalyptic dreams of Da Tong and Tai Ping – dreams for which men have struggled and fought – and began to exercise an important influence.[7]

Within the theological spectrum of Christianity itself, Needham's sensibility tended towards orthodoxy.

> It takes one back (if one is at all interested in Christian ways) not only beyond and behind the exaggerations and excesses of both sides in the Reformation period, but also behind the time of the scholastic philosophers themselves, who he feels were largely on the wrong track in trying to encompass mystical religion within the strait-jacket of Aristotelian philosophy . . . for him the political actions so replete with symbolism, which liturgiology studies, are themselves the carriers of meaning and prayer as much as anything purely mental. And evidently this is equally true of worship in all the great religions of Asia and China.[8]

To acknowledge the other, in this case the other civilisations and cultures of the vast Orient, must necessarily lead to a praxis. This praxis consists in urging on the movement of time, at the time when the 'East Wind' is blowing – not in sermonising in the name of impotent ideological schemes. We have mentioned Needham's attitude, from 1917 onwards, to the Russian Revolution and towards Marxism, and we have referred to his actions from 1938 on at the heart of the great task of renaissance under the impetus of the Chinese Revolution. In 1952, as a member of the International Commission investigating the accusations that bacteriological weapons were being used in Western China and Korea, he became convinced of the guilt of the imperialist aggressors; in this sense, he remained faithful to the spirit of the Cambridge Scientists Anti-War Group (founded in 1935 by J. D. Bernal, J. B. S. Haldane, W. A. Wooster, D. Needham and others) which was to be the driving force behind the study of science and society in the world.

A third lesson has to do with method. This cannot be other than comparative, given that there does not exist a univocal, privileged world. This very comparative method would effectively overturn the existing position on the problems. The question of knowing 'why modern science . . . has only developed in the Western world?' leads to a second question: 'why, between the first and the fifteenth century of our age did Chinese civilisation prove to be so much more effective than Western civilisation as far as the application of a knowledge of nature to the practical needs of man was concerned?' Should one look to the (Weberian) ideal-type of China, India, Egypt or Mesopotamia? 'The answer to all these questions is to be found, I now believe, in the social, intellectual and economic structures of different civilisations . . . I believe that the great historical differences between cultures are best explained through sociological studies; and I believe that someday that will be done.' He adds, 'that is why I have never felt drawn towards that current in Marxist thinking which has sought a rigid, unitary formula for the stages of social development through which all civilisations must pass'.

Only a simultaneous, comparative study of given phenomena in all the civilisations and cultures of the world can make it possible to elaborate progressively global theoretical interpretations in each field. Needham's work teems with examples of this exemplary method – notably in his study of time; in the comparison between the recruitment of the political class in the Orient and the West, where the Orient is shown patiently preparing its 'organic intellectuals', several centuries before Gramsci evolved his theory between 1920 and 1930.

We are witness here to a life's work, unfolding magnificently at the service of a great work which makes of Joseph Needham the outstanding encyclopedist of the age, standing as he does at the meeting-point of the relations between cultures and civilisations. 'Europe, its failures as well as its successes, must be seen through the eyes of that great part of humanity formed by the peoples of Asia and Africa.' At the same time, we must study the contribution of the Orient. 'Perhaps the whole question goes back to the active practice of humility and brotherly love. We have need of a true conviction in whose terms all racism, all complacent beliefs in cultural superiority constitute a denial of the world-community.'[9]

That is the road followed by the eminent master who so readily describes himself as an 'honorary Taoist'. In Confucius he finds the illustration of Anacletes's dictum: 'Behave towards every man as if you were receiving a great guest.' Then, 'he who respects the dignity of man and practises love and courtesy shall have every man as his brother'.

9

The Third World and the Orient

It is now thirty years or so (arguments about dates are not really very important) since a number of new notions entered the social and political vocabulary for the first time – notions like 'Third World', 'national democratic states' and 'development'. These were added to the body of notions dating from the period between the wars – 'culturation', 'under-development', 'modernisation' and 'national bourgeoisie'. It would be interesting here to trace the development of these terms. As we have already shown, they come into a different category of notions and concepts; we are dealing here with 'operational' concepts which must be very clearly distinguished from 'scientific' concepts, properly speaking, that is to say from those ideal forms which have generated thought and knowledge rooted in a critical analysis of social phenomena in their historical evolution and which, comparatively speaking, ensure that they continue to provide a framework of universal, or more or less universal validity.

These notions and concepts are 'operational', to the extent that they concern new phenomena. And we should recognise here that what is new is the acknowledgement in Western consciousness, both in Europe and North America, of phenomena, institutions and ideas which belong to other regions of the world. Naturally, such 'operational' notions and concepts will set themselves a double objective: to account for all that is different beyond the frontiers of the West; and to make these different phenomena intelligible by categorising them on the basis of the Western experience, that is to say in the traditional way. The history of this sequence of events, which should be accompanied by a history of the world from ,within the various cultural spheres which comprise it, remains still to be written. Elsewhere,[1] we have tried to set out the theses and the stages of development that characterise this process, thus making it possible to take on this notion of a 'Third World', whose ups and downs yield many surprises and perhaps some lessons too.

When A. Sauvy and G. Balandier use the term for the first time in 1956, they are certainly dealing with a fact, but also with the definition of that whose existence is thus asserted. The *fact* is the 'colonial' world, which the liberal spirits would have us believe is in the process of 'decolonisation' – Asia, Africa and Latin America. The expression used, however, more closely expresses the *vision* of liberal thought coming to grips with a changing world. On the level of terminology, the notion of the 'Third World' is more closely related to that of the 'Third Estate', namely that class or social sector which has no position to defend in the real interplay of forces, in the dialectic that opposes the state of the ruling class and the alternative state demanded by the dominated class. The Third Estate, the Third World, is thus conceived as a formless wilderness, virgin territory: yesterday, the scene of all colonial exploitation; today, the site of the struggle between the various imperialisms; tomorrow, perhaps, territories and populations whose personality and course of evolution will remain to be defined.

One finds this fundamental vision repeated in almost every case where the scholars and institutions of the West, whatever their ideology, approach the question of 'other' worlds. One might ask: what is the Third World? The definitions would be marked by their negativity: the poor countries as a whole; countries struggling for their national independence; the developing or underdeveloped countries. Moreover, at no time do we feel that anything else could be involved. The starting-point, and therefore the frame of reference, is the West itself, that is industrialised, capitalist Europe and North America, and equally, since 1917–45, the sector of the European socialist states. That is the real world.

Other sectors do exist outside that world, whose otherness is defined by a difference in their level of development, their economic and particularly their industrial potential, their military strength and their level of scientific and technological advance. The radical vision of the West will prefer to put the accent on the political aspects of this sector, that is on the struggle for independence and national liberation. *Grosso modo*, the 'Third World' will thus be described as the totality of the underdeveloped countries, struggling for their independence against the aggression or the exploitation of the great powers. What is called for, then, is either to oblige the societies of these countries to follow the course of evolution laid down by the two great models of development of Western societies – capitalist or socialist – or, at best, to help them to disengage from the directly political grip of the Western hegemonies. What is projected is the unfolding of the Utopian vision of a unified world, a total system, a globalisation in which, of course, the periphery as a whole, that is four-fifths of humanity, could do no other than adopt the model of today's hegemonic West.

Within this unified vision, one could distinguish three roads, three attitudes on the part of the hegemonic West towards that world designated 'Third' in the column of History.

For imperialism – both the hegemonic imperialism of the United States and the traditional imperialisms of the Western capitalist states – the movements of the Three Continents are considered essentially as a threat. As we know, these movements are undergoing a trial by ordeal to which the wars in Vietnam and Indochina, the Algerian War, the conflict in the Middle East and the struggle against racialism in South Africa, bear witness. Despite the bombs and the electronics, this so-called 'Third' world refused to be dismembered. On the contrary, it has proved capable of powerful initiatives, of an irrepressible advance despite its diversity, its contradictions, at times even its incoherence.

Confrontation had to give way to subjugation; that was and is the neo-imperialist project (or 'neo-colonialism' as it is often called, though inappropriately; it is not a matter of introducing new colonists into the countries of the dependent sphere). This second vision takes as read the continuing inexorable forward march of the dependent nations, and consists rather in penetrating to the very heart of those movements of thought and action that give impetus to this advance and induce them to conceive of this process as leading only to the reproduction of the Western models. It is accepted that a gaudy, highly coloured, exotic space must be accorded to the ancestral tradition, whitewashed with the label of 'authenticity'. Here, the 'Third World' is plied with honours. Its progress is acknowledged with realism and compassion, sometimes even with a real sympathy attributable to the personal itinerary of certain theorists.

The 'Third-Worldists', if one may call them that, directly linked to the Westernised sector of the intelligentsia and of the political class, thus take on, objectively, the role of 'compradors' on behalf of the different hegemonic powers. For a time, until the affirmation of the two great motor forces, the two great models for the transformation of the dependent world in our time – the radical-national and the socialist – these groups were to serve a useful purpose as intermediaries and allies, while at the same time accepting the vision of themselves as the West's

'Third World'. They were to be able to negotiate an occasional respite in the class struggle within national movements that were in a state of accelerated radicalisation, hoping thus to be able to prepare new pauses and transitions.

The third vision was that of the movements and ideologies of Western socialism. Here the central role would belong to the socialist states, with the support of the national parties, trade unions and popular organisations inspired by socialist ideology. Their position would be that of a strategic alliance between the socialist front in the West and the national independence movements of the Three Continents, and it has had an important role to play in many sectors of the Three Continents. But on the way it has not been able to hold back on various occasions from taking the attitude of a mentor, an intellectual guide, the historical godfather, so to speak, of the national liberation movements and the social revolutions engaged in struggle throughout the Three Continents. The 'Third World' as an ally against imperialism; but a 'Third World' which, given the primacy acknowledged to belong to the socialist states and the international labour movement, must take second place as far as the historical initiative is concerned.

On the other side of the river, the vision is quite different; the project and the will, too, are very different. In fact, beneath the mask of political terminology, that 'other side of the river' does not consist of a magma of poor countries fused in a unified and coherent whole. It consists, rather, of groups of very different societies, some of which – Egypt, China, Persia – are the oldest nations the world has known.

The better to judge this difference, it would seem useful to adopt a further division presented in the form of interpenetrating circles within a multiple dialectics: (i) *civilisations* – the Indo-Aryan (or Indo-European) circle, the Chinese circle: (ii) *cultural spheres* within each major civilisational framework; the Indo-Aryan circle (Antiquity, Egypt, Persia, the Classical world, Europe, North America, most of the Indo-European spheres of Latin America, sub-Saharan Africa – the civilisational-cultural sphere of Islam, principally in its Arab component); the circle of Chinese civilisation (China, Japan, Mongolia-Central Asia, Vietnam and South-east Asia, the Indian subcontinent, Oceania, the cultural sphere of Islam, from Persia to the Philippines).

On this matrix, the framework of what we have called the civilisations of the Orient would then be composed of the framework of Chinese civilisation with its constituent cultural spheres; the median civilisational-cultural sphere of Islam, from Morocco to the Philippines;

sub-Saharan black Africa and certain sectors of Latin America directly linked to Africa, notably Central America and Brazil.

The motor centres of the Orient thus understood are, therefore, clearly China (at the centre of the Asian circle) and the Arab world around Egypt (at the centre of the Islamic sphere). It will be obvious that within these civilisational frames and these cultural spheres is located the third circle, (iii) the *nations*, in the many senses of the term, from Antiquity to our times.

The usefulness of this grid becomes clear when it is applied to the magma of the 'Third World'. According to the Western conceptions, the 'Third World' would shrink progressively, as this or that country detaches itself, either as a result of a socialist revolution or of a sudden economic takeoff. In 1945, China in Western eyes still formed part of the 'Third World', becoming isolated from it after 1949; yet China clearly considers itself to be an integral part of the tricontinental block. Japan, on the other hand, is regarded by the West as the third most powerful industrial nation in the world, and thus forms part of that which is not the 'Third World'. Yet it is evident that socialist China and the Japan of the great capitalist monopolies are both integral parts of the Orient considered as a fact of world history. At the same time it is clear that they participate in very different ways, and that each of these nations maintains relations with the other cultural spheres of the Orient which are far from identical.

In fact, the basic use of this grid, in approaching the history of our time, stems from the fact that it allows us to distinguish clearly the group of countries, around their national state, which has constituted the hegemonic sector in world history from the fifteenth to the twentieth century, from the great maritime discoveries to Yalta. This group of countries constitutes the West, that is Europe and North America. On 'the other side of the river', another group of countries, the Orient – and it should be emphasised that the countries of the Orient represent more than four-fifths of the tricontinental sphere – are those which have been deprived of their motor role in history as a result of the rise of the front of national states of the various bourgeoisies of the West from the fifteenth century onwards. These are the countries which have been labelled the 'Third World' – with the addition of Latin America around 1945.

At this stage of what must necessarily be a schematic analysis it becomes clear that this world which has been accorded a 'Third' place in the great march of contemporary history in fact occupies a prominent place within it. In less than half a century, and particularly during the last thirty years, that is in the course of the period which has produced the very term 'Third World', the great wave of national independence movements or, if you prefer, of national and social revolutions has broken, held back and often destroyed the imperialist positions in Asia, Africa and Latin America. This action has been made possible by the priority given to the formula of the *national united front* embracing all the social forces, the political formations, the institutions and the spiritual families committed to the independence project and opposed to imperialist domination. That is the historical significance of the phenomenon which has come to be known as 'Nasserism'; and one can see today how effective and lasting are the great united fronts, in which the popular forces and the national army act in a concerted way at the service of the national project as a whole.

It is clear, then, however unwilling one is to pose the issue at the level of the general movement of world history, that it is the Chinese Revolution, from the Long March to the Cultural Revolution, that provides the most resounding confirmation of the effectiveness of the national united front, in enabling national liberation and social revolution to be joined in their role as instruments of a grand civilisational project, which in China is affirmed as a 'cultural' revolution, and in the Arab world as a 'renaissance'. In neither of these two motor centres of the Orient, however, is it a question of 'culturation', 'development' or 'modernisation'. The fundamental political objectives are political independence, the development of the national culture, nationalisation and planning. Moreover these are no more than instruments at the service of the great civilisational project, wherever they are posed; and it is that project itself which consigns the 'Third World' parenthesis to the sideshows of history. Thirty years ago, marginalisation was the issue. Thirty years were enough for the Orient to begin to seize the historical initiative in a forceful development which, it is hoped, will complement initiatives in the West itself which should not delay very much longer.

What form will they take? It is here, at the level of the *historical initiative*, that the real difficulties begin.

The analysis of the transformation of world power relations from 1956–9 to 1975 – from Suez and the creation of the Chinese People's Republic to the disintegration of US imperialism in the huge Asian arena, beginning in that crux year that was 1973, the year of the October War and one year after the victory of the Vietnamese and Cambodian peoples – reveals unexpected results with respect to traditional history, that is the history of the world hegemony of the West from the fifteenth century onwards, and with regard to the historiography developed by the principal cultural centres of the West to deal with the dominated world of the dependent sphere, principally the Orient.

Until now the nations of the dependent sphere – principally the Orient, in terms of civilisation – have suffered the effects of the initiatives, that is of the colossal historical advance of the West in every field. The great economic, political and philosophical-ideological problems, the central questions, were of course posed in the motor centres of the West. This continued to be the case throughout the prestigious stages of history: the bourgeois-democratic revolutions; socialism; the Industrial Revolution; the scientific spirit; modern technology; the globalisation of the world by imperialism and the mass media. Now this world, unified by and around the hegemonic power, presents all the symptoms of crisis. And this crisis, so blindly and insistently baptised 'the energy crisis', is in fact the *crisis of the logic of the process of social development* which the West itself had laid down – that is industrialisation, productivism and the consumer society erected as models of civilisation.

These symptoms of unease have emerged as a result of the great waves which have marked the movement towards renaissance in the contemporary Orient. China, surrounded by Vietnam, Korea, Cambodia, and itself the essence of the socialist movements of the Orient, calls into question the inexorability of the productivist model, and proposes instead a future socialist project based on the national-cultural specificity of the principal sectors of the world. In doing so, Asian socialism resolutely takes the initiative in the discussion of the difficulties and problems faced by Western socialism, a discussion hitherto circumscribed by socialist humanism on the one hand, and on the other what is called, with Manichaean simplicity, 'Stalinism' – with the result that no critical analysis has been able to address itself to the central problems of the socialist project as a whole. Is the central question how to catch up with the standard of living of the industrial capitalist countries, and the United States in particular, by transferring the appropriation of the surplus to the popular classes – the workers and the peasants? Or is it rather a matter of forging the new man of the future socialist society, moulded by a communitarian, non-Manichaean conception, thus giving priority to the deeper, long-term questions rather than the quantitative approach to the problems of socialism? This debate, which is today being undertaken on an increasingly broad scale, is posed at the very heart of socialist thought and action in our time. It is essential to recognise that the initiative in posing the problem, as well as the first elaboration of a project capable of resolving it, has been taken in the Orient. This, in a precise sense, is what is meant by the 'historical initiative'. It is the socialist Orient that has posed the problem of the socialism of the future; and it is Western socialism which must now reflect on the different courses of development that flow from those arguments, discovering in the thought of Gramsci, so long denigrated, its specifically European referent.

Simultaneously, the 'renaissance' of the Arab world in our day also sees itself as rupture with the attempts at penetration, from the Crusades to Suez; in other words, it is moved by a forceful aspiration to draw together the specificity of the national culture and the political, state power of the Arab world as a whole. In this way the Arab world has found itself objectively led towards a confrontation in depth with imperialism; it has taken four wars, launched by the Zionist state, to make the West conscious, as a result of the oil question, of the impossibility of maintaining a political course founded on the logic of contempt. Thus, objectively, the use of oil as a political weapon by the Arab Orient has obliged the West, and all its constituent spiritual families, to call into question the profound nature of the Western civilisational project. This question has certainly been on the agenda since the emergence of socialism in the nineteenth century, and of the critical philosophy of history at the beginning of the twentieth, the one concerned with the decline of the bourgeoisie, the other with the decline of the West. Yet neither approach, fruitful though they (and the socialist approach in particular) may have been, could ever have imagined that this exotic, dependent world, this world of marginal interests on the 'other side of the river' could one day carry their questioning into the very heart of the West. That, in a precise sense, is the sense of the historical initiative taken by the Orient in this domain.

We have come a long way from the first Western perceptions of this so-called 'Third' world. Yet not as far as it may appear.

It has to be acknowledged that, until now, the majority of the centres of information and the mass media in the West have persisted in presenting this 'renaissance' of the Orient, as a whole, as a threat. Seen from the Orient, that is from the 'Third World', the relations with the hitherto hegemonic West are conceived as *non-antagonistic* – though they are, and will remain for some time to come *conflictive*.

So it would seem that we should be directing ourselves towards *complementarity*, that is the organisation of great common initiatives capable of carrying forward the development of the societies of the world into the future, and inspired by the great national-cultural and civilisational spheres of the world, on a basis of equality. This process affects too many interests, however, for it to go ahead without difficulties. At the same time that is, perhaps, the challenge laid down by our age before the heart and the mind of every one of us – the challenge of this convergence of action.

10

The Civilisational Project

I(a)   We can begin by considering the history of the notion of national independence; later, at a second level, we can consider what it is that has motivated the new search, the new questions – most of which seem to have arisen in that sector which had been regarded until now as outside the problem: the liberal-capitalist states and countries of the West, and of Europe in particular.

The classical statement of the problem of national independence has been expressed hitherto in two main, and successive ways:

1. The traditional or what can equally well be called the liberal-conservative argument. This lays the stress on the notion of 'independence' itself, with reference to explicitly juridical and diplomatic criteria. Independence was to appear as an advanced form of the moves towards autonomy which became increasingly significant as the Western bourgeoisies rose to power in the principal hegemonic centres – the various 'empires', if you will. It was a matter of attaining the juridical equality at the diplomatic level which would allow them to join in the 'concert of the powers'.

That has been, *grosso modo*, the perspective of the major movements of modern Western history, from the War of American Secession to the emergence of the Austro-Hungarian and Ottoman Empires.

2. A second, radical-revolutionary position was soon to emerge, particularly in those regions which had been subjugated as a result of the emergence of these European hegemonic centres. This argument emphasised the process of 'national liberation' rather than simple 'independence'. This was from the outset a dialectical approach to the problem, based on the struggle between antagonistic centres; its objective was the

constitution through struggle of a distinct, national entity which would be sovereign in relation to the wider framework of the hegemonic political entity against which its struggle is undertaken. Such is the history of the national movements of the Orient – principally in Asia and the Arab world – later joined by those of Africa and, more recently, of Latin America. What is involved here is a rupture, an estrangement certainly akin in some of its aspects to the preceding independence process, although obviously of a more clearly defined character in both a positive and a negative sense.

(b)   How can we account for the fact that new questions are being posed within certain of the traditionally more dynamic sectors of the West itself?

It is a new, or at least a very recent phenomenon, and arises essentially in the course of the struggle of the European nations against the Hitler–fascist Axis during the world war of 1939–45, when the resistance movements assumed as their objective the conquest of national liberation through armed struggle. 1945 and Yalta mark the end of this last in a long series of attempts by one or other European state to establish military hegemony over the West as a whole. For a number of new factors had emerged to blur the traditional approach: the decline of the traditional imperialisms in the face of the growing power of United States economic imperialism, on the one hand, and on the other the establishment of a bloc of socialist states around the Soviet Union, and the long-awaited emergence of a powerful wave of national liberation revolutions in the Orient, centred on China, carried out in the name of socialism.

On the other side of the river, in Asia, Africa and Latin America, the process of national liberation appears less as a problem than as a concrete, living reality, to be accepted or actively chosen; at all events, it was an inexorable process, whose only alternative was the acceptance of a historical subjection with no future. But what of Europe? After 1945, the slogan of independence – independence and not national liberation – appeared to be aimed at maintaining the necessary distance from the hegemonic power of the United States, as well as standing aside from the balance of power between the two superpowers of the West – and this specifically at the time when the 'Cold War' has been transformed, via the period of 'peaceful coexistence', into 'détente'.

These, then, are the framework, the tone and the historical moment.

*   *   *

It is important, therefore, for those sectors of the West who are correctly concerned about their independence to understand the implications of the resurgence of the Orient.

2(a)   At the immediate level, the exposed part of the iceberg. One can see clearly the organic link, albeit at very different levels, between national independence and national liberation; it is equally clear how the latter is undertaken as a process of struggle on the one hand, and as a national revolution, a *social revolution* on the other. What is new here is that this link is now acknowledged to be *organic*, and not merely a circumstantial, tactical connection. Experience has shown that broad national fronts, activated principally by the native, so-called 'national' bourgeoisies, face growing difficulties as far as the structuring, consolidation, maintenance and hardening of their fronts are concerned; for these bourgeois leaderships seem more attached to their class privileges than to the imperatives of the national liberation movement itself. Thus a moment of radicalisation occurs, in which the sectors of the bourgeoisie that are in power opt for a process of deeper economic and social transformation, choosing to turn to the people in order to hold the nation against the occupying force: thus Nasser's Egypt and the Algeria of the FLN; Sukarno, and an emergent Indonesia; Peru, Tanzania, Sri Lanka and the body of republican states at the heart of the Arab world. Elsewhere – notably in Asia, in China, in Vietnam, Cambodia, Laos and Korea – geo-historical conditions have permitted things to develop in a more broadly based and far more profound direction, so that the socialist revolution has sanctioned and run parallel with the struggle for national liberation. For those sectors of the West concerned with independence, the consequences are many. Clearly, even at the level of the most immediate political repercussions, it scarcely seems possible to sustain the full sovereignty of the nation, when significant sectors of the population feel themselves to be unjustly ignored by political leaders with whom they feel little identification except during those flashpoints when a Churchill, a de Gaulle or a Roosevelt come to symbolise the unanimous will of the nation. Unless they are willing to open everything to question in socio-economic terms, the sectors of the European bourgeoisie concerned with independence will run away from a social dialectics which places endogenous social struggles at the centre of the stage, with the inevitable result that class struggle takes precedence over a national union whose theoretical and practical justifications seem very tenuous.

(b)   The national liberation movements of the Orient, in their two radical-national and socialist variants, still operate, or more precisely are still constrained to operate, within the straitjacket imposed by the world balance of power – a balance which has defined all the possible parameters of autochthonous action. That is the principal lesson to be drawn from a comparison between the two principal Oriental spheres which have experienced domination; if Asia has been able to achieve such a far-reaching disengagement (and it is not only the case of China), then it must be recognised too that the Islamic world, around its Arab centre, has constantly found itself in direct confrontation on a number of fronts with the various states of the hegemonic West, from the Crusades to the Zionist state. In a general sense, the given factors appear to be the same:

1. The existence of three *major power poles* in the world: the West, around the United States; the European socialist states around the Soviet Union; and Asia, centred on China. New poles are emerging, but it is logical to assume that they are unlikely to reach the same level as the three principal centres of the contemporary historical dynamic: Europe, the Arab world, Japan, Vietnam and Brazil, in particular.

2. The existence of *dynamising potentialities* which have frequently been underestimated until now: in particular, the resurgence of the Orient in its various cultural-national spheres, on the one hand, and the competition within collaboration between the capitalist and socialist centres of the Western world on the other.

(c)   The difficulty arises in attempting to compare the coefficient of dynamic potential of the various sectors seeking to achieve national independence: the tricontinental sphere, ranged around the Orient, on the one hand, and certain sectors of the West, particularly in Europe, on the other. In the first case, independence conceived as the historical objective of a struggle for national liberation organically linked to social revolutions of various kinds is quite literally a precondition for life itself. We shall return to the point. Equally, we shall set out to show that it is not at all like that in other sectors, where what appears to be both feasible and desirable is to maintain the nation and its sovereignty in the face of an overwhelming American hegemonic imperialism, and to safeguard the national entity in the *détente* between the two superpowers. In this sector, obviously, we must speak of independence. The tricontinental sphere,

around the Orient, on the other hand, will raise higher with every day that passes the banners of national liberation, not for ideological reasons but simply as the result of the totality of specific conditions within which the daily lives of men and societies develop in this sector of the world.

*   *   *

If we are to go further, the following observations are important:

3(a) The 'non-dependence' pursued by each of the two sectors – though according to totally different criteria – achieves a *mobilising influence* when it no longer limits itself to disputing the national 'market' but moves on to a global, multifaceted front of the maintenance of national identity as a whole. Certainly, in every case under study, the struggles for influence are most apparent at the heart of the market, that is of the national economy. Yet even within this economic space, it is clear that these struggles are a permanent process, a constituent factor in the economic existence of the tricontinental countries; for they represent a slowing down, an imposition of irksome blockages for an economy in full process of growth, namely that of Western capitalism.

(b) The *maintenance of national identity* appears as a problem only in the societies of the dominated sector. Outside the economic space, the national market, and beyond the forced integration into the international capitalist market, imperialism brings its weight heavily to bear in every sector: in the distortion of education; in the attempt to pervert the national culture; in the artificial divide that is established between the Western-centred elites and the popular masses; in the maintenance of the scientific and technological backwardness of these countries and in the weakening of national power both from within, and through repeated acts of aggression from without. The result is a sense of permanent destabilisation, a continuous process of threats, questionings and pressures with an eye to rupture.

(c) Where, then, do we find the cement capable of binding together in the most durable possible form that front whose aim will be the maintenance of national identity in the face of imperialism and the hegemonic powers? It is here that the argument can be posed in civilisational terms:

1. In the immediate and the middle term, it is necessary to state the problem in political, or rather politistic terms; from the tactical to the strategic level, a wide range of variables will allow the different political formations to occupy the various political and ideological sectors of contemporary political life.

2. Later, at the heart of the nation, the submerged portion of the iceberg will argue the primacy of the will, that is the primacy of political action, *the primacy of the political*. And this primacy of politics will be transformed into a project that goes far beyond political platforms, strategies or techniques, however honourable and effective these may have been.

At that point, the project becomes a national-cultural project. And this national-cultural project, itself capable of maintaining the national societies of the different nations through time, is quite naturally grouped around the great formative matrices which are the civilisations of our world.

*   *   *

4(a)   The *civilisational project* of all Western societies seems to have constituted the axis of Europe's ascent towards world hegemony between the fifteenth and the eighteenth centuries: an unbridled growth of production, set on an exponential expansion; the continuous rise in the standard of living, and the growth of consumption and of the social services; the subjugation of the different sectors of the Orient, both by fire and sword and by the exercise of cultural and intellectual imperialism, the better to sustain that hegemony. The philosophical basis of that process was to be rationalist, classical, liberal, theist or materialist at first, and later that of socialism, and socialist humanism. The world is conceived to mean Europe – or what today we would call the West – since the centre of power has shifted to North America.

The general model, the value systems, the image of man are not fundamentally different. What is at issue between the two great types of socio-economic regime which divide the West between them is the nature of that sector of the population which owes most to and derives the most from this conception of the world, and from its gains and its *fundamental strategic surplus* – itself the result of the subjection of the societies, the nations and the peoples of the tricontinental sphere, grouped around the Orient, by the hegemonic centres of the West.

(b) The source of the confusion thus becomes abundantly clear; the consolidation of national independence from the hegemonic centre, which today is the United States, will in fact require the establishment of the widest possible margin of *regional autonomy*. For, until now, none of the great autochthonous units of the West have been able to generate any alternative civilisational project to the loud and overbearing promise of the American way of life to establish its dominion over the whole world.

(c) The doggedness and persistence of this refusal to give way is exposed as soon as we pose *the problem of an alternative presented in terms of a civilisational project*. For centuries, Europe has considered 'Civilisation' to be its own; what is good for Europe is good for the world. Today, whatever originates in the West is sure to be reproduced in the areas of the periphery. And it is not a matter of the reductionism of imperialism and the various hegemonic centres only, but equally, and with an even greater insistence, of the theoreticians of anti-national cosmopolitanism, successive generations of whom have proposed the notions of 'centre' and 'periphery', of 'North' and 'South', whether in the Enlightenment Europe of yesterday, or in the international socialist movement of today in its relations with the so-called Third World. Western-centrism has taken over from Euro-centrism, and constitutes today even for Europe itself the major obstacle to the possibility of posing the problem of an alternative civilisational project.

In fact, a certain number of partial attempts and initiatives, muffled by the general reticence, do allow us to offer some reflections on this question; the renewal of religious ideologies; the affirmation of national character, both within the national political class in power, properly speaking, and in its Communist opposite number; the new consciousness of crisis among the young which at its height reaches into the urban political and intellectual elites; the ineluctable challenges flung at the Western model by the 'periphery'; and so on. Until now, no one has been prepared to recognise that these provided a source of renewal. The Western way of life, that is the American way of life, has so conditioned Western society as a whole that it has penetrated to the very heart of the body of social thought and sensibility. The time has come, therefore, for the vanguard, which aspires to shape the future of the West, to pose for themselves the possibility of achieving their own national independence, in terms of a cultural revolution. Without rupture and reconstruction, the future will necessarily be that assigned by the American centre within the confines of its empire, even though that will of course allow a wide and very liberal margin of autonomy.

(d)   We can readily introduce here the notion of *the 'transfer of the historical initiative'*, an initiative which has been loudly accorded to Europe from the fifteenth century until Yalta, but which today seems increasingly to be passing into the hands of the Orient which has, furthermore, been directly involved in the transformations caused by the birth of socialist power in the West. Out of Asia have come the arguments of the 'cultural revolution', the very core of the primacy of the political, which have imposed themselves on the attention of the world. And the radical national states in which people and army have united around oil have emerged in the Islamic-Arab sphere. Further, it is in this vast tricontinental arena that a syncretism has imposed itself between the traditional national cultures, often taking the form of important religious allegiances, on the one hand, and the action of national and revolutionary movements on the other. Thus one can see in the not too distant future the end of that strange odyssey in which reason implied the rejection of faith, universalism the rejection of the nation and power the banishment of philosophy. And that, in simple outline, introduces, moreover, another new dimension.

(e)   It seems, therefore, that it will be as a result of the establishment of dialectical relations, that is relations of confrontation, though not necessarily antagonistic ones, between those sectors of the West seeking national independence and the vast tricontinental front ranged around the Orient, that there will appear the richest possibilities of renewal, of posing the question that can lead to the constitution of the great civilisational projects for our time. The time has therefore come *to restore fully philosophy to its rightful, privileged place*; the alternative is to continue still further a process without a project.

The epigones of that mode that is entering its decline will call this a strange time, as the 'spectres' – nation, philosophical thought, the reality of civilisation – which they had believed it possible to lay to rest emerge once again. However, the time seems to have come in which human societies can struggle and unite, with an eye to thinking and carrying through the construction of modes of life which tend towards the symbiosis of the endogenous constituent parts and of the level of world integration. The privileged instrument of action, on the basis of a philosophy restored to its rightful place and at the service of various civilisational projects, continues to be the framework of the national reality.

Part III

The Concept of Specificity

11
The Notion of
'Depth of Historical Field'

1. Position of the problem

The history of sociology (now in movement again after a period of disaffection) has been essentially linked to the question of describing sequences, drawing up balance sheets and inventories, and sometimes of setting out a prospective problematic. With a few very rare exceptions this history of sociology has remained historicist, in the classical sense of the word. Constantly and quite rightly concerned to lose nothing of what they see as the living tissue of their science, and aware of the challenge of neighbouring and clearly older disciplines, the historians of sociology have not so far sufficiently stressed the sociological interpretation of sociology. The economic dimension is clearly perceived, sometimes even as directly and schematically determining; the political dimension has come to be recognised as central to any theoretical reflection in the field of the social sciences as a whole. What are not yet clearly perceived are the relations of interaction between the sociology of a society or a given national-cultural sphere at a given phase of its historical evolution, and the specificity of that society in its historical persistence and its re-emergence under the impact of contemporary society.

In this field as in many others, the reticence of the intellectuals – notably in the West – is difficult to dispel. We should like to be able to account for the differentiation and the divergences in critical terms; but we limit ourselves to the formal, structural aspect of that critique, because a critical-historicist analysis would make it impossible to ignore the national-cultural factor, the dimension of specificity – particularly in the era of the resurgence of the nationalitarian phenomenon.

Within the necessarily limited framework of this study, a sociological approach to the differentiation of theoretical sociology in the wake of the

Second World War would allow us to account for the breach between the structuralist-functionalist tendency on the one hand, and the critical-historicist on the other, where it is clearly the latter that has a theoretical vocation. This essential break is not the same thing as the ideological rupture which we have tended to see as central (to some extent out of habit) in the framework of the Cold War. Certainly the critical-historicist approach, around Marxism, is diametrically opposed to the static conceptions devoted to the conservation of society. One tendency within Marxism, though still weak, has adopted the structuralist development, for reasons of modernity and perhaps too of cultural fashion; within the other tendency, whole sections sensitive to the European cultural heritage see themselves as concerned with historical sociology. This is the general framework, briefly summarised here on the basis of a number of connected works; and it allows us to situate the literal resurgence of the concept of history and the notions that derive from it and which structure its epistemological field within the sociological theory of our time. This concept, moreover, derives essentially from the domain of the theoretical, critical-historicist tendency.

At the same time, a second movement was beginning to take shape which today has come to disturb the tranquillity of classical sociology. Hitherto, the starting-point and the foundation of every theory within the social sciences as a whole has continued to be, whether explicitly or tacitly, classical formal rationalism, particularly in its Aristotelian and positivist variants. This foundation takes the form of what we propose to call *equivalentism* – in fact, the reductionist approach of the Western-centred social sciences. The different sociological facts are perceived, theoretically, as ideally equal as far as their potential for evolution, transformation and progress is concerned.

At this point, however, the actual history of our time lays down clear and unavoidable challenges. The myth of a development progressing by continuous leaps yields its place, in many cases, to the hypothesis of the development of underdevelopment. The unilinear, continuous conception of social progress and the evolution of nations begins to fade, and gives way to a dialectical, contradictory and conflictual conception of the evolution of human societies, an evolution which must often confront breakdown, deep crisis, even regression – a stormy diachrony. Suddenly, the good conscience which allowed everything to be referred back to environmental, exogenous factors, to the contingency of history so to speak, comes into question; should one not put the stress on the endogenous factor, the internal structure of the terrain under consideration, in a word specificity in place of a universalistic and 'equivalentist' theoretical unanimity?[1]

These are unusual questions and unexpected problems – each of them testimony to the fact that we have reached an impasse; the dead end of mechanistic, formal rationalism in the field of sociological analysis and conceptualisation.

The reality is there – unavoidably so. The human societies of the real world demand to be understood; frequently, that demand expresses itself at the level of political action. Thus, in the second half of the twentieth century, the central question posed for every sociologist, for every sociology, is as follows: how can we account for the reality of the real world in our time, in the light of its disparities and contradictions?

A first approach would set to work factors of a universal kind, with attention given to the geographical framework, sometimes seen against its historical background. The play of political forces, the relations between these forces within the country under study and between it and the major international lines of force on a world scale; these will increasingly become the object of our attention. Under the influence of Marxism, an important place will be accorded to the analysis of social structures, and particularly class structures. The role of the economic infrastructure would be recognised, and in certain cases given priority in the last instance. Thus a causal interpretation based on the interaction of different orders of facts will allow us to set out the non-traditional factors of difference between societies infinitely better than in the time, now past, when equivalentism went unchallenged.

None the less, a 'residue' remains which is both important and highly variable. For the refinement over the last hundred years of the instruments of analysis does not change the nature of the analysis itself. Whether during the Enlightenment or in our own time, that analysis stemmed from the will to universalism, and was based on the postulate of the immediate reducibility of all social phenomena, all national and social totalities, to a single model.

A 'residue' remains which either confirms or undermines the expectations of one or the other. The first are located within the Western-centrist tradition, yearning for normality and refusing to recognise the different, dissimilar cultures that challenge it.

What then does one do with the fact of difference, other than take note of it, the better to keep it at a distance? This question defines the psychological and political atmosphere in which is developed the typological interpretation initiated by Max Weber, and which later has in

Alfred Weber its epigone in the field under study. If the social 'residue' is a striking reality, it is the case that the different national societies go back to different 'ideal-types'; these exist, of course, at all times, and thus are constitutionally bereft of any possibility of differential deployment or transformation; they are fixed, static and immutable *ideal-types* – *homo islamicus, homo germanicus, homo sinicus*, etc. The difference is fixed in a way that is by definition immutable, since it is structurally defined on the basis of an ideal-type. Immutable, and also incapable of movement. Thus difference becomes the negation of evolution, of transformation; there is no social dynamic, nor can there ever be. History is fixed in frozen moulds; and both have lost their legitimacy!

One can easily see why, and at what analytical turning-point, the crisis breaks. Certainly, national societies are perceived as different; but this difference is not metaphysical. To admit that would be to deny the whole body of knowledge accumulated in the human and social sciences since Ibn Khaldoun and Paracelsus, since the very emergence of modern thought in the eighteenth century. Thenceforth, the search will be for the means to mediate the specific and the universal, the differences and the identity of the constitutive mould. That will be the object of the principle of historical specificity, taken up among others by C. Wright Mills, the theory of which we have set out to analyse and whose clearly defined manifestations we have tried to explicate.

2.   Demarcation and definition of the notion

We shall not repeat here the analysis of the concept of historical specificity, but it is worthwhile to recall its major features.

Having rejected the structuralist-functionalist approach, with its emphasis on ethno-racist, fixist, 'ideal-type' notions, we must go on to isolate the factors of maintenance which provide the basis and the framework of the historical self through the movement of history: changes of epoch, of socio-economic formation, political regimes, cultural and ideological models and systems, etc.

We shall seek first of all the key factors of all social maintenance, of the maintenance of all national societies in historical time. After the long period of hegemony of the idealist or spiritualist conception, on the basis of the philosophy of history, the determining role in the last analysis of the economic infrastructure of human societies in evolution seems to have won its recognition in the light of Marxism. In our view, three other dimensions should also be taken into consideration; they are secondary, it is true, but they are also decisive in structuring the social mould around the economic core: the reproduction of social life, at whose core lie the problems of sexuality and affectivity; the social order, that is problems of power and the state; and time, shaped by death, which is the source of all religions and metaphysics.

The second moment will be concerned with studying the specific mode of maintenance within historical time of a given national society – the specific ordering of these four factors. That ordering itself will be determined by the framework of movement; first of all by geography, the physical framework within which all social life develops; the evolution of that framework, that is its historical geography; finally, the relations between this framework in movement on the one hand, and the main lines of force in the world, that is geopolitics, on the other. We need only recall the interest aroused by the theses on the 'hydraulic societies', the contrasted cases of Japan and Latin America among others, to see to what extent these approaches make it possible to identify the specific ordering of the principal factors of social maintenance.

Thus historical being is no longer ideal-type, but synthesis, the result of specificity described in this way. We are at the opposite extreme from the idealist approach to specificity; this is a critical-historicist perspective founded on the concrete dialectics of concrete societies through the concrete history of the real world.

The concept of historical specificity in sociology is naturally elaborated through the grid of time, of historical duration. It is not our purpose here to discuss the philosophical problems that arise from the question of time; but let us stress that historical time is not conceived merely as a linear, diachronic sequence of events, phenomena and structures, but essentially as a process, a slow and contradictory process interspersed with sudden, dazzling openings. This process will not necessarily take the comforting shape of the classic dialectical triad (synthesis is not inevitable, for rupture and retreat are equally characteristic phenomena of concrete history, etc.). In a word, historical time is conceived as a genetic structure.

It is now possible to establish the boundaries of the notion of the depth of historical field. In the first place, it appears as one of the constituent elements of the concept of historical specificity. But in what way?

First of all, as support within duration, a take-off point, in some sense the vertical dimension. If the maintenance of a national society through historical evolution is the deep core of the problematic of historical specificity, then it is clear that duration is directly involved – time in its continuity, rather than the time of immediate perception, of memory or a project. And this continuity, this maintenance through time is not a dotted line but a sphere of development, of movement. Hence the designation 'historical field', whose most significant quality is its 'depth'.

This is the second aspect of the notion; it is both a support and a structuring framework. Maintenance can be achieved and perceived according to different modes of density and coherence. Not all maintenance has the same significance; the variation is the result of the interaction between two orders of factors – the integration of historical duration into the movement of a given national society on the one hand, and the specific ordering of the constitutive elements of that society on the other. These are subtle relationships which show clearly that human societies cannot be fitted into the falsely universalising, reductionist approach.

In other words, the depth of the historical field is the face of the concept of time that is seen when one grasps the maintenance and the density of social dialectics in the history of human societies. This is the general framework in which the general historical specificity of a given national society within a given cultural sphere, itself a component of *one* among the great civilisations of the world, takes form.

3.   Dynamics of the notion: outline for a research programme

The object of this introductory analysis is to set in motion a programme of research rather then to present theses by way of conclusion. Such research should have three major lines of orientation, as follows.

3.1   General theory and epistemology

The central problem here will be to deepen and define the relations between the concept of time and the constellation of notions concerned particularly with the density of time in the domain of the history of human societies. The emergence of the non-Western world (Africa, Latin America, Asia above all) into the field of vision of the social sciences half a century ago considerably diversified and enriched the fund of materials that research had at its disposal at its first stage, covering in part the field of secondary analysis: inventories and calculations; categorisation; and an outline of method.

At a second stage this should make it possible to realise in the epistemological field of time the same process of critical restructuration, this time on the basis of an authentic world vision, and no longer simply as from the realities and traditions of the successive hegemonic centres of Western civilisation. The 'different times', the schematic opposition of the West and the Orient will appear not as ideal entities, disparate by nature, monads with neither transcendence nor social dialectics, but as the different modes through which temporality is manifested and grasped; a temporality determined by the concrete social rhythms of a specific history within the frameworks of different geographical and cultural circles.

The third stage will consist in realising a new synthesis, carrying this restructuration of the concept to its conclusion. The research that needs to be undertaken, now and in the future, is located at the second stage; its results should make it possible to move to the third level – the level of the completed theoretical formulation – in the middle term.

3.2   Sociological theory

On the level of *sociological theory*, research should be concerned with the kernel, the central contradiction between identity and movement, that is between the following two orders of factors:

3.2(a)   The propensity to change, which is the direct result of a high coefficient of effective presence of the depth of historical field at the heart of the society under study, of the density and significance of the social dialectics unfolding within its national or regional framework. The elements of this level are social and national cohesion and integration; the matrix of the national power of decision; cultural unity; national identity; the capacity for dissemination and influence at the level of the superstructures, beyond the measurable, immediate, objective poten-tialities; the effectiveness and the radical character of the will to change, when that will has been held back both among the masses of the people and at the level of the state, etc.

It will be clear that it is the most ancient nations and national formations that have at their disposal the most important fund of endogenous resources with which to think, desire and bring about change.

3.2(b)   The resistance to change concomitant with the factors of change within the same type of societies. Here the factors are national tradition and sectional traditions in every domain of social life; adherence to the collective self-image, the popular national identity through time; the existence of classes, social groups, centres and apparatuses of power with significant instruments at their disposal and devoted to conservation, to maintenance – they are able to find in the implicit ideology of the deep country significant allies, whose active repercussions at times of crisis tend to be disconcerting and profound.

Here too, as in the first group, the most ancient civilisations, national cultures, and national formations are also those in which the very abundance of endogenous resources can hold back most effectively and for the longest period the process of change.

The prioritised analysis of this fundamental contradiction – of this knowledge of fundamental contradictions – should lead us to the subjective factor (subjectivity and subjectivism) in the field of social dynamics: vision, will, a shared view, action.

Here exists a number of blockages; and equally great are both the myths of subjectivism and the disparagement that greets the necessary critique of the role of the individual in history. Are we in a better position to consider the problems on the basis of the factors we have outlined? It would appear that the collective subjectivity – which is an objective reality and should be treated as such – can only move effectively in the direction of the dynamic of social change, to the extent that it is rooted in a precise scientific knowledge of the particular specificity of a given society, and thus of the nature, and the coefficient of specificity of social dialectics appropriate to that society.

Thus it becomes clear how the choice of factors, of levels, of key points can be made on which to concentrate the act of rupture which can provoke or accelerate a profound change, and modify in depth the existing manner in which the key factors of social maintenance are ordered. It is clear that the dynamisation as markedly different as France and Ethiopia, Egypt and the United States, China and Great Britain among others cannot be seen in the same terms – except, of course, within the reassuring framework of the reductionism of left and right, both equally disdainful of the real.

3.3   Comparative sociology and political science

On the level of *comparative sociology*, as well as in political sociology and *political science*, the use of the notion of the depth of historical field should enrich our study of the two major orders of problems:

3.3(a)   The typology of national formations, on the one hand, which in our view must be elaborated on the basis of the resurgence and contemporaneity of the non-Western world in the course of the last two centuries, of the historical reality lived by the majority of human societies.

We know how the problem of the historical formation of the conceptual apparatus of the social sciences has been posed . . .

Within the typology of national formations which we have outlined elsewhere, the notion of the depth of historical field has a literally *central* role in elaborating, refining and diversifying the typology and thus the very concept of nation that is to be restructured.

3.3(b)   On the other hand, there is the question of the relations between this notion and the potential both of the most recent national formations, those with the weakest historical roots, and of those which have found themselves marginalised by historical geography. This brings us to the heart of the problematic of the so-called 'new nations', and above all of the so-called 'a-historical' societies. This in turn will bring us again to the functionalist vision of sociology: reductionism and social manipulation in the case of the 'new nations' and structuralism in the case of the marginalised societies on the basis of which panstructuralism attempts to establish its fixist extrapolations through sharply intuitive descriptive inventories.

These seem to us to be the major lines along which it will be possible to define the depth of the historical field, and to locate its role and its possibilities within the new sociology of our time.

12

The Concept of Specificity

1. Orientations

There is an almost indisputable need – for both the human and the social sciences on the one hand, and societal practice on the other – for a conception capable of relating the particular to the universal, the sectoral to the general, in order to unify our vision and comprehension of the world. Never before, in truth, have we witnessed or participated in such an intensely varied range of societal units and processes. And this at the very time when gigantic strides in scientific discoveries and their technological applications are coupled with global systems, in the guise of ideologies, blue-prints for world systems, prospective Utopias and the like.

This need is particularly felt in the hitherto non-participant areas of the world, that is, in Asia, Africa, Latin America, or in what we can define in civilisational terms as the Orient (the Asian circle, around China; the Islamic circle, around the Arab world and its aura in Africa, and parts of Central and South America). It is there that the quest for authenticity and national identity is most forceful, for obvious reasons directly linked with the rise of national movements throughout the hitherto dependent area, against the hegemony of the West imposed upon them since the fifteenth century. Yet, a parallel concern with the contents of the major types of social systems now existing in the advanced countries is pushing to the fore the normative quest in that sector of the world too. This second aspect, that is, the resurgence of the normative quest in the West, has been accelerated, in a real sense, by the rise of the Orient during our century. Thus, the need to investigate the field of the interrelations between the particular and the universal, the sectoral and the general, can be said to be a universally felt need in human societies in our times.

A wide range of problems and questions arise: How can we relate to them, if at all, and to what degree? The structure of power in new states (Papua-New Guinea, Guyana, Jamaica, etc.); federal or confederal states; instances of the modern national states; ancient nation-states? Can there be a bridge capable of linking, in a comprehensive manner, the definition of cultural policy in France, Brazil, Egypt, Australia, Japan and Mexico, *inter alia*? Can we reach a consensus on a comparativist approach to, say, political pluralism, and identify the capacity for societal change and transformation in societies as different as Canada, Paraguay, Indonesia, Madagascar, etc? What would be the potential capacity for intellectual creativity, scientific and technological innovations, resistance to change, the interplay of archaism and modernity in nations like Mongolia and Italy, Hungary and Chile, Peru and India, etc?

Key problems now relegated to the area of 'exceptionalism' seem to be deeply perplexing to the traditional mind: the role of the army in politics; the resurgence of the national dimension, specifically under the guise of the nationalitarian phenomenon; the subtle evolution of religions towards the cultural-ideological dimension, and vice versa; the growing awareness of the convergence of formally very different patterns of societal maintenance, such as the autocratic state, political pluralism, populist or tribal consensus – *inter alia*. There is hardly a major field of the sciences of man and society in our times which remains immune from such ambiguities, and the quest for a relevant solution.

The following points aim at bringing together a number of positions, here summarily posited, with a view to clarifying the major issues around what we submit to be the key conceptual tool: the concept of specificity.

2. The framework of comparativism

The first and preliminary step in engaging upon the new path we have been advocating is to introduce some form of coherent *typology of the macro-societal units* to be compared. In other words: before comparing, we ought to know what it is that we are comparing. Three major interwoven types of circle constitute the frame of comparativism:

2.1 Civilisations

This is the outer, more general, circle, to be defined on the basis of Needham's approach: (i) the circle of Indo-Aryan civilisation;(ii) the circle of Chinese civilisation. This leaves Latin America unaccounted for, at that level of analysis. We shall return to this point.

2.2 Cultural areas

The mediating circle, often confused with the civilisational circle, as in Arnold Toynbee's work, whose successive attempts at typologies can be followed. Broadly, the following cultural areas can be delineated:

(*a*) in the Indo-Aryan civilisation circle:
  Egyptian, Persian, Mesopotamian Antiquities;
  Greco-Roman Antiquity;
  the European cultural area;
  the North American cultural area;
  major parts of the Indo-European cultural area in Latin America;
  the sub-Saharan African cultural area;
  the Islamic cultural area, partially: that is, the Arab-Islamic and Persian-Islamic cultural areas (to the exclusion of the Asian-Islamic cultural area, linked with the Chinese civilisational circle).
(*b*) in the Chinese civilisational circle:
  China proper;
  Japan;
  Mongolia–Central Asia;
  the Indian subcontinent;
  Oceania (with the exception of Australia–New Zealand);
  the Asian-Islamic cultural area (from Persia to the Philippines).

These two, outer major circles ought to be interpreted as from the introduction of the historically fundamental difference between the two worlds of mankind: the Orient and the West.

In fact, 'Orient' can clearly be seen as composed of the following constituent parts:

(*a*) the circle of Chinese civilisation, and its cultural areas;
(*b*) the circle (civilisational-cultural) of Islam – which clearly appears as the one major link between the circle of Indo-Aryan civilisation and the circle of Chinese civilisation; both a mediation and an area of maximal tensions;
(*c*) parts of the Indo-European cultural area of Latin America, directly linked with Africa, that is, specifically Brazil, and the Caribbean too;
(*d*) the sub-Saharan African cultural area.

The 'West' is therefore made up of the major sections of Indo-Aryan civilisation.

2.3 Nations (or 'national formations')

These are the basic units for the very existence, continuity, unfolding, evolution of macro-societal process. We have suggested a typology in five categories:

(*a*) the fundamental nations, also to be described as renascent nations (Egypt, China, Persia and Turkey; Vietnam, Mexico, Morocco);
(*b*) the European, then Western, type of nation-state;
(*c*) the new nation-states heading towards unification. Both the new nation-states strictly speaking (Ethiopia, Ghana, Mali, Burma, Thailand, etc.); and the national formations within the framework of multinational *ensembles* (Armenia, Georgia, Ouzbekistan, etc.);
(*d*) the dualistic Indian, then European, nation-state, mainly in Latin America;
(*e*) the new states with a national vocation (mainly in several parts of sub-Saharan Africa, and a minor portion of Central and South America).

2.4 Key distinctions

The key distinction between the three circles cannot be dealt with here except in very broad outline.

(*a*) Civilisational areas would be defined by the general conception of the interrelation between cultures, nations, societal formations on the one hand, and the time-dimension on the other hand. More than a strict vision of the world, it is this philosophic relation to 'time, the field of human development', and its consequences, which can be said to distinguish Orient from West.

(*b*) Cultural areas can then be seen as societal *ensembles* sharing a common *Weltanschauung* (more in terms of historical-geographical determinism through history (both ecological and geo-political) than in terms of philosophy proper), a conception of the world expressed in a limited set of main languages, sometimes in a single language (Arabic; Chinese; English; Persian; Japanese – in each one of the cultural areas concerned).

(*c*) Nations – or national formations – are easier to delimit, once agreement is reached on the indispensable structuring typology.

Yet, once we thus posit these three major interwoven types of circle – the framework of comparativism – we have posited what is really a topographical description (anatomy) of the field of comparativism. We now have to relate dialectically the different units within each of the three circles to the surrounding (wider and narrower) two circles. This, precisely, is the purpose of introducing the concept of specificity.

3. The concept of specificity: structure and dynamics

We would propose to take our tentative position on the concept of specificity from its first global formulation in 1970: 'The analysis of the concept of specificity can be attempted at three levels/moments.'

1. The level/moment of general definition, from the origins. In order to reach for the specificity of a given society, one should seek what has been the pattern of societal maintenance obtaining in a given socio-economic national formation through a critical study of its historical development. The particular pattern of this societal maintenance is simply the pattern of structuration of and interaction between the four key factors in every form of societal maintenance: the production of material life in the geographic and ecological framework (the mode of production *stricto sensu*); the reproduction of life (sexuality); social order (power and the state); the relation to the time-dimension (the limitedness of human life, religions and philosophies). In that group, the production of material life occupies the decisive place in the structuration of the whole pattern of maintenance, but only in the last instance. By applying this model to different societies, we would be in a better position to clarify the general picture, to qualify and to give colour, adding tone and nuance to the first analysis undertaken on the basis of socio-economic criteria.

2. The level/moment of the emergence of spatio-temporal factors to conscious awareness. The study of specificity is not undertaken in the outer world of pure epistemology – but within the framework of the concrete evolution of given societies. This evolution puts the time factor in the forefront; hence the central importance of the notion of 'depth of historical field'. There is no specificity in a temporary society – a jamboree, student movement, a state artificially established for show purposes. To talk of societal maintenance is to address oneself to the long historical duration that moulds events – not to contingency. So one can validly speak of specificity in the old social-national formations – the

ideal terrain for specificity – and in those formations which have not yet reached the level of national evolution *stricto sensu* – in the 'new nations', to use the term coined by Thomas Jefferson in speaking of the United States of America. One can thus see how vast the field is – the immense majority of nations and peoples in our time. The social sciences will feel less at ease with the 'space' factor – because one form of geo-politics has fallen out of favour. However, the historical evolution of societies does not take place in the abstract space of the dialectics of the mind – 'History' in place of 'history' – nor does it unfold in the secluded field of epistemology.

Societies – but only within the framework of their geographical conditions, considered under two aspects: (i) the aspect of location, which enables one to assess the importance of location to each society and its state as compared with others, that is, geo-politics; (ii) the aspect of internal conditioning, that is, ecology, which indicates and quantifies resources and potentials, which then had to be tempered by taking the demographic factor into consideration.

3. The moment-dimension of the dialectics of the factors of maintenance and the factors of transformation, on the basis of the ultimately decisive action of the mode of production and in extreme cases of the progress of techniques of production. To disentangle that which is maintained from that which maintains (which is a very different thing from speaking of 'invariables' – of much later origin), distinguishing each according to their pattern from that which was not, but is becoming, and that which is, but shall be no more. To distinguish the four linking factors, whatever their relative weight at any given stage of historical evolution.

4. The concept of specificity will apply to both the hegemonic and the dependent area, where several factors can be isolated that merit consideration, as they constitute the structuring framework of specificity at the nodal point of meaningful social theory. These problems can be divided into two groups: (i) the uses of the concept of specificity, that is, its relevance in different types of society; (ii) the definition of priority areas for comparativism, using the concept of specificity as the main conceptual tool.

4. Specificity and authenticity

From 'universalism' to specificity, a path to be charted by comparative critical studies, yet remaining still within the field of exceptionalism. For the hitherto prevailing assumptions of a self-assured Western theory, reductionism, cannot be expected to wither away in our fluctuating world, simply as a result of the emergence of the cultures and nations of the Orient, coupled with the growing sense of crisis in the advanced industrialised societies of the West, with their consumerist ethos. Yet specificity is here to stay. What remains, however, is a question; where does specificity belong?

As a universally valid concept, it would seem to work for and be relevant to all existing societies. A glance at the literature, however, suggests something rather different. For there it emerges clearly that the accepted or acceptable concept of specificity has been developed to deal, above all, with the non-Western, non-industrialised national societies: China, the Indian subcontinent, Asia (with the exception of Japan), the Arab and Islamic worlds, Africa, the hinterland of Latin America. There does seem to have been some attempt to bring theory up to date, from the now defunct 'colonial sociology' to the still favoured 'sociology of development' (or 'underdevelopment', of 'the Third World', etc.). Ethnism in sociological garb. That is the current conception of the concept of specificity, and the way it is being used. Several terms have been adopted or coined to show how ideally relevant it is to marginal societies. Thus the Arabic substantive *al-assalah*, that is, authenticity, has here and there been introduced to serve as a synonym for specificity.

Let us look at it more closely. What, in a sociological perspective, can be considered to be authentic? Manners and customs, social and ethical values, patterns, tradition, etc. – in a word, the whole gamut of phenomena belonging to the past, long ago in terms of historical development, and yet still more or less intact, homogeneous and relevant, to our times. Thus, in the *'assalah'* vision: the values of Bedouinism, as the Arabic form of nomadism, stand side by side with the Arab concepts of honour; sensuous love; political rhetoric; the patterns of Andalusian home architecture; the mystic-cum-erotic musical and vocal genre of the *muwasshahat*; the capacity for cultural dialogue and, simultaneously, cultural irredentism; *inter alia* – these comprise the Arabic-Islamic type of authenticity. Similar attempts have been made to delineate the authenticity of other national-cultural areas and national societies, of which amusing or cynical catalogues have been written.

Now, what we are getting at really is the sum total of the major different characteristics of one given societal grouping (civilisations; national-cultural areas; national societies), as compared with other such groupings. And yet, when such catalogues are established, they are mainly about non-Western societies. Attempts to compare catalogues referring to two or more non-Western societies set out to evaluate the *quantitative* load of each case – not to reach for the interpretation (*critical-historical*, or *historical-dialectical*) of their continued existence, and even less to understand the variations in their existence, effective impact, style of evolution, as elements developing within one given framework of societal maintenance; not as component parts, or factors, of that framework itself – thus eluding the comprehension of the pattern of societal maintenance of the unit under scrutiny. What we have amassed is a sort of sophisticated list of 'manners and customs', under (non-Western) national flags, a compendium for the educated traveller, businessman, diplomat.

As to the field of general, normalised, comparativism, catalogues are taking extreme statistical shapes, that is, statistical computations without historical, or analytical-objective background, as exemplified in current 'data programmes'.

Thus we reach a stage where 'new' conceptual tools serve mainly to negate the vigorous process which is opening up the hitherto sectoral, Western-centred vision of the whole world.

And yet, the whole world is here for us to ponder, challenging us to readjust our theoretical tools to a global theory. This is precisely the intellectual climate which has provided the vital inspiration to delimit, define and gradually to elaborate the concept of specificity. For, in our view, the time is not right for restrictive, reductionist approaches. What we are in need of, both in the field of visions and ideas, and in the realm of politics, is an instrument capable at one and the same time, simultaneously:

(*a*) of accounting for the persistence and evolution of any and all given societies – what we have proposed to call the *'pattern of societal maintenance'* – on the one hand;
(*b*) of doing so on the basis of common, ascertainable factors, pertaining to any and all national societies and at work in each and every one of them in varying degrees and shapes, as from the historical-geographical framework of existence within which each society has functioned, and is functioning to this day, on the other hand.

Let us revert to the type of instance illustrated by the above-mentioned problem of *'al-assalah'*. As we know, literally dozens of such instances and denominations can easily be traced.

Sometimes they refer to the prevailing ethnist assumptions, here and there, more or less racialist and nearly always ethnocentrist, that is, Western-centred. More recently, and in a more sophisticated manner, such shades of interpretation have derived their credentials from the Weberian 'ideal-type' conception: particularism was deemed to have its roots in the objectively different types of societies and social formations; and these differences were to be ascribed to the unfolding through history, as it were, of different ideal-types of social formation, different historical personalities, defined from their structural, intellectual and spiritual characteristics.

To many social scientists and thinkers, the Weberian approach appears more like a progressive rational one than the usual pot-pourri of pre-assumptions and prejudices. Yet, it meant, at one and the same time:

(*a*) a recognition of the differences in all societies as against the reductionist assumption of universality, and the subsequent policy of compulsory universality;

(*b*) the unbridgeable gap between such different social formations, mainly in the form of nations or national-cultural groupings – each unit being now non-reducible to other units, having been fully credited with its particularity, and this particularity itself defined as structurally different from other such particularities – structurally, and not as a *result of the objective course of its historical development.*

Examples here abound to follow the so-called '*assalah*'. We could cite in a tentative list: the accusation of militarism levelled against several nations and national-cultural *ensembles* of both Orient and West; the dreamy and sentimental character of, say, the Mediterranean grouping; the elusive relation to the time-dimension in Latin America; the non-integrative tendency said to obtain in sub-Saharan Africa; rationalism in France; the historical and philosophical mind in Germany; pragmatism and experimentalism in the Anglo-Saxon world; the drive for new frontiers in the United States and the USSR; symbiotic, integrative visions of the world in the oldest nations (Egypt, China, Persia, etc.)

A tentative list – and one can easily think of more examples. Yet, even at this modest level, one can see how irreducible we are all deemed to be. Different, and condemned to remain so; separate, and incapable of joining hands. The recognition of differences, the right to be different, lead to segregation, isolation, non-communication. Our one world would appear to be a constellation of monads, unrelated and alien to each other, because of their very differences, as defined by ideal-types.

Is there a way out of this mechanistic nightmare?

5.   Understanding the global depth-reality

The concept of specificity can, and ought to be used to chart the path for a meaningful and relevant comparativism leading to the restructuration of social theory. And it can do so by locating the priority areas for comparativism.

According to what criteria?

5.1

Let us accept, and allow for, the widest possible range of pluralism: priorities and criteria in the social sciences are clearly defined, or delineated, under the direct influences stemming from the nature of political power at the helm, while socio-economic factors appear to exert their influence in an indirect, secondary manner throughout, never in a direct, mechanical way. There are also obviously legitimate institutional and personal scientific preferences and choices at work. The question of *priorities and their criteria* remains to be scrutinised.

Let us begin from the above statements.

A first range of priorities for comparativism, and therefore of criteria leading to the positing of such priorities, will obviously lie in the immediate and medium-range fields, that is, in the *project* – socio-economic, political, cultural – defined by any one national society at a given stage of its historical evolution. The common characteristic of such an approach – inevitable and useful, for practical purposes – is that it addresses itself to the field of the feasible, to social praxis and practical politics, using mainly quantitative tools, inasmuch as the long historical perspective seems of little immediate relevance here. Such appears to be what we would propose to term *operational comparativism* – or functional, tactical, comparativism.

The depth layers remain unexplored, where, from a cross-civilisational perspective, the raw materials of social theory lie. This is precisely where the concept of specificity can be best deployed, inasmuch as the *'depth of the historical field'* constitutes the very stuff of which this concept is made, the source from which it stems; without it the very thought of developing such a concept could not have arisen. Should we accept this approach, we would then have at our disposal a whole set of factors leading to definite priorities and criteria, on this level/form of comparativism, which we would propose to term *fundamental/meaningful* or *civilisational, strategic comparativism*.

5.2

The four key areas would be those that constitute the mode of societal maintenance itself: production of material means of life; reproduction of human life; social power; relations with the time-dimension. A large number of phenomena and factors could be grouped under those four headings. But there still would remain an immense number of such factors and phenomena of a historically transient nature.

Several questions emerge:

1. Are all four areas equal in their importance for the development of fundamental comparativism?

Here, we would have to look into the direct patterns of interrelations between each one of these areas on the one hand, and the necessities of social praxis on the other. The area of production of the material means of existence cannot be separated, at any one moment, from the very nature of practical politics, of immediate and continuing social praxis, at any time and place in history –hence, perhaps, the Marxian selection of this area/factor as the ultimate and decisive factor in social dialectics. And this is so, in spite of the fact that there is a specific mould of, say, a capitalist socio-economic formation and development in different national societies and national-cultural groupings (Japan and Canada; Sweden and Egypt), etc., itself the expression, or actualisation, of the particular specificity of each of these societies, the front of its historical evolution.

2. The other areas, or groups of factors, seem to be more permeated with specificity. They seem to constitute the level of superstructure proper, though the reproduction of human life – that is, the whole field of sexuality – stands at the crossroads between economic production on the one hand, and the power-cum-culture *ensemble* on the other hand. One could note that a notable evolution has taken place in that complex balance: for whereas sexuality could be said to have been more directly linked with economic production in the pre-capitalist societies, where self-awareness was not magnified by the mass media or the ethos of productivism and consumerism as it is, in our days, in the more advanced industrialised societies. Conversely, sexuality can now be said to be

immensely more attuned to, and permeated by, the changing images of the human condition, and particularly by its relations with the time-dimension, philosophy, ideology, metaphysics, religions, mysticism, as well as its transformation, literally, through the mounting struggle for the transformation of woman's condition in the advanced societies of our day.

3. Power in societies has recently vividly manifested its structural links with the hidden part of the iceberg, that is, the depth roots of national-cultural specificity, notably in the diverging paths of socialism as exemplified mainly by the Soviet Union and China: the role and place of the army at the centre of political power in the varieties of Nasserism (Egypt, Algeria, Peru, Argentina, Portugal, *inter alia*) as against the hitherto traditional reactionary obscurantist putschism prevalent in regions with weak national traditions; the fortunes of liberalism in Western capitalist countries; the post-colonial phase, embarked upon by the traditional ex-colonial powers (Great Britain, France, Portugal, Belgium notably), and American hegemonic imperialism (in Vietnam, as the most extreme case).

4. Nowhere more than in the fourth area, or component part, of the pattern of societal maintenance, as defined above – that is, relations with the time-dimension – do we meet the same density of manifest, explicit specificity. For we are here at the very heart of the realm of culture and thought; even more so, at the level where culture and thought reach their apex, in the delicate network of the sophisticated and systematic constructions of religion and philosophy. Here, we experience only a limited need to explain different styles, shapes, moulds, characters. For, obviously, we are treading upon the familiar ground of ethnicity, coming to grips with the exposed part of the iceberg.

Yet the significance of this massive evidence is not always sufficiently perceived. If culture and thought – revolving around the relation of man with the time-dimension, as expressed in religions and philosophies – can show such a weight of differences, such explicit types of specificity, then it must be that they thus express the sum total of societal maintenance, the *global depth-reality*, the achievements, the balance sheet as well as the prospective potentials of a given society. Hence the relevance of the evidence of such an exceptional weight of specificity in that very domain – a revealing phenomenon of paramount importance.

It follows, therefore, that the field of the combined aesthetic-intellectual superstructure proper – which expresses itself in religions, philosophies, metaphysics, ideologies, meta-psychological and mystical forms – is that field in which fundamental/meaningful or strategic civilisational comparativism can best deploy its resources and reap the widest harvests. For here, more than in other fields, we can see the all-pervading central constitutive influence of the time-dimension, of the depth of the historical field.

5.3

Thus, a preliminary attempt to define the priority areas for comparativism shows:

1. that the area/field/level of the greatest and most explicit differences – that of cultural and aesthetic-intellectual superstructures, as exemplified in philosophies, religions, ideologies – can usefully serve as the major starting-point for fundamental/meaningful comparative research and enquiry;

2. that, as from that point, we ought to be able to benefit from the work done at that level to clarify aspects of specificity in the two other superstructural areas – reproduction of physical life; power in societies – and to shed some light on the economic infrastructural domain;

3. that the broader and richer area could be defined as encompassing both the factor of man's relation to the time-dimension and the factor of power in society. For power seldom hesitates to relate itself to given religions, philosophies, ideologies – whereas it often conceals its organic links with the economic infrastructure, itself heavily permeated with technological advances easy to generalise in their broad lines to different national-cultural areas.

5.4

One major example could perhaps shed some light on this highly complex field. Let us consider the range of societies which have come to be known, over a generation or so, by the name of 'hydraulic societies'. As we know, such societies are those which depend on artificial irrigation for the production of their food supplies in the absence of a natural irrigation provided by regular rainfalls, such as we find in the temperate areas of the world. These societies would therefore be found mainly in the tropical, subtropical and equatorial areas of the world, and thus are deemed to have been the oldest sedentary regions where the oldest societies, and therefore civilisations of the world, have sprung up: Egypt, Mesopotamia, China, Central and North India, Central America, Central Africa. According to this theory, the use of artificial irrigation – that is, the erection of dams, irrigation canals and drains – was the only means to control the colossal course of the major rivers such as the Nile, the Yang-Tsê Kiang, the Ganges, the Tigris, the Euphrates, the Congo, etc. This need for persistent, continuous and systematic control of natural water resources inevitably compels sedentary societies in these regions to create an instrument for central unified control of this immensely complex network, as against a series of regional/or subregional units. Such is deemed to have been the case of new centralised states in Africa, and it can be easily understood that century after century, in fact several hundred years extending to a maximum of several thousand years, gave an inevitably autocratic character to these states. Well and good. Yet immediately, two major questions can be posed:

1. If the autocratic nature of state power in these regions of our world can account for such a range of societies, how could we account for the autocratic nature of state power all over the world and throughout the range of human history, except for brief interludes in restricted areas of the world, and of a temporary sort? Would it not be, perhaps, more proper to consider that the functions of the state are, *per se*, those of societal control, of the rationalised use of violence for the maintenance of a given social order? To be sure, there are different degrees of autocracy. Yet, to this day, the role of violence seems to have been constant throughout the history of mankind.

2. If we take the range of societies, as indicated above, could we really say that social and cultural institutions, phenomena, processes are identical in, say, Vietnam and the Sudan, Pakistan and Morocco, Iraq and Cambodia, etc.? And, if this is not so, how could we account for the differences, unless we make do with superficial generalities. We must plunge into the depths, and use the concept of specificity, here very briefly sketched, to explore the dimension of the maintenance and transformation of each one of these societies and national-cultural groups?

*   *   *

This could end parochialism. No one advanced industrialised society is either in need of negating, or hiding, its authenticity, its *assalah* so to speak, or averse to considering its 'manners and customs' as constituting its specificity. And the same goes for less industrialised, mainly non-Western societies. Thus, the concept of specificity appears as the integrative conceptual tool *par excellence* – aiming as it does to discover that which makes societies different, through the whole course of their historical evolution to this day. Integrative and dialectically unifying – but not reductionist. Instead of data banks, valuable if and when used to inform basic critical-historicist analyses, the instrument for integrating the quantitative-statistical approach into a synthetic global view of our world, reaching in two major directions – vertically (historical evolution) and horizontally (civilisations, cultural areas, national societies) – is the concept of specificity.

13

On the Dialectics of Time

> Thought will only begin when we have learned that what has been so magnified over the centuries – Reason – is the bitterest enemy of thought.
>
> Martin Heidegger: *Roads that Lead Nowhere*

The very position of the problem we are discussing here suggests that the whole direction of social development, our methods and conceptual approaches to the problematic of social development in the world, are basically at fault. At the very least a growing number of thinkers, and particularly in the Orient, have called them into question.

Briefly (we shall develop the point later) the question before us is this. How can we situate the problem of social development within the framework of the transformation of the contemporary world? For the traditional formulations, the traditional framework of socio-economic positions on the problem of development and the relations between civilisations, cultures and nations in our world, are clearly restrictive, marred by reductionism, leading only to blind alleys and irrelevant to the future of mankind. We are suggesting, too, that there is an alternative way of posing the problem which, it is hoped, would open new avenues for the relations between civilisations and cultures conceived as a dialectical process.[1]

1. Reductionism: the quest for an alternative

The traditional position of the problem can be briefly summed up as follows:

(a) 'Development', as a means whereby the hitherto marginalised

societies – mainly of the Orient, Asia and Africa, but also later and in a rather different way, Latin America – can catch up with the 'developed societies' of the West, including, for reasons of state, Japan.

   But what is the objective? In a word, to present as the optimal goal a tolerable combination of a growing GNP and an area of civic and personal liberty within a broad access to culture, communication and, above all, the pleasures of life – the fruit of a hedonistic, social-progressive belief in processual social evolution. The model suggested is already in existence in the advanced nations of the Western world, in Europe and North America, where the pleasures of life, social and individual hedonism have reached their climax in human history. In that respect, it is relevant to point out that the analysts of the Orient and the West alike have stressed the massive, powerful and protracted contribution of the scientific, technological and economic infrastructure to the global impact of Western thought and social institutions. This planetary impact is no longer seen as a product *ex nihilo* of the assumed superiority of the Western mind, but rather in terms of a combination of material advancement and cultural creativity. This global vision of the problem of the predominance of Western thought is itself indicative of the new mood prevailing in the human and social sciences in our times in both the Orient and the West – as we have repeatedly pointed out.

(b)   If this predominance is so marked, however, and undisputed, what would be the purpose of and the means for achieving something different, namely national-cultural and civilisational identities? Under what heading would it take place? Here we enter the realm of specificity. Given the existence of several different civilisations and national-cultural areas, however, how can societal maintenance and historical continuity be assured and carried forward, and to what end? How can we escape reductionism?

(c)   The traditional answer is that the way to ensure the persistence of authenticity, the maintenance of civilisational and cultural identity – in a word, of the historically defined specificity of the different societies that comprise today's civilisations and cultures as we know them – is through socio-economic transformation and social revolution. If you want to be yourself, to avoid the Western road, and to escape reductionism, then the only path is to transform your own national society.

   This process can be seen to consist of two conflicting aspects:

1. On the positive side, the social transformation of any national society, of any nation, usually leads to both a growth in production, in the GNP, and to a better, more equitable distribution of the benefits of development throughout society leading at best to the kind of advanced social reformism that already exists in many countries.

2. But where does this lead? Here a question arises, or has arisen, as to the conjunction of two major trends of development: (i) in the West a crisis of faith in the civilisational value of the Western development model, which is labelled, or explained, as the crisis among youth, the generation gap, neo-Utopianism, etc.; (ii) the emergence of the Orient, the access and emergence on to the contemporary scene of the Three Continents of Asia, Africa and Latin America. This marks the end of the traditional empires, the dead end of failure reached by hegemonic imperialism in Vietnam, the October War of 1973 and the (so-called) 'energy crisis', etc.

A planetary impact certainly. Yet on 16 September 1977, the US President's Commission on Mental Health, under Dr Thomas Bryant, published its bewildering report, which estimated that 'between 20 and 32 million Americans require some kind of mental health care at any one time'; according to the estimates of the majority of the Commission, the real figures reached 40 million.

(d)   It is appropriate here to consider the global political framework within which this homogenisation of the world under the globalising effect of Western culture and civilisational values is achieved.

Since 1945, the world has gone from the Cold War, through peaceful coexistence towards '*détente*' – which is now itself in deep crisis. Yet *détente* was more than a passing international arrangement, or a convenient, mutually agreeable strategy. With *détente*, the two systems of the West – the liberal or monopoly-capitalist, and the autocratic socialist system – were in effect making it clear that the hegemony, or historical precedence of the West was an inescapable fact, the starting-point and the real basis of social and human evolution for all societies in our time. Further it indicated that no crisis that led to breakdown would ever be tolerated, except to the extent that it might actually meet the needs of the existing superpowers.

For the Three Continents, this represented a dead end, above all as far as the civilisational sphere of the Orient was concerned. Permanence equals conformity, and conformity was the only guarantee of survival. The deadlocks, crises and blind alleys, from which the Orient could not escape, nor its societies fail to live out, were the result of the lack of infrastructural resources in the Three Continents and the Orient. Thus the process would evolve towards its inevitable and negative outcome. Hence the search for alternative solutions. But how, and in what direction, should the search progress?

At the macro-level, on a more theoretical plane, the search took as its guide the concept of the *civilisational project* with its accompanying civilisational strategy. A civilisational project, and not just a societal project, though still, in the here and now, essentially socio-economic and with populist overtones.

At the micro-level or rather at an instrumental and topological level, the search was and is for the instrument and the locus for the necessary distancing which would open the basic space in which to elaborate, formulate and begin to implement the alternative pattern(s) of civilisational development. Yet the urgency of history has imposed at the same time an unrelenting action towards national development in the more traditional sense of the term.

2.   'Time, the unending river'

The key is to be sought in the time-dimension. For we are dealing here with the depth of the historical field, with duration, with societal maintenance through history, with civilisations and cultures facing the problem of their identity, continuity and evolution; in a word, the problem of the dialectics of specificity within the global framework of mankind.

Time, the field of human development, the unending, refreshing river, the very content and texture of evolution itself.

We could, of course, have chosen other meaningful, formative factors in the dialectics of civilisations and cultures: political power; the quality and capacity for resistance, and the transformation of socio-economic infrastructures; the capacity of different civilisations and cultures to react to the impact of foreign, exogenous factors; and their capacity to promote intellectual creativity under pressure, that is amid the influence and impact of exogenous factors, of converging hegemonies.

3. Time – a unified vision?

It would seem so. Both the *Encyclopedia Britannica* and the *Encyclopaedia Universalis* seem to have no doubt about this. The entries under 'time' and 'temps' speak of this concept as a given, unified and solidly entrenched Western approach in philosophy and physics, with the stress on the Aristotelian-Kantian tradition. Nowhere in the major Western reference works do we get the impression that it would be worthwhile to devote some attention to the historical structuration of the concept of 'time', to say nothing of the different conceptions and visions of time in the many splendoured cultures and civilisations of mankind. We return to the postulation of universality as a *de facto* approach to culture, theories, and the whole realm of intellectual endeavours.

We know the Western vision of time.[2] It is above all an *operational* view, whose aim is to locate and point the way to an analysis whose programmatic aim will be to develop through action. In fact, it is Aristotle who plays the key role here, as in the whole range of philosophy and logical thinking in the West. This is not the place to provide an historical interpretation of the motivations of Aristotelianism. It will suffice to note that the rise of formal logic, the hegemony of analytical thinking, the very constitution of the whole system of formal logic linked to Aristotle, were designed to accompany the temporary unification of the previously separate and feuding city-states of Greece into one state under the rule of Macedonia and Alexander. Operationality, efficacy, action were the demands made of thought at that time. And it was precisely to meet these requirements that the Western vision of time came to be formulated as a tool for action, not as a conception of man's place in historical duration, in the wanderings of the human species through the universe, nor its location in one unit of this unknown universe – our globe.

From then on, the Western vision of time proceeded along the same operational, analytical lines. Nothing arose in the concrete historical process to challenge the West between, say, Alexander and the Islamic conquests of the ninth century. It is no accident that critical reflection on time started precisely after the wave of Islamic conquests, through the fifteenth and sixteenth centuries, with Galileo and the prolegomena to the European Renaissance. Meanwhile, the rise of Western hegemony, the rise of the West and its assumption of the central historical initiative in world history at the time, did ensure the continuation of the Aristotelian analytical-operational tradition exemplified in the whole trend of Western philosophies, from the eighteenth century to our time, from Kant to Einstein.

For here, as before, the concrete processes at work in history failed to provide the challenges capable of promoting an alternative vision of time.

Thus time became one among several instances of the analytical-operational conception which constitutes the major tradition in Western philosophy from Aristotle to our time. After all, time was but one instance of existence in the real-concrete world. Man, conceived or rather conceiving himself as demi-urge, master and creator of the universe, faced what was described as the alienation of religions, ideologies and establishments. In the itineraries of rationalism and scientific thinking, man as demi-urge could only be man as master and user of time. Thus gradually in everyday language, men appeared to 'have' or 'lack' time, 'not to have enough' time, as if time were a kind of private property, like a chariot, a car, a writing pad or a washing machine – the corned beef, as it were, of existence. The issue was how to use time, rather than how man was used by time itself. How to use time to achieve something, rather than considering the significance of actions and achievements through the dimension of time. It can and should be argued, of course, that the best thing we can do is make the best of time; that is the basic psychological-intellectual atmosphere in which the positivist conception of science, rationalism and thus of time, was gradually historically structured in the Western world.

Achievements, an apparently irrepressible forward impetus, were there to confirm and to confront; nothing could usurp the place of the prevailing visions. Nothing, that is, until history began to change direction.

On the other side of the river, the conceptions of the Orient were structured through a different process realised in a totally different environment.[3]

If we study the historical-geographical constitution of the nations and societies of the Orient – Asia, around China; the Islamic area in Afro-Asia – it will be clear immediately that we have before us the oldest sedentary and stable societies or socio-economic formations in the history of mankind. A group of societies came to be established around the major rivers, facing wide openings to the ocean and sea, thus enabling the pastoral groups to move towards a more stable, agricultural-sedentary mode of production and societal existence. These were the objective conditions for the constitution of the oldest nations in our world, gradually regrouped into cultural areas within the two major civilisation frameworks of the Orient. This stabilisation was possible as a result of a plentiful water supply – often regulated by hydraulic societies – temperate weather, and ample access to the sea. It is crucial here to consider the relevance of 'durability', of 'societal maintenance' through centuries and millenia to these objective basic elements; for we must beware of an inclination to turn to Weberian, 'ideal-type' interpretations of an idealistic or spiritualist kind.

A second factor of major importance serves to underline and deepen this dimension of durability, of societal maintenance, national-social cohesion and centripetal convergence in the Orient. At this stage, we must introduce into our analysis the history of geo-politics. The nations of the Orient were for the most part located at the crossroads between continents, and seemed to hold the key to networks of commerce, of economic and human exchange, in the face of wider circles where there existed non-sedentary ethnic groups, mostly of a pastoral, tribal sort. These outer circles, quite naturally, felt drawn towards the more privileged regions where the nations of the Orient existed and prospered. Thus began the history of the repeated waves of conquests, invasions, looting and occupation, from Antiquity through colonialism and imperialism to our own times, mainly concentrating on parts of the Eastern Mediterranean and Western Asia (what had come to be described by geo-politicians during the 1914–18 war as the 'Middle East'). Obviously this long series of historical struggles could only have effect, since they were threatening the very existence of the prosperous nations of the Orient – namely to strengthen and deepen the tendency to continuity, societal maintenance, centripetal convergence and national unity of these nations.

Thus it happened that the objective historical framework of the Orient itself underlay the paramount importance given to time conceived as the wider formative frame of national existence itself. Gradually, time became the key to the whole *Weltanschauung*, the converging visions of the Orient. Time, the all-encompassing dimension, the master of human history itself, the climate in which were to arise the three great monotheisms, as well as the philosophical and mystical traditions of Asia and Africa.

Time is master. Therefore the conception of time can be said to have developed as a non-analytical vision, as a unitary, symbiotic, unified and unifying conception. Man could no longer 'have' or 'lack' time; time, the master of existence, could not be apprehended as commodity. On the contrary, man was determined and dominated by time. His existence, and his understanding of it in the world, passed through time in a syncretic, and sometimes circular way. Time, in short, became the unified vision of the Orient; and that is how it appears today more than ever, as the subtle texture of the civilisational difference between patterns of thought and action throughout the world, on both banks of our common river.

Where, then, do we go from there?

4.   Elements towards strategy

The Oriental vision of time, the Oriental conception of time, will now lead us directly to the dialectics of time.

(a)   The primacy of time thus established, it is an inescapable conclusion that there is no other way for man or society to tackle the time-dimension, other than by submitting to its paramount hegemony, its decisive role in the formative framework of life and human action. It follows that we cannot avoid granting to objective time, the time of historical duration, primacy over subjective time, the time of individualised perception, the time of man. Thus only by playing the game of time, as it were, by 'releasing' time, can it be made a positive factor. Freedom, in that sense, is the understanding of necessity. This can be said to be the negative moment, or component, of the dialectics of time.

(b)   Positivity – the negation of the negation – is the possibility for the nations of the Orient to pass through time, and in doing so draw upon their own potential and resources (as we have explained). Only thus can they establish the distance without which there is no hope of escaping from Western reductionism and hegemony for a very long time to come.

We have thus reached the level of action, of the means and instruments of action – in a word, the realm of the political.

The conception we have outlined here has as its aim to enable the nations of the Orient to take action, after a necessary distancing. Thus they can begin to address themselves to the elaboration of their own specific civilisational project, joining hands in a meaningful way with other nations, cultures and civilisations, and marching forward together into a future world.

The primacy of the political requires us to consider the following problems. To begin with, there are two levels of national action:

1. The exogenous-oriented sector of the national establishment; it should be stressed here that by 'exogenous-oriented' we do not mean those groups and sectors in any Oriental nation which are organically linked to, and representative of, the interests of the power centres of the Western world, that is, the compradors. Rather it is used to refer to those groups and sections of the national establishment which are by tradition, vocation or circumstance more knowledgeable about the contribution, internal problematic, historical specificity, promises and problems, achievements and failures of the major cultural traditions of the West.

2. The endogenous-oriented national establishment; at the decision-making level, these are the essential sectors, in that they represent the permanent spiritual families of the nation. This element, it should be pointed out, is not a backward-looking, archaic, reactionary sector. In fact the past two centuries, and particularly recent decades, have shown that this is the sector most acutely aware of the need to restructure the national entity in a contemporary way, in order to meet the growing challenges, conflicts and tensions directly imposed by the converging hegemonies of the Western world.

The second major area is that of the state, as unifier and provider of orientations. Here, it is important to take stock of the transformation of the role of the state in our times, for it has come more and more to act as the major organisational and directive power structure in all modern societies, albeit, of course, as representative of the hegemony of the political front in power. This is everywhere true, but nowhere more so than in the states of the nations of Asia, Africa and Latin America. This suggests that it is urgently necessary to reconsider the question, if we are to benefit from the immense potentialities which are now coming to the fore in a dialectical way.

What is, or could be the role of these sectors of the national establishment?

1. The role of the exogenous-oriented sector of the national establishment is, above all, to serve as a bridge between the nations of the Orient and the West. It must be able to provide the national establishment as a whole with a variegated vision of the impact of the outer world, while always being prepared to act as mediator between the endogenous-oriented establishment and the Western world. None the less, this sector

is not and cannot be the formative sector in decision-making at a national level.

The central role, therefore, will fall to the endogenous-oriented sector, whose historical role can be defined as the utilisation of the dialectics of time to elaborate the civilisational project, and define the civilisational strategy. The aim will be to disentangle itself from the obligation to deal with the problem of the future in the terms posed by the West, by taking into account both the current impasse and crisis situation, on the one hand, and the immense promise and potential of the Orient on the other.

2. The endogenous-oriented sector will therefore concentrate on areas like: power and culture; the model of production and consumption; and the preservation of the national potential and resources, etc. In doing so, this nucleus must take into account the scientific definition of national-cultural specificity as defined in the course of the evolution and constitution of the nation under study. Then and only then will this formative group be able to resolve the problems of power and culture, of production and consumption, of potential and its utilisation, etc., of the uses of the past in the future, in a decisively non-reductionist way. This will draw out the widest range of intellectual creativity among a large majority of the population of a nation united, in the optimal case, in the united national front for liberation, democracy and social progress.

The role of the centre of political power – the state – will be decisive; but in order to be so, it must be something very different from the rational use of coercion for the maintenance of any given social order. The state must literally assert the primacy of the political, that is the primacy of thinking and action for the common good of the global society, for the elaboration of a future in terms of a positive historical vision.

This is precisely the place of philosophy in the city. Now, more than ever before since the European Renaissance, since the end of the Islamic empire and the decline of China (from the late fourteenth to the early sixteenth century), the philosophical search plays a central role in forming the minds, inspiring the hearts and moderating the action of both the leading elite and the broad masses of the population at one and the same time. The problematic is not really that of 'political science', but of the primacy of political philosophy within the city, at both central state and popular levels. And it is here that the Oriental visions of time, outlined above, can prove to be the central instrument, enabling the Orient to face the problem of its future development in terms of renaissance and meaningful evolution. If this can be accomplished in time, before the effects of the inevitable counter-thrust, the generalised strategic counter-offensive of the Western world, under way since 1973, grow sharper and more penetrating, then the renaissance of the Orient need not be neutralised.

In conclusion, one can ask why this neutralisation would be a negative development in world history?

In reply, we must return to the crisis in Western civilisation, and the rising promise of the Orient, to see how and why the promise of the future of mankind in this one world of ours can only be tackled through a meaningful interaction between the civilisations and cultures of the Orient and the West.

Yet this interaction does not occur in a void, in a mythical world, but in the real world, the world of conflicts and tensions and competition, and at a time (since 1973) when the patterns of world power are being restructured. That is why we must consider this meaningful interaction as a dialectical process, in the terms of the dialectics of civilisations – and not simply a dialogue between them. For it must be understood that the aim and object of this dialectical process is to achieve a non-antagonistic yet contradictory dialectical interaction between the two banks of our common river.

If the Orient wishes to become master of its own destiny, it would do well to ponder the old saying of the martial arts in Japan: 'Do not forget that only he who knows the new things while knowing the ancient things, can become a true master.'

Notes and References

Chapter 3

1. Compare, *inter alia*, the absence of an entry on 'theory' in the (American) *International Encyclopedia of the Social Sciences* (1968) or Unesco's *A Dictionary of the Social Sciences* (London, 1964), where one is referred to 'Model (theoretical model)', an intricate and distinguished piece of philosophical erudition by E. A. Gellner (p. 435), with the basic, precise and clear article 'Theorie' in A. Lalande's classic *Vocabulaire technique et critique de la Philosophie*, 8th edn (Paris, 1960) pp. 1127–8.
2. The theses outlined in this chapter are based on our sustained work in the fields of social and political theory between 1960 and 1972, and represented in the present volumes.
3. *Science and Civilisation in China* was launched as a major project in 1942; the first volume appeared in 1954, published by Cambridge University Press. The completion date is 1980, and about two-thirds of the work has been published so far, in seven volumes. Three accompanying volumes to the encyclopedia proper have also been published: *Clerks and Craftsmen in China and the West* (1970); *Within Four Seas – the Dialogue of East and West* (1972); *The Grand Titration – Science and Society in East and West* (1972).
4. Cf. our publications in Arabic: *Dirasat fil-Thaqafah al-Wataniyyah* ('Studies in National Culture') (Beirut, 1969) and, more specifically, 'Min agl stratijiyyah hadariyyah' (For a civilisational strategy) in *Al-Thaquafah al-Arabiyyah*, Beirut (April 1973) pp. 116–31.
5. As defined in 'The Concept of Specificity', pp. 160–74 below.

Chapter 4

1. Cf. *University Grants Committee: Report of the Sub-Committee on Oriental, Slavonic, East European and African Studies* (London, 1961). Latin America remains outside the scope of this report as the linguistic factor does not hinder research. Yet the nature of the problem is similar to that of Asia and Africa.

2. A. W. Small, *Adam Smith and Modern Sociology*, vol. I, pp. 235, 238, in H. Becker and H. E. Barnes, *Social Thought from Lore to Science*, 3rd ed. (New York, 1961), vol. II, pp. 523–6.

3. *Economie politique*, trans. A. Posner (Paris, 1962) vol. 1, p. 379.

4. Cf. E. Roll, *A History of Economic Thought* (London, 1962) pp. 11–17, 303–18.

5. Asa Briggs, 'History and Society' in *A Guide to the Social Sciences*, ed. N. Mackenzie (London, 1966) pp. 33–53.

6. There is an abundance of literature by indigenous social scientists, especially from Latin America, viz. the work of Raul Prebisch, Celso Furtado, etc. See too the issue of *Partisans*, nos 26–7 (1966).

7. Cf. the collected theses and discussions, especially those of T. Balogh and H. Myint in *The Teaching of Development Economics*, ed. K. Martin and J. Knapp (London, 1967): and the general Introduction by C. Issawi to *The Economic History of the Middle East, 1800–1914: A Book of Readings* (Chicago–London, 1966) pp. 3–13.

8. Cf. Abdel-Malek, 'La vision du problème colonial par le monde afro-asiatique' in *Cahiers Internationaux de Sociologie*, XXX (1963) pp. 145–56; and 'Sociology of National Development', *Social Dialectics*, vol. 2 (London, 1981).

9. This concept has been refined and applied recently by M. Rodinson, particularly in *Islam et capitalisme* (Paris, 1966).

10. For example, on the basis of the purchasing power of the US dollar in 1924–33.

11. J. Weiler, 'Le passage de l'analyse à la sociologie économique' in G. Gurvitch, *Traité de sociologie* (Paris, 1962) vol. I, pp. 357–82. He mentions similar criticisms by J. Nef.

12. Cf. his introduction to *Les étapes de la pensée sociologique* (Paris, 1967) pp. 9–22.

13. C. Wright Mills, *The Sociological Imagination* (Harmondsworth, 1970) pp. 13–14. J. Berque's approach to Arab studies has opened new perspectives for specialists by the use of what I would call 'prospective intuition'.

14. 'Histoire et sociologie' in G. Gurvitch, *Traité de sociologie*, vol. 1, pp. 83–98.

15. Wright Mills, *Sociological Imagination*, p. 164. For a survey of this subject as a particular field of sociology in the nineteenth-century classical style, see H. E. Barnes, *Historical Sociology: its Origins and Development* (New York, 1948).

16. Wright Mills, *Sociological Imagination*, pp. 163, 165, 168. It is significant that the two phenomena that Mills selects should be the army and nationalism.

17. Ibid., pp. 166–7.

18. 'Sociology' in *A Guide to the Social Sciences*, pp. 79–94.

19. Wright Mills, *Sociological Imagination*, p. 172.

20. Ibid., p. 174. This case is argued, *inter alia*, by both Asa Briggs and T. Bottomore in their contributions, quoted above.

21. Ibid., p. 171.

22. A. Briggs, 'History and Society', p. 49. Cf. A. Abdel-Malek, 'Orientalism in Crisis', below, and I. Sachs, 'Du Moyen-Age à nos jours: Europecentrisme et découverte du Tiers-Monde' in *Annales*, XXI (1966) pp. 465–87. This typological approach reaches its peak in the work of J. Austruy.
23. Primitive classless society, slavery, feudalism, capitalism, socialism and communism. The gradual publication of Marx's *Grundrisse* (Harmondsworth, 1973) has stimulated discussion of pre-capitalist economic formations of the non-European type, among them the so-called 'Asiatic mode of production'. Cf. E. Hobsbawm's illuminating introduction to K. Marx, *Pre-capitalist Economic Formations* (London, 1964) pp. 9–65.
24. *Al-tatawwor al-iqtisadi fi Micr fi-l'acr al-hadith* (Cairo, 1944) pp. 27–8. Leading centres at the time were 'Dar al-Abhath al-Ilmiyyah' and 'Lagnat Nashr al-Thaqafah al-Hadithah'.
25. *Al-tajdid fi'l-iqtisad al-Misri al-hadith* (Cairo, 1962) pp. 431–41.
26. *Al-ard wa'l-fallah, al-mas'ala al-zira'iyya fi Misr* (Cairo, 1958). Other studies paying special attention to this field are by Shuhdi A. al-Shafii and F. Jirjis. The whole discussion has been studied in A. Abdel-Malek in *Egypte, société militaire* (Paris, 1962) pp. 15–91.
27. C. Issawi, *Egypt at Mid-century* (New York, 1954) chs 2 and 3; G. Baer, *A History of Landownership in Modern Egypt 1800–1950* (London, 1962); A. A. I. el-Gritly's *The Structure of Modern Industry in Egypt* (Cairo, 1948) starts from a slight historical background, in sharp contrast to his very interesting *Al-sukkan wa'l-mawarid al-iqtasadiyya fi Misr* (Cairo, 1962).
28. This is the formulation adopted in my *Egypte, société militaire*.
29. The first figure is from 'The U.A.R. Budget Estimates 1962–3', *National Bank of Egypt Economic Bulletin*, vol. XV (1962) pp. 108–25: the last item is taken from P. O'Brien, *The Revolution in Egypt's Economic System from Private Enterprise to Socialism 1952–65* (London, 1966) pp. 325, 317.
30. A. Abdel-Malek, 'Nasserism and Socialism' in *The Socialist Register 1964* (London, 1964) pp. 38–55.
31. *L'Egypte nassérienne* (Paris, 1964).
32. Op. cit., p. 316, and also 'As a document, the first Five-Year Plan suggests, however, that almost all economic activity is centrally planned, but as implemented Egyptian planning includes no more than investment expenditure by the public and private sectors and the allocation of foreign exchange' (p. 319).
33. In *Pour Marx* (Paris, 1965).

Chapter 5

1. On the general history of traditional Orientalism up to 1962, and particularly as regards the Arab and Islamic world, there is an abundant bibliography, notably: V.-V. Barthold, *La découverte de l'Asie histoire de l'Orientalisme en Europe et en Russie* (Paris, 1947); there is nothing in the *Encyclopédie de l'Islam* nor the *Encyclopedia Britannica*; 'Orientalistika', *Enclyclopédie*

soviétique, vol. IX (Moscow, 1951) pp. 193–202; G. Vacca, 'Orientalismo', *Enciclopedia italiana di scienze, lettere ed arti* (Rome, 1935) XXV, p. 537; G. Levi della Vida, 'Per gli studi arabi in Italia', *Nuova Antologia* (Dec 1912) pp. 1–10; A. Bausani, 'Islamic studies in Italy in the XIX–XXth. centuries', *East and West*, vol. VIII (1957) pp. 145–55; Z. M. Holt, 'The origin of Arabic studies in England', *Al-Kulliyya* (Khartoum, 1952) no. 1, pp. 20–7; A. J. Arberry, *Oriental Essays* (London, 1960); M. Horten, 'Die probleme des Orientalistik', *Beitrage zur Kenntnis des Orient*, vol. XIII (1916) pp. 143–61; G. Germanus, 'Hungarian Orientalism – past and present', *Indo-Asian Culture*, vol. VI (1957) pp. 291–8; L. Bouvat, 'Les hongrois et les études musulmanes', *Revue du monde musulman*, vol. I (1907) no. 3, pp. 305–24; Nagib Al-'Aqiqi, *Al-moustashriqoun* (Cairo, 1947); Youssef A. Dagher, *Dalil al-A' areb ila ilmal-koutoub wa fann al-makateb* (Beirut, 1947); *Faharess al-maktabah al-Arabiyyah fil-khafiqayn* (Beirut, 1947) pp. 105–12; *Massader al-dirasah al-abadiyyah*, vol. II, 1800–1955 (Beirut, 1955) pp. 771–87; J. Fueck, *Die arabischen Studien in Europa* (Leipzig, 1955); and so on.
2. 'Orientaliste' in *Grand Larousse encyclopédique* (Paris, 1963) VII, 1003–4.
3. We are referring to the celebrated book by the master from Berlin, *Paideia, Die Formung des grieschischen Menschen*, vol. I (Berlin-Leipzig, 1934), thus summarised by M. Guidi: 'No broadening of the historical horizon can change the fact that our history begins with the Greeks .... This history, obviusly, can not take the whole planet as its arena, but only the "Hellenocentric" peoples ... since it is they who have taken from the Greeks the conscious principle of the true Kultur .... It is not difficult to draw the practical consequences of this theoretical formula: the absolute and central value of Antiquity as the eternal and unique source of the constituent principle of our culture and thus as a force of formation and education. A total humanism' (Guidi, 'Trois conférences sur quelques problèmes généraux de l'orientalisme' in *Annuaire de l'Institut de philologie et d'histoire orientales – volume offert à Jean Capart* (Brussels, 1935) pp. 171–2).
4. Our italics. They mark clearly the reference to self, that is to Europe.
5. M. Guidi, 'Trois conférences', pp. 171–80. In 1954 he defined Orientalism thus: 'The scholar of the Orient, or the Orientalist worthy of his name is not he who limits himself to knowledge of certain unknown languages or can describe the strange habits of certain peoples; rather he is someone who can bring together a knowledge of certain aspects of the Orient and a knowledge of the great spiritual and moral forces which have influenced the formation of human culture, a person nourished by the teachings of ancient civilisations and who has been able to evaluate the role of the different factors involved in the constitution of the civilisation of the Middle Ages, for example, or the Renaissance' ('Ilm al-Sharq wa tarikh al-oumran', *Al-Zahra*, rabi'awwal 1347 H. (Aug–Sep 1928); quoted by Dagher, *Massader*, p. 771).
6. On the definition of 'Euro-centrism' cf. among others J. Needham, 'Le dialogue entre l'Europe et l'Asie', *Comprendre*, no. 12 (1954) pp. 1–8; and our preface to *Egypte, société militaire* (Paris, 1962) pp. 9–13.
7. R. Schwab, 'L'Orientalisme dans la culture et les littératures de l'Occident moderne', *Oriente moderno*, vol. XXXII, no. 1–2 (1952) p. 136.

8. A. J. Arberry, *Oriental Essays*.
9. Dagher, *Massader*, pp. 779–80.
10. J. Berque, 'Cent vingt-cing ans de sociologie maghrébine', *Annales*, vol.XI, no. 3 (1956) pp. 299–321.
11. 'Higher studies, and Oriental, philological and historical studies in particular – are they not the most treasured collaborators in Italy's policy of colonial expansion?' (A. Cabaton, 'L'Orientalisme musulman et l'Italie moderne', *Revue du monde musulman*, vol. VII, no. 27 (1914) p. 24). We know of Lawrence's extraordinary epigraph to his *Seven Pillars of Wisdom* when, caught in his own game, he wrote; 'Damascus had not seemed a sheath for my sword when I landed in Arabia: but its capture disclosed the exhaustion of my mainsprings of action. The strongest motive throughout had been a personal one, not mentioned here, but present to me, I think, every hour of these two years. Active pains and joys might fling up, like towers, among my days: but, refluent as air, this hidden urge re-formed, to be the persistent element of life till near the end. It was dead before we reached Damascus'. And 'The French Nation works, accumulates. From its adventurous consuls to the Utopians who built the railways, to its emotional travellers – Lamartine, Barres – she builds in the Orient a work for which Champollion, Sacy and Renan provide the scientific counterpoint. At that time the Arabs neglected their own past and stammered their noble language. Contemporary Orientalism was born of that absence. The exploration and resurrection of all that moral wealth was the opportunity given to the erudite Christian, as well as the Christian from the Bank, to revivify the barbarian spaces and restock the warehouses.... Look, for example, at the Arab tribes, the Bedhouin in general. Orientalism exposed them to three great political thrusts: the phase of our "Arab Bureau" in Algeria, to around 1870; the phase of the "Revolt in the Desert", triumph of the British agents in the Near East; and the contemporary oil-based expansion' (J. Berque, 'Perspectives de l'orientalisme contemporain', *Ibla*, vol. XX (1957) pp. 220–1). In 1822 the founders of the Société Asiatique' proposed to 'allow historians to explain the Antiquities of the Oriental peoples', to gather 'precious documents on diplomatic operations in the Levant and commercial operations throughout Asia'. Among the questions posed for Orientalists at Lyons were these: 'Have Europeans an interest in demanding that their treaties give them the right to residence in the interior of China, in order to buy there directly from the producers of cocoons and silkworms, to establish branches there and generally to trade there? What are the advantages and disadvantages in bringing Chinese coolies to a foreign country?' (Texts quoted by J. Chesneaux, 'La recherche marxiste et le Réveil contemporain de l'Asie et l'Afrique', *La pensée*, no. 95 (Jan–Feb 1961) pp. 4–5.
12. On ethnist typology see M. Rodinson, 'L Egypte nassérienne au miroi marxiste', *Les temps modernes*, no. 203 (April 1963) pp. 1859–65.
13. J. Berque and L. Massignon, 'Dialogue sur les Arabes', *Esprit*, vol. XXVIII, no. 280 (1960) p. 1506. On the relations between Orientalism and colonialism see these words of L. Massignon: 'I myself, strongly colonial at the time, had written to him of my hope of an early armed conquest of Morocco, and he had replied approvingly ... (letter no. 1 from In-Salah.

2nd Oct. 1906). It is true that Morocco was then in a terrible state. But fifty years of occupation, without Lyautey and his high Franco-Moslem ideals, would have left nothing of note' ('Foucauld au désert devant le Dieu d'Abraham, Agar et Iesma', *Les mardis de Dar-es-Salam* (1959) p. 59).

14. Precise criticisms in *UGC Report of the Sub-committee on Oriental, Slavonic, East European and African Studies* (London, 1961) under the chairmanship of Sir William Hayter: 'Modern Far Eastern studies are a closed book in almost every other history or social science faculty' (38). 'The more inward looking characteristics of the language departments and their lack of interest in modern studies and languages have contributed to a number of unfortunate results' (46), etc. A recent volume *Etudes d' orientalisme dédiées à la mémoire de Lévi-Provençal* (Paris, 1962, 2 vols) collects 61 articles, only 8 of which deal with the modern period, and three of a bio-bibliographical character that include it.

15. Chesneaux, *La recherche*, p. 5.

16. Omar al-Dessouqi, *Fil-adab al-hadith*, 3rd ed. (Cairo, 1954) pp. 325–6; Dagher, *Massader*, p. 779; N. Al-Aqiqi, *Al-moustashriqoun*, pp. 207–9; Mohammed Hussein Heykal, *Hayat Mohammad*, preface to 2nd ed., 6th ed. (Cairo 1956) pp. 60–1; Anouar al-Guindi, *Al-adab al-Arabi al-hadith fi marakat al-mouqawamah wal-tagammo minal-mouhit ila'l-khalig* (Cairo, 1959) pp. 621–4, and then *Al-fikr al-Arabi al mouacer fi ma'rakat al taghrib wal-tabai-iyyah al-thaqafiyyah* (Cairo, 1962) pp. 271–85, etc.

17. Notably the Institute of Arab Manuscripts directed by Pr. Calah Eddine al-Mounaijed at the Arab League, the journal *Magallat al-makh toitat al-Arabiyyah*, published in Cairo since 1955; the creation of the new Institute for Islamic Research at the University of El-Azhar, directed by Pr. Abdallah al-Arabi, *Al-Ahram*, 23 Nov 1961; one should also mention the efforts at restoration undertaken by the Ministry of Culture and National Orientation, particularly under Fathi Radwan, Hussein Fawzi and Sarwat Okashah. Similar efforts in Syria and Iraq notably. In Egypt, the existentialist philosopher Abd al-Rahman Badawi had set in motion, from 1940, a gigantic effort at updating, inspiring many works on Islamic thought; while the great philologist Mourad Kamel deciphered authoritatively the Coptic, Ethiopian and Semitic domains.

18. J. Berque developed an extended critique both in his *Le Maghreb entre les deux guerres* and his classes at the Collège de France. See too J. P. Naish, 'The connection of Oriental studies with commerce, art and literature during the XVIIIth and XIXth centuries', *Journal of the Manchester Egypt and Orient Society*, vol. xv (1930) pp. 33–9; J. Chesneaux, 'French historiography and the evolution of colonial Vietnam' in D.G.E. Hall, *Historical Writing on the Peoples of Asia – Historians of South East Asia* (Oxford–London, 1961) pp. 235–44.

19. Cf. M. Khalidi and O. Farroukh, *Al-tabshir wal-instimar fil-bilad al-Arabbiyyah* (Beirut, 1953).

20. On this notion cf. R. Makarius, *La Jeunesse intellectuelle d' Egypte au lendemain de la deuxième guerre mondiale* (Paris, 1960) and our 'La vision du problème colonial par le monde afro-asiatique' (1972).

21. J. Berque, friend of the Arab renaissance and mediator between the two

cultures, has paid homage to many of our intellectuals. I myself have to thank him for mentioning my work on several occasions (notably my work in collaboration with Mahmoud al-Alem) and the writers of the Egyptian realist school, both in his classes at the Collège de France and in his 'L'Inquiétude arabe des temps modernes', *Revue des études islamiques*, vol. XXVI, no. 1 (1958) pp. 87–107; and *Les arabes*, p. 102, etc.

22. However it is E. Renan who, in France, has theorised the difference between Semitism and Aryanism, the peoples of the first group being inferior on all levels to those of the second group (cf. *Histoire générale et système comparé des langues sémitiques*, pt 1 (Paris, 1855). D. Kimson takes his inspiration from Renan in his *Pathologie de l'Islam et les moyens de le détruire* (Paris, 1897). This theory has been unceasingly contested by the thinkers and scholars of the Arab world.

23. Pp. 10–11. It is not our purpose here to provide a critical analysis of this book.

24. *Le Maghreb*, p. 8.

25. *Perspectives*, p. 237.

26. Exposition of theoretical results in 'Expression et signification dans la vie arabe', *L'Homme*, vol. I, no. 1 (1961) pp. 50–67.

27. *Report of the Interdepartmental Commission of Enquiry on Oriental, Slavonic, East European and African Studies* (London, 1947); commentary by A. J. Arberry, *Oriental Essays*, pp. 240–9; analysis in *Hayter Report*, pp. 6–40.

28. *Hayter*, pp. 45–52.

29. Ibid., pp. 53–63. General P. Rondot who looks at the attitude of the United States to the contemporary Orient in *Orient*, no. 2 (1957) pp. 19–52 and no. 3, pp. 31–80, points to the role of the foundations, the schools of languages and regions of the Near East, at the American Embassy in Beirut, and at the two American Universities of Cairo and Beirut (this latter, be it noted, the only foreign institute of education permitted in the UAR). The motives put forward by the University of Michigan (Ann Arbor) as to its reasons for expanding its programme of studies on the modern Orient are described as: '1) to make the Near East known to the greatest possible number of Americans; 2) to encourage the idea the US has a vital interest in the present and future developments in the area; 3) to constitute an intelligent group of American experts on the Near East'. The author is reluctant to judge the completed work, however. Cf. R. Bayly Windsor, 'Arabic and Islamic studies in the US', *Middle East Forum*, no. 31 (June 1956) pp. 19–22.

30. 'An interpretation of Islamic history', *Cahiers d'histoire mondiale*, vol. I (1953) pp. 39–62.

31. 'Pour l'étude des sociétés orientales contemporaines', *Colloque sur la sociologie musulmane-Actes*, 11–14 Sept 1961 (Brussels, 1962): 'It is anomalous that we should be gathered here to discuss the societies of the Orient in the absence of our Oriental colleagues . . . and that merits some thought. For their interpretation, I believe, takes us beyond the political conjuncture to a questioning of the methods and object of our study.' (85) 'The regretable absence of our Oriental colleagues does not respond as one might think, to a political conjuncture, but to a deep malaise in the very

nature of the society whose relations with our own we are currently studying'; however, 'we are not wrong to describe ourselves thus'.

32. 'Arawa shatahat anna wa an tarikhina', *Al-Ahram* (21 Dec 1962).

33. We should point particularly to 'Le problème des échanges culturels', *Etudes Lévi-Provençal*, vol. I, pp. 141–51, which provides a résumé of the volumes edited by the author, notably *Unity and Variety in Moslem Civilisation* (Chicago, 1955) and with W. Hartner, *Klassizismus und Kulturverfall* (Frankfurt, 1960); 'An analysis of Islamic civilisation and cultural anthropology', in *Actes, op. cit.*, pp. 21–71.

34. On the page where the author writes 'Alas, semantic anarchy is only too real. And evasion of the facts through verbalism is only too frequent', one finds the following errors; *al-hiyad al-igabi* (positive neutralism) is substituted after 1959 by *adam al-inhiyaz* (non-engagement); the first expression was not rejected because it was 'judged outmoded' and the second 'seen to be more satisfactory', but rather because of the new orientation of Egyptian politics after Bandung, at the time of the 1959 repression (cf. our *Egypte*, pp. 219–42). 'Cadres', called *itarat* in North Africa, are not called *milak* in the Orient but quite simply *kadr*; 'structure' is translated as *tarkib* in philosophical terminology, never by *haykal*, *gihaz* or *nizam*. One is astonished to learn that this is the speech of M. Abdallah Ibrahim, on 'April 1959, to 'open the way to a modern Arabic where words express realities' (what happened before?); and to quote *niqabat* (trade unions) used since 1908 in Cairo, *al-gihaz al-assasi* (infrastructure) in Egypt, *al-tarkib al assasi*, while *al-tarkib al-ilwi* is used to designate the 'superstructure', these two terms have been in use since 1939–45 among Marxist intellectuals in the Orient at grips with the struggle for national liberation and reconstruction (*L'Arabe moderne* (Paris, 1960, p. 360). Cf. M. Rodinson in *Cahiers de l'Orient contemporain* (1950, 1962).

35. 'Those countries that seek access to history and the right to make it,' says Berque, 'probably do not yet have chairs of modern history in their Universities' (*Dialogue*, p. 1508). One should point out the work in modern and contemporary history carried out in the University of Cairo for the last two generations, as well as at Damascus, Baghdad and Alexandria. In a single number of the *Proceedings of the Royal Society of Historical Studies*, vol. I, Cairo 1951 (published 1952), 77 pages out of 194 are devoted to contemporary history (articles by M. M. Safwat and G. E. al-Shayyal). Chairs of modern and contemporary history exist in faculties of letters and political science particularly. Of course, these are little more than sparks – they do not pretend to be exhaustive. Cf. the critique of contemporary Arab historiography in 'The uses of history by modern Arab writers', *Middle East Journal*, vol. XIV, no. 4 (1960) pp. 382–96.

Let us note that a great effort at understanding has been made in the European countries not directly involved in traditional colonialism: on Germany See L. Rathmann, 'Zur Widerspiegelung des antiimperialistischon Befreigunsbewegung des arabischen Volker in der burgerlichen deutschen Historiographie', *Zeitschrift fur Geschichtswissenschaft*, Berlin, vol. X, no. 3 (1962) pp. 548–74; on Spain, F. Cantera Burgos, 'Los estudios orientales en la España actual', in *Oriente moderno*, vol. xxxv, no. 1 (1955) pp. 236–47.

36. *Perspectives de l'orientalisme*, pp. 218–32. The same thesis at the Brrssels colloquium: 'Orientalist sociology should aspire to integration with Oriental societies, not through knowledge, elsewhere tied to colonialist expansion, but through its contribution to analysis and thus to internal construction' (*Actes*, pp. 458–9). H. Jraus-Elbeshausen, 'Islamic studies in post-war Germany', *Islamic Culture*, vol. xxxvi, no. 2 (1952) pp. 51–6; on Spain, Cantera Burgos, 'Los estudios orientales'; on Belgium, G. Ryckmans, L'Orientalisme en Belgique', *Revue générale belge*, no. 23 (1947) pp. 724–38; on Italy, E. Rossi, 'Near Eastern Studies in Italy', *Middle Eastern Affairs*, vol. viii, no. 2 (1957) pp. 57–60; on Finland, P. Aalto, 'Les études orientales en Finlande', *Archiv orientalny*, no. 19. (1951) pp. 79–84; A. Abel, 'Approches critiques d'une étude sociologique du monde musulman contemporain', *Etudes*, Brussels, vol. i, nos 1–2 (1962) pp. 3–16, etc.

37. *Islam and Modern History* (Princeton, 1960), in the same spirit: 'A number of Christians, apart from the author, would be happy to see a Moslem writer undertake a similar study of contemporary Christianity.' This book is full of interesting analyses, and gives a general view of the Islamic reality in Africa and Asia.

38. The budget of a single institution in the United States – the 'Near Eastern Center' at the University of California, Los Angeles – is six times greater than the annual budget of a small European state.

39. Several Arab professors hold teaching posts in several American universities, while others direct research departments.

40. The analysis of 'articles and studies', of the table for the years 1957–62 in the new modernist journal *Orient* is instructive on this point. Four native authors out of some 75; a large proportion is in fact made up of texts on literature, thought, religion and politics in our countries. But these are the materials of study for the analyst, who remains transcendent.

41. 'Problems of Middle Eastern history' (Washington, 1956) in *Studies on the Civilisation of Islam* (London, 1962) pp. 342–3; the author chooses not to take into consideration historical and sociological research undertaken in the Middle East, other than *Introduction to the History of Education in Modern Egypt* by J. Hepworth-Dunne (London, 1938). W. Montgomery Watt's *Islam and the Integration of Society* (London, 1961), based on the theories of Mannheim, is greeted with silence in recent Arab work; see M. Rodinson, 'Bilan des études mohammadiennes', *Revue historique*, fasc. 465 (Jan-March 1963) pp. 169–220.

42. On the 'university' level, two works by J. Austruy, who theorises about *homo Islamicus* on the basis of a total ignorance of Arab language and culture: *Structure économique et civilisation* (1960) and *L'Islam face au développement économique* (Paris, 1961). On the journalistic side, J. and S. Lacouture pronounce judgement on culture and religion: 'Will the author be forgiven for broaching the subject without reading Arabic?'; later, pointing to certain omissions, 'it is not a matter here of "national" culture' (*L'Egypte en mouvement* (Paris, 1962, pp. 306–43). The work abounds in interesting

morsels. At the same time, S. Lacouture published *Egypte* (Paris, 1962) where literature, thought, aesthetics are judged in peremptory terms, pride of place being given to foreign writers living in Egypt, but totally unknown to the public. Of course, there are many more such examples . . . 'Consider only the question of literatures. A non-European finding himself in the Reading Room of the British Museum or the Bibliotheque Nationale in Paris, and asking what in the end was the value of that great mass of books, would be considered a savage. But there are worlds of other literatures of more or less equal depth, like Chinese literature for instance, of which the ordinary educated European understands not a single word. Is he not equally a barbarian? ' (Needham, *Le dialogue*). C. Bremond in a brief study of mass communications in the developing countries (*Communications*, vol. II (1962) pp. 56–67) judges the issue on the basis of reports from European experts, with no reference to a single indigenous work, from any country at all.

43. A first stage of this work is given in *Islam et capitalisme* (Paris, 1966).

44. 'When at the time (1950) I decided to direct my research to the history of the Chinese proletariat and working class in the wake of the October revolution and the first world war, it was for me a sort of Pascalian wager, an expression of my conviction that it was both possible and necessary to establish as a truly scientific discipline the study of contemporary Chinese history' ('Recherches sur l'historie du mouvement ouvrier chinois', *Mouvement social*, no. 41 (Oct 1962) pp. 1–12). The central theme chosen – that of the 'workers' movement' rather than the 'national movement' – refers back to the problematic of European Marxism.

45. The author disposes both of a library of works and documents relating to science and technology unique in the world, and of a plethora of collaborators at his side at Caius College, where he is Master: Wang Ching-Ning, Lu Gwei-Djen, Ho Ping-Yu, Kenneth Robinson, Rs'ao T'ien-Ch'in).

46. W. Z. Laqueur notes that the new journal of Soviet Orientalism *Sovetskoe Vostokvedenea* first appeared in April 1955, the month of Bandung. He stresses the decisive role of A. I. Mikoyan, B. G. Gafurov (member of both the Academy of Sciences and the Central Committee of the CPSU), N. A. Mukhtidinov and A. F. Sultanov, all leaders of non-European origin, and mentions certain publications which seem to him to be important, notably E. A. Lebedev's book on Jordan, *Contemporary Persia*, *Contemporary Syria* (1956), A. N. Kotlov on the Iraqi Revolution (1958), I. P. Belaev's *American Imperialism in Saudi Arabia* (1957) and M. F. Gatavlin's *Agrarian Relations in Syria* (1957) and *The Soviet Union and the Middle East* (London, 1959) pp. 168–86. The principal publications on neo-Orientalism in the socialist countries (up to 1962) are: M. Perlmann, 'The study of the Islamic Middle East in the Soviet Union 1940–56', *Report on Current Research* (1957) pp. 17–26; B. G. Gafurov, 'Immediate tasks of Soviet Oriental studies', *Vestnik Akademit Neuk*, vol. 9 (1957); N. A. Mukhtidinov, *K Novym Uspekham Sovetskogo Vostokvedenea* (Moscow, 1957); M. Guboglu, '40 ans d'études orientales en U.R.S.S., 1917–57', *Studia et Acta Orientalia*, vol. I (1958) pp. 281–316, where he speaks of the 'collapse of the

Trotskyist "Asiatic mode of production" in 1934' (p. 295); 'La prima conferenza Pansovietica degli Orientalisti, Tachkent, 4–11 juin 1957', *Oriente Moderno*, vol. 38 (Feb 1958) p. 202; W. Z. Laqueur, 'The shifting line in Soviet Orientology', *Problems of Communism*, vol. 5 (1956) pp. 20–61; R. Loewenthal, 'Russian materials on Islam and Islamic institutions, a selective bibliography', *Der Islam*, vol. XXXII, nos 1–2 (1958) pp. 208–309; and 'Russian materials on Arabs and Arab countries, a select bibl.', *Der Islam*, vol. XXXIV (1959) pp. 174–87; 'Dix ans d'études orientales en Pologne', *Roesnik orjental Istyczny*, vol. 20 (1956) pp. 7–14; D. Sinor, 'Dix années d'orientalisme hongrois', *Journal asiatique*, vol. 239 (1951) pp. 211–37; *Les actes des journées scientifiques d'orientalisme* (Praha-Dobris) (20–25 June 1949); J. Reychman, 'Les études orientales (islamiques) en Pologne', *Studia et Acta Orient Ealia*, II, 1959, pp. 161–87; J. Kabrda, 'Les études orientales en Yougoslavie', *Archir Orientalny*, vol. 25 (1957) pp. 146–55; J. Blaskovic, 'Les buts, l'organisation et l'activité de l'école orientalistique tchécoslovaquie', *Studia et Acta*, vol. II (1959) pp. 61–9; K. Petracek, 'Les études arabes et islamiques et la semitologie en Tchécoslovaquie', *Archiv orientalny*, vol. 19 (1951) pp. 98–107; J. Rypka, 'L'Orientalisme en Tchécoslovaquie', ibid., pp. 15–26; M. Guboglu, 'Contributions roumaines/aux études orientales', ibid., vol. 24 (1956) pp. 459–75; D. Zbaritel, *Die Orientalistik in der Tschechoslowakei* (Prague, 1959).

47. 'Christianity and the Asian cultures', *Theology*, vol. LXV (1962) pp. 1–8.
48. 'There have been long centuries of preparation during which Europe has assimilated Arab education, Indian thought and Chinese technology'; 'Europe is not concerned about the inventions that made the explorations possible: the compass and the stern rudder from China; the multiple masts from India and Indonesia; the mizzen-mast sail, derived from the Arab sailors.' 'We often hear it said that the Europeans discovered the rest of the world. This is a limited and not entirely correct conception up to the Renaissance. The Bactrian Greeks did not discover the Chinese, but vice versa (in the person of Tchang Tchien in 125 B.C.). Two centuries later, Kan Ying reached the Persian Gulf, that is further towards the West than any Roman had gone towards the Orient. At the end of the Ming dynasty, the Chinese flag was everywhere to be seen, in the Pacific and the Indian Ocean, from Zanzibar to Borneo, and from Borneo to Kamchatka.' 'The idea, often expressed, that the sense of history is the result of European civilisation alone is totally false. The honour would rather fall to Chinese civilisation, whose 24 dynastic histories, beginning in 90 B.C., form a body of historical writing that is without par.... Even if one insists on reading "sense of history" to mean "philosophy of history", Europe's contribution was not the first even in this field, for Ibn Khaldoun lived three centuries before Vico.' 'We cannot accept the thesis that Europe brought forth the idea of making a single society of the whole human race. The Confucian proposition that "across the seven seas, all men are brothers" dates from the 6th century B.C. In India, Kabir was only one of a chorus of poets and prophets proclaiming human solidarity.' 'Some European scholars consider modern science and technol-

ogy, in their victorious march across the world, to have been accompanied by a secularised and partly mutilated form of European civilisation. They notice, not without sadness, that the European system of values has been rejected by all the national independence movements of Asia and Africa. For these thinkers, Christianity is inseparable from the spirit of modern science; it was so to speak, the intellectual context of its evolution. In accepting such theories one would be only a step away from predicating a new Crusade, in order to impose European religious ideas on other cultures. Their pennants might carry the sign of the Cross, but it would be capitalism and imperialism that were carrying them into battle. What no one has yet been able to determine is exactly what are the indispensable intellectual elements of science and technology?' (*Le dialogue*). Later, the profoundly human encyclical of Pope John XXIII showed Catholicism's will to bring an end to this vision of things.

49. 'A. I. Mikoyan: Speech to the 25th Congress of Orientalists', *Problemi Vostokvedenea*, no. 5 (1950) pp. 3–6. The 'disinterested' aim of Orientalism is that 'which the military engineer proposes in examining the enemy's defences and offensive preparations: destruction' said Goguyer in his translation of Ibn Malik's *Alfiyya* (quoted in Massignon, *Les mardis*, vol. IX (1958) p. 59).

50. K. Mueller, 'Des Ostblock und die Entwicklungslander', *Das Parlament* (12 July 1961) pp. 397–411.

51. As expounded in *Colloque sur les recherches des instituts français de sciences humaines en Asie*, organised by the Singer-Polignac Foundation (23–31 October 1959) (Paris, 1960) pp. 39–41.

52. The theses expounded in *Oriental despotism* have been forcefully criticised by, among others: E. E. Leach, 'Hydraulic society in Ceylon', *Past and Present*, no. 15 (1959) pp. 2–29; J. Needham, 'The past in China's present', *Centennial Review*, vol. IV, no. 2 (1960) pp. 164–5; J. Chesneaux, *Les recherches*, vol. 12, no. 5; a recent lecture by the Hungarian scholar F. Tokei on the Asiatic mode of production (CERM, Paris, 1962, June 1962) 35 pp., on the basis of a recent text of Marx, *Formen die der kapitalistischen Produktion vorhergehen*. The *Grundrisse* opens a new phase in Marxist research in the problem, which since then has enjoyed a considerable interest.

53. Marx–Engels, *The First Indian War of Independence* (Moscow, 1960). It is something very different from the 'mutual errors' based on a so-called 'reciprocal' theory. Recently, S. Avineri has provided a useful anthology of *Karl Marx on Colonialism and Modernisation* (New York, 1969).

54. Our ideas on the subject are developed at length in *Idéologie et renaissance* (Paris, 1969).

55. In our view the *theoretical* basis of the Sino-Soviet divergence is to be found in the Chinese leaders' refusal to accept any perpetuation of 'Euro-centrism' in Marxist theory or revolutionary strategy. In 1955, Lukacs had already written: 'In their march towards modern civilisation, in their effort to eliminate the relics of their own Middle Ages, countries like India are following a path which is, at least in part, taking the place of socialism. It is

infinitely obvious that the original nature of these social transformations will be expressed through new literary forms that will not be reducible to abstract schemes.' *Die Gegenwartsbedeutung des kritischen Realismus* (Hamburg, 1955)°

56. Chesneaux, *La recherche*, pp. 11–16.

57. 'The 21st Congress of the CPSU and the tasks of Orientology', *Problemi Vostokvedenea*, pp. 18–25; and M. Mancall, 'The 21st Party Congress and Soviet Orientology', *Journal of Asian Studies*, vol. XIX, no. 2 (1960) pp. 18–25.

58. Enrica Collotti-Pischel in *Cina, India ed Egitto e la 'fase di transizione'* rightly points to the geographical and historical affinities between Arab and Moslem researchers and their European colleagues, while the gulf grows deeper as far as China is concerned. (*Problemi del Socialismo*, vol. VI, no. 2 (1963) pp. 193–213). Her book *La rivoluzione interrota* (Turin, 1962) is one of the most lucid Marxist attempts to understand the Chinese vision of history.

59. *Colloque*; see note 51. In 1966 he was to add as a conclusion to *L'Asie orientale aux XIXe et XXe siècles* (Paris, 1966): 'The originality of the history of modern Asia does not at all mean, quite the contrary, that the general comparative history of human societies is no longer valid. The history of Asia does not unfold in isolation. But it has its own rhythm – which does not mean it was irreducible to the level of the West in theoretical terms. It is on the basis of a study of Asia, historically liberated from Europe as it tends to be historically, that one can build at a higher level than in the past and in a more solid way, the soundly based unity of human history'.

60. This last in his remarkable course at the Sorbonne on *L'Orient philosophique* (roneo, Paris, 1960–2).

61. Fung Yeou Lan, *History of Chinese Philosophy* (Peking, 1937 and Princeton 1952–3) 2 vols; and J. Needham, *Science and Civilisation*, vol. 2.

62. Under the impetus of Sheikh Moustafa Abd al-Razeq (1882–1947) the method of Moslem history of philosophy has been renewed, notably in his *Tamhid ila tarikh al-falsafah al-Islamiyyah* (Cairo, 1944). Cf. works by Abd al-Rahman Badawi, Abbas al-Aqqad, Osman Amin, Mohammad Youssef Moussa, Ibrahim Makdour, Ismail Mazhar, Mohammad Abd al-Hadi Abour Ridah, Omar Farroukh, Cadeq Galal al-Aazm Hassan Cab *et al.* Cf. *Al-fikr al-falsafi fi miat am* (Beirut, 1962) nos 9–70, 102–241, 298–392; our review of 'How Greek science passed to the Arabs' by De Lacy O'Leary (London, 1951) in *Al-Magallah*, vol. I, no. 4 (1957) pp. 125–7.

63. P. Sweezy, *The Present as History* (New York, 1953).

64. Report of the Conference, *Probleme des Neokolonialismus und die Politik des beiden deutschen Staaten gegenuber dem nationalen Befreiungs kampf der Volker* (5–8 April 1961, Leipzig) 2 vols. The text quoted is by M. Mancall.

65. Chesneaux offers (in *Recherches*) the following approximative table of the XXth Congress of Orientalists (Paris 1948) to the XXVth taking place in Moscow in 1960:

Number of papers	Total	'Modern' topics	Authors from Asia or Africa
Paris	299	23	37
Istanbul	185	17	51
Cambridge	404	55	62
Munich	438	80	86
Moscow	767	287	197

66. 'The past in China's present', *Centennial Review*, vol. IV, no. 3 (1960) p. 308.
67. The *Revue d'histoire économique et sociale de l'Orient* (Leiden, 1957 onwards) edited by C. Cahen, is principally concerned with the Classical periods. In the main historical journals of a Marxist or neo-Marxist character in Western Europe – *Past and Present* (Oxford), *Recherches internationales* (Paris), *Studi Storici* (Rome) – the contemporary Orient continues to occupy a very secondary place. The English Marxists (notably publishers Lawrence and Wishart) give it more attention, notably R. Palme Dutt, *The Crisis of Britain and the British Empire* (London, 1957), *Problems of Contemporary History* (1963), the work of J. Woddis on Africa, etc.
68. Frequently quoted in preceding notes.
69. On this institute see *Problemi Vostokvedenea*, no. 6 (1960) pp. 221ff.
70. *Colloque . . .* , see note 51.
71. H. Passin, *China's Cultural Diplomacy* (London, 1962) pp. 107–15.
72. An interesting work of recent scientific Orientalism – Andre Miquel's *L'Islam et sa civilisation* (Paris, 1968) notably book IV, pp. 315–401 – takes this direction; while D. and J. Dourdel continue the pre-sociological tradition in *La civilisation de l'Islam classique* (Paris, 1968).
73. In the United States, it is interesting to note, 'the accent has been put on 6 "critical" languages – Arabic, Chinese, Hindi, Japanese, Portuguese and Russian; eighteen other Slav and Asiatic languages have been singled out for support' according to the *Hayter Report*, which formulates its own conclusions for Great Britain.

Chapter 6

1. This explains the blossoming in many countries (Mexico, Argentina, India, Indonesia, etc.) of a number of unknown or misunderstood works on socialist humanism, and particularly Marxist humanism. Only one (by L. Senghor) is included in the thirty-five in Erich Fromm's interesting compilation *Socialist Humanism* (London, 1967). On the relations between war and civilisation, see the interesting contrast established by B. H. Liddell-Hart between Sun Tzu (4th century B.C.) and Clausewitz, entirely favourable to the former, in *Strategy, the Indirect Approach* (London, 1967) and Sun Tzu, *The Art of War*, trans. S. B. Griffith (London, 1963): 'What is of supreme importance in war is to attack the enemy's strategy. Thus, those

skilled in war subdue the enemy's army without battle. They capture his cities without assaulting them and overthrow his state without protracted operations.'

2. Cf. the articles on 'Ethnology' (J. Beattie) and 'Social anthropology' (John L. Fisher) in Gould and Kolb (eds), *A Dictionary of the Social Sciences* (London, 1964) pp. 245–7 and 644–6; and Paul Mercier, *Histoire de l'anthropologie* (Paris, 1967).

3. On these writers see *Les origines de l'exogamie et du totémisme* (Paris, 1963), which marks a renewal of contemporary Marxist ethnology.

4. *Social Evolution* (London, 1951) p. 161.

5. Retained in the latest edition (1963), vol. v, pp. 824–31.

6. See *Kulturgeschichte als Kultursoziologie* (Munich, 1950).

7. This dimension, an unsuspected one for Europeans, is clearly illuminated in all recent works on the history of national movements and on the culture of the main Afro-Asian countries.

8. Introduced by J. W. Powell, director of the Bureau of American Ethnology, in *Introduction to the study of Indian languages* (Washington, 1880) p. 80.

9. In his introduction to F. Ortiz, *Contrapunto cubano del tabaco y del azúcar* (Havana, 1940).

10. On Marxism and the theoretical problem of the nation, see the theses of S. F. Bloom, *The World of Nations* (New York, 1960) and Horace B. Davis, *Nationalism and Socialism* (New York, 1967). A conference of the Paris Centre for Marxist Studies and Research in November 1965 on 'the notion of civilisation' took as its starting-point that 'the idea of "civilisation" has not been elaborated in classic works on Marxist thought . . . Where one might expect to find it, the concept of "nation" stands in its place' (Jean Boulier-Fraissinet). This lack is not attributed to the civilisational framework in which Marxist thought evolved.

11. Notably in A. Gramsci, *Letteratura e vita nazionale* (Turin, 1954) and the interesting issue of *Critica Marxista*, quaderno, no. 3 (Rome, 1967) on 'Prassi rivoluzionaria e storicismo in Gramsci'.

12. As exemplified by Paul. H. Lazarsfeld, William H. Sewell, Harold L. Wilensky (eds), *The Uses of Sociology* (New York, 1967).

13. Accompanied by Talcott Parsons's 'Grand Theory'.

14. R. Aron, *Les étapes de la pensée sociologique* (Paris, 1967) pp. 497–583; E. Fleischmann, 'De Weber a Nietzsche', *Archives Européennes de Sociologie* vol. v, no. 2 (1964) pp. 190–238.

15. In the case of Brazil I would mention particularly the remarkable special issue of *Les Temps Modernes*, vol. XXIII, no. 257 (October 1967) pp. 577–760) edited by Celso Furtado.

16. Respectively: G. Gurvitch, *Traité de sociologie* (Paris: PUF, 1960) 2 vols: Gould and Kolb, *A dictionary of the social sciences* (London, 1964); T. B. Bottomore, *Sociology, a Guide to Problems and Literature* (London, 1962); I.S.A. *Annual Report 1966* (Geneva, 1967).

17. Armand Cuvillier, *Manuel de sociologie*, 4th edn (Paris, 1960) pp. 666–86.

18. An excellent study in *Traité*, vol. II, pp. 315–30, which links up with Bastide's work as a whole. Cf. also the *Contributions à la sociologie de la connaissance* (Paris, 1967) published under his direction.

19. India is the only country in the colonial world that Marx – and Weber – mention in a few scattered works. As far as India is concerned, one sociologist devotes a general manual to centring its sociological problems in the United States (H. T. Muzumdar, *The Grammar of Sociology, Man in Society* (London, 1966)).

20. 'Note sur la notion de civilisation', *L'Année Sociologique*, vol. XII (1909–12) pp. 46–50.

21. *A Study of History*, 12 vols (London, 1934–56). In his recent *Change and Habit, the Challenge of Our Time* (London, 1966), the author lists between 15 and 30 civilisations, depending on the criteria adopted (p. 69).

22. The author gives the theoretical basis of his work in 'The Past in China's Present', *The Centennial Review*, vol. IV, no. 2 (1960) pp. 145–78. Cf. also Raghavan Iyer (ed.), *The Glass Curtain between Asia and Europe* (London, 1965), and the precursory essay by Chang Tung-sun, 'A Chinese Philosopher's Theory of Knowledge', *Yenching Journal of Social Studies*, vol. I, no. 2 (1939). The integrationism of the right is aptly expressed by General Golberi de Couto o Silva, one of the principal theoreticians of the Military Institute of Brazil, who bases himself on T. S. Eliot ('If, tomorrow, Asia were to be converted to Christianity, that would not mean that it was converted into part of Europe') and the Lusitanian ideology of Coimbra: 'the West as ideal, the West as object, the West as programme . . . that current of ideals, propelled by history, that source of all creative energy . . . science as an instrument of action; democracy as the formula of political organisation; Christianity as the highest ethical model of social life.' After Islam, the Moors and the Turks, then Stalin's Russia, it is 'the China of Mao which, by relying vigorously on the one hand on a surprising degree of accelerated technological and scientific progress, and on the other hand upon an enormous demographic potential gathered together under a totalitarian system, has made of it the standard-bearer of a fulminating counter-offensive and a principal arm against the West, already so shaken in its fundamental beliefs by Marxism' (*Geopolitica do Brasil*, ed. Jose Olympio (Rio de Janeiro, 1967) pp. 226–34). It would be impossible to express more clearly the deepest thought of a whole spectrum of key European thinkers, from right to left.

23. Cf. in particular disparate articles by C. Cahen in Wilfred Cantwell Smith, *Islam in the Modern World* (Montreal, 1960) in which there are Marxist elements; and M. Rodinson, *Islam et capitalisme* (Paris, 1967).

24. Particularly those of Nyazi Berkes, *The Development of Secularism in Turkey* (Montreal, 1963); Jacques Berque and Jean-Paul Charnay *et al.*, *L'ambiguité dans la culture arabe* (Paris, 1967); Mohi Eddi Caber, *Al-taghayyor al hadari wa tanmiyat al-mougtama* (Sir-el-Layan, 1962); Abdallah Laroui, *L'idéologie arabe contemporaine* (Paris, 1967); etc. The June 1967 war produced a series of new critical works.

25. T. B. Bottomore, *Sociology*, pp. 125–16. Several comprehensive works, particularly M. Mauss, 'Civilisation. Le mot et l'idée', *Semaine du Centre de la Synthèse* (Paris, 1930) pp. 31–106; A.L. Kroeber and C. Kluckholn, *Culture: a Critical Review of Concepts and Definitions* (Papers of the

Peabody Museum of American Archaeology and Ethnology, vol. XXXXVII, 1952, no. 1).

26. 'W. W. Rostow's non-communist manifesto *The stages of economic growth* (1960) proposes five "stages" which are really no more than a nominal antithesis to the Marxist stages. The five stages in fact concern *one* transition only, and not as the Marxist series does, the whole history of the race' (E. Gellner, *Thought and Change* (London, 1964) pp. 129–30).

27. M. Rodinson, *Mahomet*, 2nd edn (Paris, 1968).

28. A. Lalande, *Vocabulaire technique et critique de la philosophie*, 8th edn (Paris, 1960) pp. 768–70.

29. 'The approach to the study of human affairs in the time-dimension is necessarily genetic, and its form of expression is therefore necessarily narrative . . . In comparing and analysing a number of parallel life-streams, we must take care still to keep them all moving. If we mentally arrest their movement in order to study them in cross-section, we shall be denaturing them and consequently distorting our view of them. Life does not stand still. It has to be studied on the run' (*Change and Habit*, pp. 88–9). Strong words which, on this point, connect with the Marxist method.

30. In his recent book *Anthropologie politique* (Paris, 1968): 'All human societies produce politics and all are permeable to historical fluid. For the same reasons' (p. 230).

31. C. Wright Mills, *The Sociological Imagination* (Harmondsworth, 1971) pp. 166, 171.

32. Ibid., p. 172. Cf., amongst others, in the case of Africa G. Balandier, *Sociologie actuelle de l' Afrique noire* (Paris, 1955); M. J. Herskovits, *The Human Factor in Changing Africa* (London, 1962).

33. Wright Mills, *The Sociological Imagination*, p. 175.

34. Ibid., pp. 163, 167, 168.

35. 'History and Society' in N. Mackenzie (ed.), *A Guide to the Social Sciences* (London, 1966) p. 49.

36. See our 'National formations . . .', *Social Dialectics*, vol. 2 (London, 1981).

37. M. Rodinson, 'L'Egypte nassérienne au miroir marxiste', *Les temps modernes*, no. 203 (April 1963) pp. 1859–87. The same remark, on a theoretical level, appears in George Lukacs, Wright Mills, Maurice de Gandillac, etc.

38. *Theses on Feuerbach* in Marx/Engels, *The German Ideology* (London, 1965) p. 652. By 'this-sidedness' one must understand the rootedness of thought, its connection with the 'here and now'. We read with interest J. J. Goblot's 'Pour une approche théorique des "faits des civilisations"', *La pensée*, no. 133 (June 1967) pp. 3–24; no. 134, pp. 3–34; no. 136 (Dec 1967) pp. 65–88.

Chapter 8

1. This quotation comes from the masterly spiritual biography by Henry Holorenshaw, 'The Making of an Honorary Taoist' in Teich and Young, *Changing Perspectives in the History of Science: Essays in Honour of Joseph Needham* (London, 1973) p. 3. Cf. also P. Morrison, 'Science and

Civilisation in China' and R. Boston, 'Joseph Needham, the Real Thing', *New York Review of Books* (20 June 1971) pp. 1–2; 'On a Slow Boat from China: Chinese Inventions and European Plagiarists', *Times Literary Supplement* (7 Jan 1972) pp. 1–3; 'The Making and Progress of an Honorary Taoist', *Times Higher Education Supplement* (1 June 1973) p. 15.

2. Holorenshaw, 'The Making of an Honorary Taoist', p. 9.
3. Text of the dedication to the French edition of *The Great Titration*, *La Science Chinoise et l'Occident* (Paris, 1973).
4. The following are the volumes that have been published, since 1954, by the Cambridge University Press: *Introductory Orientations*, vol. 1 (1954); *History of Scientific Thought*, vol. 2 (1956); *Mathematics and the Sciences of the Heavens and the Earth*, vol. 3 (1959); *Physics and Physical Technology*, vol. 4, Part 1: *Physics* (1962); Part 2: *Mechanical Engineering* (1965); Part 3: *Civil Engineering and Nautics* (1971).
5. Ed. Hermann (Paris, 1971).
6. Holorenshaw, 'The Making of an Honorary Taoist', p. 18.
7. See 'Le temps et l'homme Oriental', *La Science Chinoise et l'Occident*, pp. 145–222.
8. Holorenshaw, 'The Making of an Honorary Taoist', p. 19.
9. To 'know for certain that the dialectics of assent and dissent, of offensive and defensive, can make a key to understanding of the Cartesian categories of which the West is so proud'; this is the just comment of General Georges Buis (in 'Mao le magnifique', *Le Monde* (20 Sep 1973) p. 4). Despite which Radovan Richta, author of the powerfully Western-centrist *La civilisation au carrefour* (Paris, 1968) ignores the whole of Needham's work, even in the very exhaustive bibliography.

Chapter 9

1. We have set out these theses in *Social Dialectics*, vol. 2 (London, 1981).

Chapter 11

1. That is the basic inspiration of our *Idéologie et renaissance nationale: l'Egypte moderne* (Paris, 1969), as summed up in its theoretical conclusions (pp. 485–517).

Chapter 13

1. The theses presented in preliminary form here are further developed in the following writings: *Ideologie et renaissance nationale: l'Egypte moderne* (Paris, 1969); *Spécificité et théorie sociale* (Paris, 1977); and the essays in the present volumes of *Social Dialectics*.
2. Examples of the traditional, reductionist conceptions of time in the Western tradition can be found, *inter alia*, in: Alexander Szalai (ed.), *The Uses of Time* (The Hague-Paris, 1972); Milic Capek (ed.), *The Concepts of Space*

and Time, their Structure and their Development (Boston, 1976); Jeanne Hersch and R. Poirier (eds), *Entretien sur le temps* (Paris, The Hague, 1967).

3. There are a few works that deal with Oriental conceptions of time, within a more general treatment of other fields, for example: Charles A. Moore (ed.), *Philosophy and Culture – East and West* (Honolulu, 1962); Hajime Nakamura, *Ways of Thinking of Eastern Peoples* (Honolulu, 1964); the series edited by Michel Chodkiewicz, *Sources orientales*, 6 vols (Paris, 1959 on). There have, however, been occasional attempts at meaningful comparativism– though even then within a limited scope – as in P. Tillich and R. Niebuhr, *Indo-Hellenism v. Judaeo-Christian. The Glass Curtain between Asia and Europe* (edited in 1965 by R. Iyer) took the correct path, under Toynbee's inspiration. It remained for the master encyclopedic thinker of our time, Joseph Needham, to chart the course for future intellectual endeavours with his towering and seminal *Science and Civilisation in China*.

Index